Geddington Church

The history, architecture, and stories of a hidden medieval gem

by John Bennett

FOREWORD

What John Bennett has achieved in this wonderful publication is quite extraordinary. Notwithstanding centuries of family connection, my own appreciation of the rich layers of narrative that can be taken from this complex, fascinating building, at Geddington's heart for over a thousand years, has been transformed. One cannot enter Geddington Church without feeling an immediate connection with history. The architecture, images, craftsmanship and the very stones themselves all speak of the skill, ingenuity, piety, and devotion of generation upon generation of people. All kinds of person - from kings and queens to artists and artisans; from Catholic abbots to puritan ministers; and from famous architects to unknown masons - have left legacies in this place. It is hard to grasp the span of its story: as patrons, my own family's direct association with St. Mary Magdalene, Geddington goes back more than 300 years, so it is humbling to think that this is less than one-third of the time since the church was founded!

A few short histories and guides to this wonderful building have been written before, but there has not so far been an attempt to create a comprehensive account of its history, art and architecture alongside the various people, beliefs, and influences, both local and national, that have helped shape it. In a period where there is, perhaps, less understanding of the Christian Church and its central place in our nation's history than at any previous time, this new work is a very timely reminder of the priceless riches we risk losing if we fail to understand and care for our heritage.

For that reason alone, this book is worth having but, for anyone with a more than passing interest, it provides a wealth of detail and a few mysteries waiting to be solved. Boughton House and Estate have been intimately associated with Geddington for centuries, so I'm especially delighted that Crispin Powell and the Buccleuch Archive have been able to provide several items that give extra colour to particular features, episodes and actions that form part of the story. I hope you will enjoy visiting this magical place and salute John Bennett whose book will help you travel back through the centuries of devotion lavished on it by our ancestors.

The Duke of Buccleuch
Patron of St. Mary Magdalene, Geddington

For Christians, 'the Church' means the body of believers rather than any particular building; but nobody can visit an ancient church and fail to feel the presence of the many thousands of people for whom it framed their weekly routines. And so it is with St. Mary Magdalene, Geddington, where the very stones seem to be trying to speak to us of past people and events – if only we could find the language to understand.

Every Vicar seems to have been captivated – as I have most certainly been – not just by the beauty and heritage of this church, but also by the special place it holds in the affections of Geddingtonians. So I feel a special responsibility, not just to safeguard this precious building, but to ensure that knowledge and understanding of it is passed on to everyone and spread widely in surrounding communities and beyond.

I am therefore delighted that a grant from the National Lottery Heritage Fund has enabled us not only to carry out long-needed conservation work to one of the great glories of the church - our medieval reredos – but to mount a programme of heritage interpretation and education work, of which this Guide Book forms a part.

I do hope you enjoy visiting this lovely church and find time to reflect on what it has meant to so many of our ancestors down the centuries; on what it means to you and your family; and on what this place will mean to our descendants in the centuries to come. We are but the latest stewards in a long line of people entrusted with its care. It is our responsibility to pass it on, together with the knowledge of its past, in good shape to the next generation. This Guide Book is part of that effort. By buying it and encouraging others to visit, you will be playing your part in helping that to happen. Thank you. With every blessing,

Rev. Gillian Gamble
Priest-in Charge, St. Mary Magdalene, Geddington

VISITOR INFORMATION

ACCESS & OPENING TIMES

The church is approached from Grafton Road via steps through the churchyard gate. Wheelchair access is available via Church Path, which is near the junction of Grafton Road and Wood Street, or from the top of Church Hill

The church is normally open every day (including weekends) between 10am and 3pm, although there will sometimes be things happening in the church, such as weddings, funerals or other activities and events. Please check our website for details, especially if coming from a distance.

Church Services are normally held on Sunday mornings at 9.45am and on Friday mornings at 10am – please see our website for details. Services normally last upto an hour.

GUIDED TOURS

If you would like a guided tour of the church, either for yourself or for an organised group, we will be happy to arrange this for you - just contact us via email or use the '*Book a Tour*' facility on our website, giving as much notice as possible please.

CONTACTING US

Address: St. Mary Magdalene, Church Hill, Geddington, NN14 1AH
What3Words: ///sketches.acquaint.pose
Email: geddingtonweekley@gmail.com
Web: http://geddingtonchurch.org.uk/
Facebook: www.facebook.com/StMaryMagdalenechurch
Phone: 01536 742200 (Vicarage)
[Please note the Vicar may not always be able to reply quickly to messages left]

ACKNOWLEDGEMENTS

This book could not have been written without the collaboration, assistance, and support of many people. The research of past generations of scholars forms the bedrock, most of whom are well-known including, for example, William Dugdale, John Bridges, Richard Gough, Nikolas Pevsner, Bruce Bailey, Bridget Cherry, Alexander Thompson, and Paul Barnwell. As so often for authors in this digital age, I have also resorted to *Wikipedia* for background or contextual material on several topics, with some adapted passages finding their way into a few sections, though none of them are specific to Geddington church.

Local historians have given invaluable service by drawing together and presenting older material for a modern audience and providing much-needed context, as well as by bringing the story up to date - none more so than the late Christopher Markham, whose 1899 book drawing on and supplementing the researches of Rev. T.C.B. Cornwell remains essential reading for anyone interested in the history of Geddington and its Church.

Other local historians have each added crucial pieces to the jigsaw puzzle, notably through the published works of Monica Rayne, Melvyn Hopkins, Burl Bellamy, Vic Crouse, and Rev. Thomas Woolfenden. I am most especially indebted to Melvyn Hopkins, not only because his *Diary of a Village 1086-1914* took all the sweat out of researching local newspaper and royal archive sources quoted here; but also for his generous gift of many photographs he took during the 1980s, and for passing on an academic paper written by PJ Ellis in 1986 on the architectural development of the church, which contains some details and insights not found elsewhere. A full list of the sources consulted in the writing of this book is given at the end.

The help and support provided by a number of individuals has been at least as important as published sources, because they have added a considerable amount of previously unpublished material that gives a book like this more colour and interest. In particular I am most grateful to Crispin Powell, Archivist to the Duke of Buccleuch who, in addition to researching and providing some delightful items from the Duke's extensive archive, has given generously of his time in reading and commenting on various iterations of this book, to its great benefit. I am also much indebted to Vic Crouse, who, in addition to being the author of his work on King John's connections with Geddington, *The Magna Carta King*, kindly let me have an extensive set of notes compiled by the late Rev. Richard Dorrington, together with his researches into the Launcelyn family and a copy of an aerial photograph of the site of the former palace. Another hugely helpful person has been Jim Harker who, as well as providing me with copies of several of Edward Bradley's sketches and paintings (including his brother Trevor's copy of 'Old Stumpy') and material collected over many years by his late father, Matthew Harker, has been an immense source of encouragement and support that has helped make the task of writing this book so enjoyable.

I am also most grateful to several people who have helped with specific items of information and with their thoughts and recollections. These include the Church's architect/surveyor, John Barker, Karen Morrissey and Mackenzie Higgins of Hirst Conservation Ltd., Bryony Dorrington, Brian and Margaret Leaton, Anthony Lawton, Kam and Karen Caddell, and Edward Coulson for his transcriptions of Geddington Manorial Court Rolls. Lastly, and not least, I am grateful to Prof. David Stocker for his expertise in relation to the dating of the reredos and thoughts on its provenance.

Whilst this book would not have been possible without all these contributions, any errors, omissions, or other deficiencies are entirely my own. Whatever shortcomings there may be, however, I hope that this book will nevertheless provide anyone who reads it, regardless of their previous level of knowledge, with some enjoyment and fresh insights into this lovely old building, where so many generations have found solace, joy and a deep connection with both God and their neighbours.

John Bennett
April 2024

Introduction

St. Mary Magdalene
Geddington

Most experts tell us that the original stone Geddington Church dates from sometime between AD 800[1] and 970. The later date seems more likely since this was a very turbulent time in English history. Between 865 and 875 the 'Great Heathen Army' led by 'Ivar the Boneless' had overrun all the English kingdoms except Wessex, and for decades Geddington was surrounded by Danish-held towns, including Kettering (Cytringan), Northampton, Leicester and Stamford. It was not until 942 that English control was firmly re-established over the area, enabling a mid-10th Century revival of Christian worship to spread rapidly.

The church was probably a 'daughter' church of St. Andrew, Brigstock, and indeed was dedicated to St. Andrew[2] for roughly the next 600 years. Parts of the original church stand to this day – evident in still-visible corner-stones, lines left scarred into walls by steeply-sloping roofs; a blocked-up window; and triangle-headed arcading on what were once outside walls.

St. Andrew, Geddington (as it then was) gained in size and importance in the high medieval period as it was closely associated with a royal hunting lodge (later a castle or palace) that once stood just north of the church. When Edward I's Queen, Eleanor of Castile, died at Harby near Lincoln in December 1290, the cortege bearing her body stopped at Geddington on its way to London - a measure of its significance. The King commanded that stone crosses be built at each of the 12 overnight resting-places, and Geddington's cross, built in 1294-95, is the best-preserved of only 3 Eleanor crosses to survive.

Whether due to neglect or the Black Death of 1348-49 (or both) the royal palace was a ruin by 1374; and responsibility for the church had passed in 1357 from the Crown to nearby Pipewell Abbey, whose monks had custody of the church until the suppression of the monastery in 1538.

Figure 1: Geddington Church in winter
Photo by KC Evans Photography

Major alterations and additions were made to the church building in each of the 12th to 15th centuries and we can see the evolution of English church architecture written in the stones – from Saxon arcading; the massive walls and rounded arches of the Norman period; the elegant arches and windows of the Early English Gothic phase, through to the later refinements of the 14th and 15th Centuries, seen in the upper clerestory windows, the tower and the reredos.

Although the church structure was essentially complete

---

1 See *Anglo-Saxon Architecture*. By H.M. and J. Taylor, (1965), pp 248-50, which dates the Nave to between 800 and 950. NMR, NBR No. 107318, suggests an early eleventh-Century date.

2 *The Parish Churches and Religious Houses of Northamptonshire : Their Dedications, Altars, Images and Lights*. By R. M. Serjeantson, MA. F.S.A. and the Rev. Henry Isham Longden, M.A. in Archaeological Journal Vol LXX No. 277 (March 1913) p 326. See also *Transactions of the Leicestershire Archaeological and Historical Society Vol. X: Notes on Buildings visited by Leicestershire Archaeological Society in June 1907* (led by Prof. A.H. Thompson), p. 157. Also *The Architectural Development of Geddington Church*, PJ Ellis (1986)

by the mid-1400s, there have been numerous superficial changes over the succeeding 600 years, many of which have been influenced by changes in the religious life of the church – most notably the break with Rome in the 1530s. The church we see today is highly unusual in still having three Chancel Screens and has gained some wonderful artwork in its windows and monuments. Although lacking the colour of its medieval plasterwork, the church's bare stonework reveals to us many of the past structural changes, so that we literally have a story – a very complex story - written in its stones.

Whilst Queen Eleanor is the best-known person associated with the church, there have been many other fascinating characters whose lives have touched, or been touched by, this place – including a mysterious medieval priest, prestigious architects, larger-than-life vicars, and people whose untold stories lie behind cold stone memorials waiting to be discovered.

So, let us begin our story.

THE SETTING OF THE CHURCH

Occupying an elevated position in the heart of Geddington, the church has been a dominant feature of the village landscape since Saxon times. Located on the road from Stamford to Oxford, and set within the ancient Rockingham Forest with its plentiful deer and boar, Geddington's royal palace just north of the church became a favourite retreat of Plantagenet kings from Henry I to Edward I.

The church is immediately surrounded by its churchyard, and a small village green backed by the south-western wall to the churchyard provides an attractive setting for the southern approach and entrance to the site. To its southwest, the church overlooks the Eleanor Cross (Scheduled Ancient Monument and Grade I Listed). Dating from 1294-95, this is the best-preserved and finest of the three surviving original crosses. At its base is the Conduit House[3] over a well reputedly used since the Roman period and, until the mid-19th Century, the village stocks stood next to the cross, where lawbreakers would be subjected to public humiliation and ridicule at the hub of village life. The church is often pictured with the cross in the foreground.

Not far from the church and cross, a 13th Century stone bridge that probably owes its existence to Geddington's

Figure 2: Geddington Cross by Edward Bradley: dedicated to his sponsor, Duchess Elisabeth Buccleuch

royal patronage crosses the River Ise. There are also many fine stone buildings from the late and post-medieval period along the route of West Street and Grafton Road to the south of the church, including the Old School[4], Church Farmhouse, and several other houses on Church Hill and Bakehouse Hill. Geddington Priory[5], dating from 1588 with 17th Century additions lies south-east of the church across Grafton Road.

The wider landscape around Geddington is framed by Boughton House (a seat of the Duke of Buccleuch and Queensbury) with its park and gardens; by the higher ground of Geddington Chase (a substantial remnant of the medieval Rockingham Forest); and swathes of attractive rolling and fertile farmland still mostly held by Boughton Estates. The church sits as a visual and historical focal point in this historic and beautiful landscape.

---

3 The Conduit House also forms part of the Scheduled Ancient Monument designation.

4 The Old School was designed by Benjamin Ferrey, an important London architect.

5 A private residence.

INTRODUCTION

THE STRUCTURE OF THE CHURCH

In terms of its structure, if not all its internal finishes and monuments, St. Mary Magdalene, Geddington was substantially complete some 200 years before the English Reformation of the 16th Century, with relatively superficial changes occurring thereafter. It is therefore a building whose essential features would have been recognised by our medieval ancestors.

ARCHITECTURAL STYLES

The church bears witness to the evolution of architectural styles over roughly 500 years – styles heavily influenced by advances in building technology and artistic trends across western Europe, with five commonly-recognised styles identifiable over this time, all of which can be found in St. Mary Magdalene, Geddington (dates are approximate only):

Saxon (597-1066): Characterised by semicircular arches, in this style doorways are usually tall and narrow. Windows usually have small external openings but are deeply splayed through to the inside. Walls are usually no more than 75cm thick. Herringbone stonework can be found in the late Saxon/early Norman period. At Geddington, there are several Saxon features, including a blocked-up window in the Nave, and triangle-headed arcading in the North Aisle.

Norman (1066-1189): Sometimes known as 'Romanesque', the most obvious characteristic of this style is its reliance on sheer bulk. Everything is larger, more solid, and carries with it an air of permanence compared with earlier Saxon work. It has semicircular arches, deeply recessed doorways, thick walls, massive round pillars, and ornaments such as zigzag moulding and bird & animal forms. The bulky rounded arches and columns of the northern arcade are good examples of this style.

Early English (1189-1307): The first of the three Gothic periods, in this style rounded arches gave way to lighter, pointed arches in windows, doorways and arcades. Sometimes called "Lancet" and "First Pointed" style, the key features are pointed arches, four-sided ribbed vaults, lancet windows (tall and narrow with a pointed arch at the top) and clustered shafts of tall, narrow piers replacing the massive rounded ones of the Norman style. At Geddington, this is evident in the quatrefoil piers and pointed arches of the southern arcade, for example.

Decorated (1307-1377): The simple geometric shapes of the Early English period gave way to complex curves; the ogee arch being the most obvious. The ogee combines a convex and a concave curve in the same arch. This double-curve is the basis of most of the curvilinear tracery which became so popular during the 14th Century. This style also features wider windows giving better lighting and richly-coloured stained glass. The magnificent reredos is an example of this style at Geddington.

Perpendicular (1377-1530): As its name suggests, the chief characteristic of Perpendicular architecture is the emphasis on strong vertical lines, seen most markedly in window tracery and wall panelling. Roof vaulting became elaborate and ornate, with a multitude of vaulting ribs spreading outwards in a fan shape, ornamented with pendants and cross-ribs that served a purely decorative function. Very large windows with elaborate tracery are a particular feature of this style. Though less elaborate, Geddington's upper clerestory windows are of this period.

MATERIALS

The Saxon elements of the church are constructed largely of stone rubble, except at its quoins (corner-stones) which are in larger, shaped, blocks. The rubble is probably of local origin, whilst the quoins may have come from the quarries at Barnack (Cambridgeshire), some 20 miles to the north[6]. Stone for the Norman and later building work came from Stanion[7], some 3 miles north. Both Barnack and Stanion stone are limestones. Weldon stone was also probably used in work from the mid-13th Century onwards, and some later repairs were carried out using local ironstone from Geddington's quarries, perhaps for reasons of economy. The earliest roofs were most likely made of thatch, although it's possible that Collyweston slates (from the village of that name some 18 miles north of Geddington) were used. Such slates may be seen on today's porch

---

6   *The Architectural Development of Geddington Church* (1986) - a draft of an unpublished academic paper by PJ Ellis given by its author to Mervyn Hopkins, who in turn kindly gave it to the author of this book.

7   Morton, *A Natural History of Northants*, p.110 quoted in Victoria County History of Northamptonshire Ed. By Rev RM Serjeantson & Sir WRD Adkins (1906), Vol. II p. 295

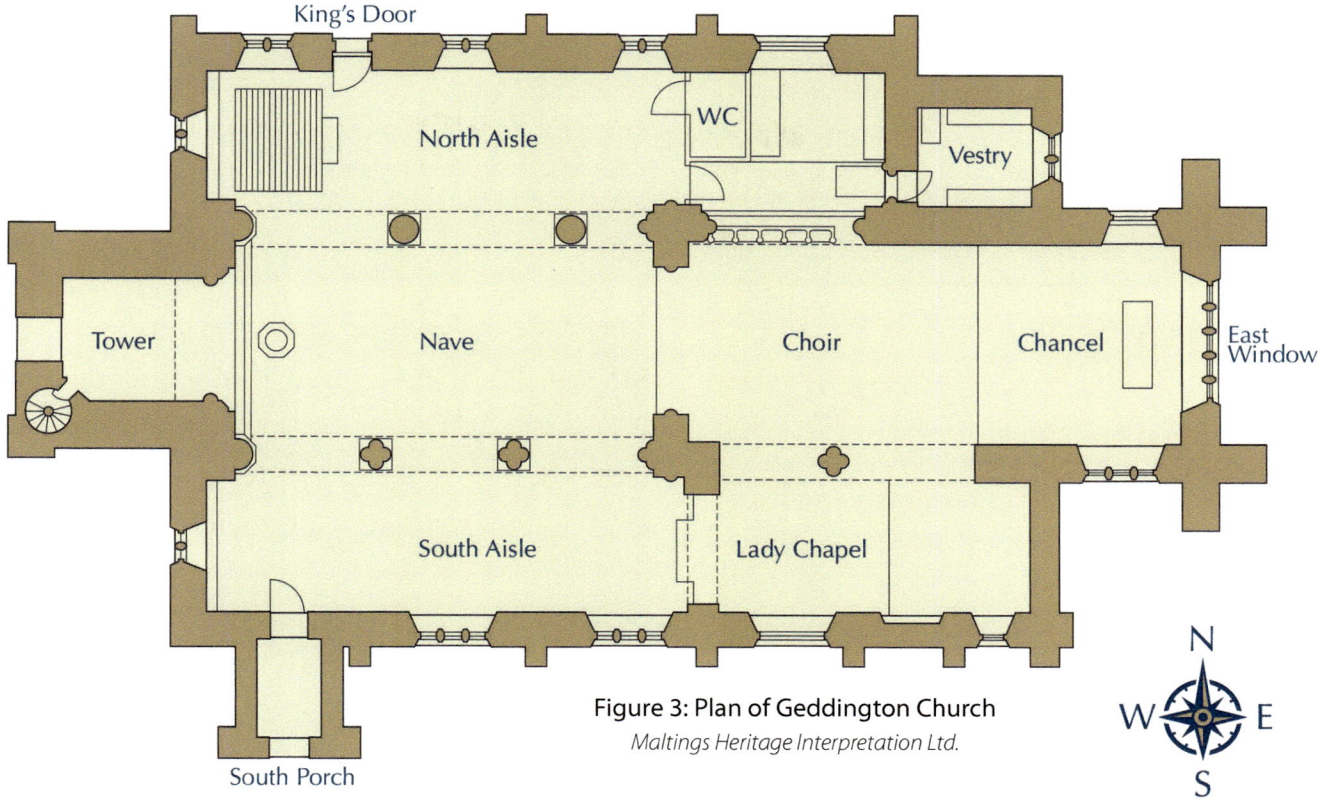

Figure 3: Plan of Geddington Church
Maltings Heritage Interpretation Ltd.

THE LAYOUT OF THE CHURCH

The earliest churches were based on the plan of the pagan Roman basilica, or hall of justice. The plan generally included –

a. a nave, or hall, with a flat timber roof, in which the crowd gathered;

b. one or two side aisles flanking the nave and separated from it by a row of regularly spaced columns used for processions;

c. a narthex, or entrance vestibule at the west end, which was reserved for penitents and unbaptised believers; and

d. an apse of either semicircular or rectangular design, located at the east end and reserved for the clergy.

This basic pattern gradually evolved over the centuries to include a Chancel, sanctuary, side chapel(s), a Vestry (where the clergy and choir put on their robes) and an entrance porch. An apse is still often found at the eastern end of a Chancel; and less commonly, a narthex is sometimes found at the western end of a nave.

Geddington Church, as with all churches, has several distinct areas within it, each of which is known by a specific name, and each having a particular origin, purpose, and significance. *Figure 3* shows the principal areas of the church. The length of the nave and Chancel together is 28m, with the base of the tower adding a further 3.5m. The north-south width of the nave with both aisles is 17m.

St. Mary's, like almost all traditional churches, is aligned from west to east with the high altar at the eastern end. This probably originated with the practice of praying eastwards towards Jerusalem. It is possible that the original Saxon church at Geddington was cruciform (cross-shaped) with small side wings, each with its own entrance, to the north and south.

Part I: A Tour of the Church

THE SOUTH PORCH

We enter the church via the South Porch, which dates from 1857 and was designed by George Gilbert Scott[8]. Built in stone with a steeply-pitched roof of Collyweston slates, it has stone bench seats and small leaded windows on each side which were glazed in 1908, having previously been open[9]. The porch once housed a triangular timber buffet designed to hold the 'Dallington bread' – loaves provided according to the Will of Sir Robert Dallington (q.v.).

The porch leads to the main south door (**Fig. 5**), which is an exact replica[10] of the previous door, set in an arch with 13th Century[11] stone moulding. An earlier 16th Century porch once had a room above known as a ***parvise***[12], used for various purposes, including possibly the occasional overnight stay of a curate or a visiting priest. Edward Bradley's sketch (**Fig. 4**) shows a more Romanesque-style entrance, suggesting the Tudor porch had been re-built or modified sometime in the 18th Century.

The blocked-up Tudor archway that once led to the parvise can still be seen immediately behind the entrance door (to the right of the door as you stand inside facing outwards); and a blocked-up squint can also still be seen on the internal wall above the entrance door, that would have given a view into the body of the church for the occupant above.

In medieval times, the porch was not considered part of the church, and penitents - who were not allowed inside - could do penance and receive absolution there. Just inside the

Figure 4: The Old South Porch in 1847 by Edward Bradley
Courtesy of Jim Harker

Figure 5: The South Door.
Photo by M. Hopkins

church door to the right as you enter, there is a recess that would have held a stoup (normally a stone bowl) for the holy water with which people crossed themselves on entry. The brass stoup found there today is modern. Immediately behind the door to your left as you enter is a brass plaque inscribed:

"THE FLOODLIGHTING OF THE TOWER AND SPIRE WAS DEDICATED ON NOVEMBER 7TH 1993. TO THE GLORY OF GOD AND AS A THANKSGIVING FOR THE LIFE OF HENRY D. KNIGHT 1905-1992."

---

8   Scott was later knighted.

9   *Kettering Guardian* 24 April 1908.

10   This replica dates from 1857. Source: Correspondence between Rev. WMH Church and the Duke of Buccleuch [Buccleuch Archive]

11   A.H. Thompson, 1907 (op. cit.)

12   Originally meaning an open space in front of a church, '***parvise***' later came to mean a room over the porch of a church.

THE NORTH AISLE

From the South Door we now make our way across the Nave to the North Aisle on the other side of the church. The word *aisle* comes from the Latin 'ala' meaning *wing*, and an aisle is a sideways extension of the Nave, from which it is separated by an 'arcade' of arches. Aisles were built originally for processional purposes, and often housed small side chapels. At Geddington, the North Aisle dates from about 1150 to 1170, and probably owes its origin to the patronage of Henry III, who in 1129 had established a hunting lodge that later became a 'palace' or 'castle' immediately to the north of the church. In pre-Reformation times, the North and South Aisles would have held the 14 'Stations of the Cross' in the form of either carvings or paintings mounted on the walls, but there is now no trace of them at Geddington.

SAXON STONEWORK

Once into the North Aisle, turn and look upwards above the arcade of Norman arches, where we can see triangle-headed arcading (*Fig. 6*) on what would have been the external face of the Saxon church. Below this, we can see the external stonework of a blocked-up Saxon window: look for the much wider inner face when we move into the Nave. And, at the junction of the wall with the modern timber screen, we can see large 'long and short' stones that once formed the north-east corner of the Saxon Nave

THE KING'S DOOR

Turning back to look at the north wall, set within an opening, we see a timber door stranded approx. 1.3 metres above the floor level: the steps were removed in 1855.

Known to this day as 'The King's Door', it once gave access to and from the former Royal palace. The external stonework suggests that the medieval door was probably set at a lower level, and there have clearly been several alterations to the entrance over the centuries.

The doorway was 're-arched' in 1857 (see *Appendix 6*), and behind the organ there remains a piece of carved masonry (*Fig. 7*) approx. 30cm wide that may have been removed when this work was carried out. Of Norman date, it shows typical saltire-cross motifs of the same design as the frieze around the tympanum of the north doorway of St. Botolph's, Barton Seagrave.

Figure 6: Triangle-headed Saxon arcading in the North Aisle

PART I: A TOUR OF THE CHURCH

Figure 7: Norman masonry with saltire motifs, held by the late MJ Harker

THE TOWNDROWS' WALL PLAQUE

Immediately to the right of the King's Door is a modern memorial plaque that reads:

Remember ALFRED TOWNDROW and his sister MARJORIE who in 1985 made a generous bequest to this Church.

Alfred was born on 8 October 1900, and later took over his father's harness-maker's and saddler's business at 51 High Street in Kettering, which he ran for most of his life. He also made the crib that is still used in the church today. He died on 23 December 1985. His sister Marjorie was born on 23 June 1902 and taught for many years at St. Mary's School in Kettering. She died on 23 September 1978. They both lived at 35 New Road in Geddington for many years, and their extremely generous bequest enabled several major repairs and improvements to be carried out in the following years.

TRESHAM LEDGER STONES

To the right of the King's Door, further along the north wall, we see two very large stone slabs standing vertically against the wall. According to a letter dated 1809[13], they were once located in the floor of the Chancel, but were moved to the North Aisle in 1857 and later raised vertically against the wall in order to accommodate the Mulsho Brass and Tresham Alabaster (see below) that were removed from St Faith's Church, Newton in 1974. They can be glimpsed very faintly in Bradley's painting of the church in the early 19th Century (see the cover picture).

They display the arms of the Tresham family, one branch of which had their manor house at Newton, and commemorate Maurice Tresham of Geddington (who gave the screen between the South Aisle and the Lady Chapel) and his wife Muriel.

The inscriptions are shown below:

> reliquie maurith tresham
> [Crest]
> ostentat clipeus foliis languenti bus herbam
> qua refeunt vitam signa caduca meam at
> cum iustitia phabus radiaueret orbem herba
> haec recrescens uere perennis erit *
>
> + + +
>
> So good kind courteous husband her ffriend
> that earth and heaven about him did contend
> earth was desirous here to have him rest
> heaven was ambitious here to have him blest
> to please them both himself he thus divides
> on earth his corps in heaven his soule resides
> Anno domini 1646

> here lyeth interred
> the body of meuriel
> tresham wife of mau
> rice tresham of ged
> dington esq. who de
> ceased   day of
> september

* Latin Translation: The remains of Maurice Tresham. The shield bears the limp leaves that refresh my fading life-signs and with justice its fruit will spread around the world and this plant's re-growth will truly be perennial.

Many members of the Tresham family were Roman Catholics. If Maurice did hold secret Catholic sympathies, we might speculate that this Latin inscription is expressing a belief that, 'with justice' the 'true faith' symbolised by the limp-leaved trefoil of the family crest would be rejuvenated and its fruit spread.

---

13   *Letter from Edmond Vialls dated Nov. 1809.* [Northamptonshire Record Office]. Vialls was a Solicitor, a partner in law firm Ironsides, Ray & Vialls of Oakham.

Figure 8: The Mulsho Brass (1400).
Rubbing by Robert Downing, Monumental Brass Society

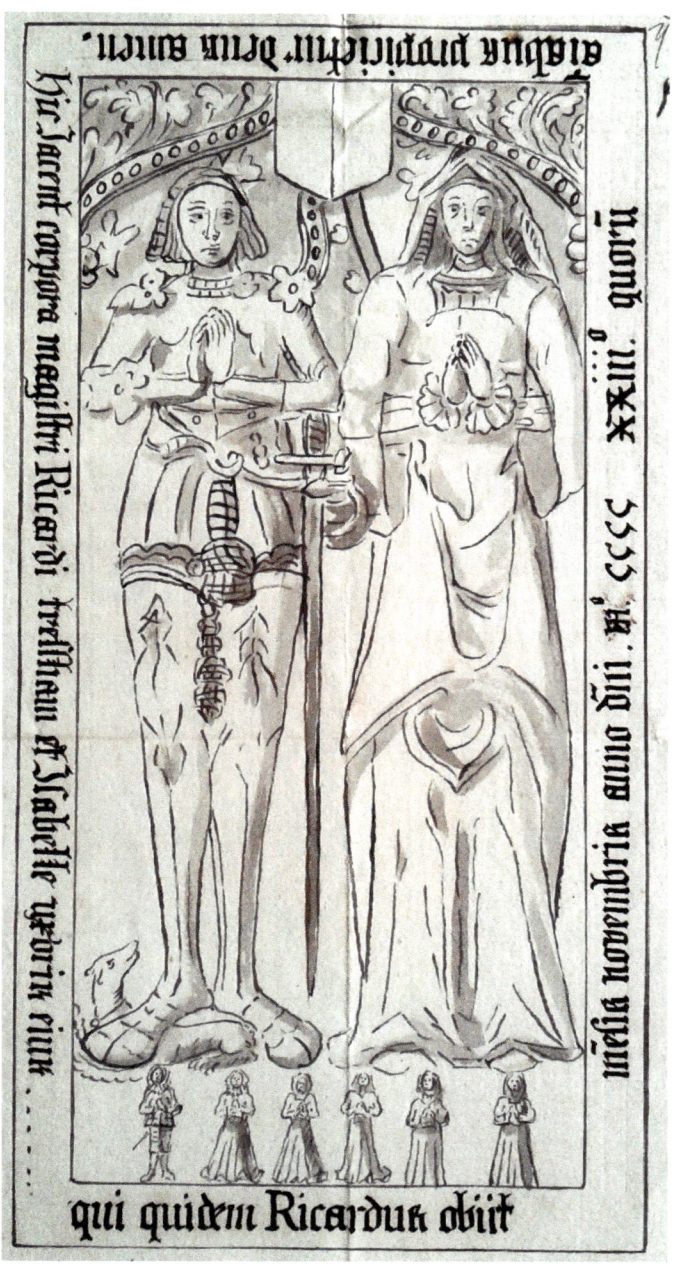

Figure 9: The Tresham Alabaster (1533).
The Buccleuch Heritage Trust

THE MULSHO BRASS

Looking down now, we find the first of two memorials set into the floor that came from Newton Church. It is a stone slab (Fig. 8) inlaid with exquisitely engraved London brass and known as the Mulsho Brass, which once lay at the Chancel step of St. Faith's Church, Newton. Around its edge is inscribed on brass:

Hic iacet Johannes Mulsho Armiger qui obit die mensis Anno d'ni mill,o CCCC Et Johanna uxor eius que obiit Nonas Maii Anno d'ni millo CCCC Quor aiabs picitur Deus. Amen

[Here lies John Mulsho, Armiger, who died on the ? day of the month of the year 1400, and also his wife Johanna who died on the Nones (7th) of May, of the year 1400. Wherefore God is seen. Amen]

NOTE: 'armiger' literally means "arms-bearer". In high and late medieval England, it meant an esquire attendant upon a knight, but bearing his own unique armorial device.

The female figure of St. Faith inside the cross wears a crown, has a halo and holds a gridiron. Saint Faith was a young girl from Agen in France who c.AD290 was tortured to death with a red-hot brazier.

Inscribed on her right side is: **S'ca fides** [St. Faith]; and on her left side: **virgo + Mr** [virgin and Martyr].

PART I: A TOUR OF THE CHURCH

At the foot of the cross, a man with cropped hair kneels alongside a woman wearing a veil and mitten sleeves. From the man's mouth a brass label (signifying prayer) rises to the saint, inscribed:

𝕱𝖎𝖉𝖊𝖘 𝖛𝖎𝖗𝖌𝖔 𝖕𝖎𝖆 𝖋𝖎𝖘 𝖒𝖎𝖍𝖎𝖎 𝖕'𝖕𝖎𝖈𝖎𝖆 [Faith, o pious virgin, please make propitiation for me].

And from the woman's mouth:

𝕸𝖆𝖗𝖙𝖎𝖗 𝖌𝖗𝖆𝖙𝖆 𝕯𝖊𝖎 𝖙𝖚 𝖒𝖊𝖒𝖔𝖗 𝖊𝖘𝖙𝖔 𝖒𝖊𝖎 [Martyr, by the grace of God may you remember me].

THE TRESHAM ALABASTER

The second monument, from the Nave of St. Faith's Church, Newton, is an alabaster slab depicting a knight with cropped hair, wearing plated armour over a coat of mail, and a very large sword by his side, his head inclined on a helmet and a dog at his feet. His lady is by his side, wearing a mantle and kirtle with sleeves puffed and slashed ending in something like 18th Century ruffles. Under their feet are the figures of one son and five daughters with their pet dog. The sword and certain other features appear black – being the residue of bitumen once used to fix decoration into the slab. The drawing (Fig. 9) depicts the slab in its original state. We know from 18th Century drawings[14] that the substantial cracks now seen occurred at some time before about 1780.

The inscription around the edge reads:

𝕳𝖎𝖈 𝖎𝖆𝖈𝖊𝖓𝖙 𝖈𝖔𝖗𝖕𝖔𝖗𝖆 𝖒𝖆𝖌𝖓𝖎𝖋𝖎𝖈𝖎 𝕽𝖎𝖈𝖆𝖗𝖉𝖎 𝕿𝖗𝖊𝖘𝖍𝖆𝖒 𝖊𝖙 𝕴𝖘𝖆𝖇𝖊𝖑𝖑𝖊 𝖚𝖝𝖔𝖗𝖎𝖘 𝖊𝖏𝖚𝖘 𝕼𝖚𝖎 𝖖𝖚𝖎𝖉𝖊𝖒 𝕽𝖎𝖈𝖆𝖗𝖉𝖚𝖘 𝖔𝖇𝖎𝖎𝖙 𝖎𝖓𝖊𝖘𝖎𝖆 𝕹𝖔𝖇𝖊𝖒𝖇𝖗𝖎𝖆 𝖆𝖓𝖓𝖔 𝖉'𝖓𝖎 𝕸𝕮𝕮𝕮𝕮𝖃𝖃𝖃𝕴𝕴𝕴 𝖖𝖚𝖔𝖗𝖚̃ 𝖆𝖙𝖆𝖇𝖚𝖘 𝖕𝖗𝖔𝖕𝖎𝖈𝖎𝖊𝖙𝖚𝖗 𝖉𝖊𝖚𝖘. 𝕬𝖒𝖊𝖓

[Here lie the bodies of the great Richard Tresham and Isabelle his wife. The said Richard fell asleep in November of the year 1433, by which God shall be justified. Amen]. NOTE: Historical records tell us that the date 1433 was wrongly-inscribed and should be 1533.

AN ARCHAEOLOGICAL INVESTIGATION

The graves under the memorials removed from St. Faith's, Newton, were excavated in 1970, and in 1998 Leicester University carried out a detailed analysis of the exhumed remains.

Together with historical and genealogical research, this identified the bones examined as belonging to Joan Mulsho (died c.1400); Richard Tresham (d. 1533); Isabelle Tresham (d. 1533); Margaret Tresham (1538 – 1604); a female, probably either Dorothy or Bridget Tresham, daughter of Maurice Tresham who gave the 1618 Chancel screen; and an unidentified infant.

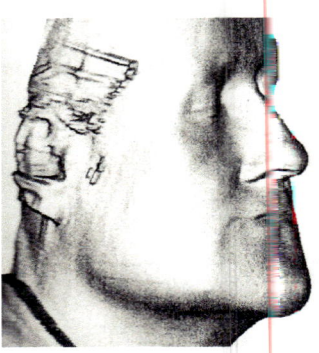

Figure 10: Isabelle Tresham (d. 1533)
facial reconstruction by Leicester University.

These remains were given a Christian burial in Geddington churchyard. The University also carried out computer-generated facial reconstructions from the skulls of Isabelle (*Fig. 10*) and her great granddaughter, Dorothy/Bridget.

THE ORGAN

To the left of the King's Door is the organ. Installed in 1867 at a cost of 150 guineas[15], it was built by Bevingtons of London, and was enlarged in 1900[16]. Originally located in what is now the Choir Vestry, it was moved to its present position in 2006. Two brass plates on the organ's keyboard cover are inscribed:

"This organ was the gift of Mr John Brown to the Parish of Geddington, November 10th, 1867"

and below it:

"It was enlarged and dedicated on Easter Day 1900 to the glory of God in memory of the Diamond Jubilee".

The relocation of the organ is commemorated with a third brass plate on the southern side, reading:

"2006. This organ was restored thanks to the efforts of many in this community, inspired by a generous bequest from Margaret McLaughlin".

WINDOWS

The one easily-visible window in the North Aisle is, like those in the South Aisle, of 15th Century origin, but an 1845 sketch by Edward Bradley shows what appears to be an 18th Century arched window of greater width in the north

---

14   E.g. see p194 of *Sepulchral monuments in Great Britain: applied to illustrate the history of families, manners, habits, and arts, at the different periods from the Norman Conquest to the seventeenth Century* by Richard Gough Vol. II, Part II, (1796)

15   *Northampton Mercury* (16 November 1867). Mr. A Bevington himself played the organ at the dedication service.

16   *Kettering Guardian* (13 April 1900).

wall alongside the organ's present position. A copy of this drawing is held privately within the parish. However, Tillemans' drawing (*Fig. 67*) of the church's north prospect (10 July 1719) does not depict such a window, but rather one similar to the others, so it appears to have been fitted in the 18th Century, as its style suggests. This was, presumably, replaced by the present (plain glass) window in 1855-57. A similar window lies behind the organ.

A 17TH CENTURY GALLERY

At one time there was an "open-fronted gallery" bearing the date 1630 situated in the North Aisle. We can only speculate on the size, nature, and purpose of this gallery, but it may have been for musicians, or perhaps it simply provided seating for members of the congregation. As it was still extant in 1809[17], it was presumably removed as part of the changes made by GG Scott in 1855-57.

THE NORTH CHAPEL

From the North Aisle we move through the door into the area behind the modern timber screen, which now houses a WC (installed in 2009) and a small room used as a Choir Vestry and for storage. Originally part of the 12th Century North Aisle, this area became a side chapel and was probably larger than we see today. It is thought that, in medieval times, the chapel may have been dedicated to St. John the Baptist – e.g. the Will of William Downhall (1504), asks for his *body to be buried in the chapell of Seynt John Baptiste in the church of Geydyngton*.[18] It is separated from the Chancel by a single arch of very similar design to those on the south side of the Chancel and in the South Aisle, suggesting it is from the same mid-13th Century period, perhaps having been rebuilt from one of earlier date[19]. After the Reformation, the chapel was sponsored by the Maydwell family of Geddington Priory, but fell into dereliction[20] and was demolished, before being re-built in its present form in 1857.

Figure 11: Trefoil window above the Vestry door

TREFOIL WINDOW

Above the door to the Clergy Vestry is a trefoil stained-glass window (*Fig. 11*) that, according to Markham[21] was the gift of Mrs. Sophia Sarah Sutton in memory of her husband, Rev. John Lucas Sutton (Jnr.). However, since Mrs. S.S. Sutton pre-deceased her husband, her gift was probably in memory of her father-in-law who was, rather confusingly, also Rev. John Lucas Sutton, the Vicar of Weekley from 1818 to 1870[22]. There is a faint inscription in the gold circle of glass but only the following words are legible:

In memory of john

It is believed that there was a pump organ in this chapel before the Bevington organ (see above) was installed here in 1867. Its position is marked on George Gilbert Scott's 1852 plan (*Fig.71*).

---

17   A letter dated Nov. 1809 from Edmond Vialls (op. cit.)

18   *The Parish Churches and Religious Houses of Northamptonshire : Their Dedications, Altars, Images and Lights*, p 326. (op. cit.)

19   A.H. Thompson, 1907 (op. cit.)

20   According to the Faculty petition seeking authority for the 1856-57 re-ordering (Northamptonshire County Record Office). It was clearly no longer standing by 1719, and the arch was blocked up when Peter Tillemans' drew his 'north prospect' of the church (*Fig.67*).

21   *The History and Antiquities of Geddington, Northamptonshire*, by Christopher A. Markham (1899)

22   There had been 3 generations each named Rev. John Lucas Sutton. The last of these – who gave the pulpit to Geddington – became Vicar of St. Andrew's Allesley in Warwickshire, and died in 1915 aged 89. His wife Sophia Sarah died sometime between 1901 and 1911 [details via *Ancestry. com*]

PART I: A TOUR OF THE CHURCH

NORTH CHAPEL MONUMENTS

On the wall near the Clergy Vestry door, to the left of the arch, some 3 to 4 metres above floor level, is an oval-shaped mural monument that reads:

> Beneath Lies the Body of
> Mr Joseph Edmonson
> Who died Septr. ye 21st 1790
> In the 22 year of His Age.

On the floor in front of the Clergy Vestry door is a stone slab inscribed:

> HERE LYETH ELIZABETH
> THE WYFE OF MAVRICE TRESHAM WYDOW OF
> THOMAS CAWOOD ESQUIRE
> WHO DYED BLESSEDLY THE 7 OF AUGUST 1616

Next to this slab is another that reads:

> Here lyeth ye body of Richard Hopkin
> Who departed this Life
> July ye 10th 1690

Another stone slab is inscribed (now all but illegible, but still visible when Markham wrote in 1899):

> Beneath lies the body of
> Mrs. jane campbell
> Who died the 20th of May 1794
> she lived -----
> and
> Richard Lockwood, esq.
> aged   Years

And beside the modern WC compartment is another slab whose inscription is today almost completely illegible but which was recorded by Markham in 1899 as reading:

> ---- e neath
> are deposited the remains of the R ------
> formerly ---
> of --------
> ------- c is R
> who -----
> …ing ----------
> He died ------ -----
> -------- -----
> as a ------ ------

THE CLERGY VESTRY

The Clergy Vestry is normally locked and contains little of interest to the visitor apart from a wardrobe for priests' vestments made of panels taken from old high square pews that were said to be the oldest dated pews in England[23], and which were removed as part of the changes in 1855. Two panels bear the arms of the Tresham and Maydwell families respectively, whilst a third is inscribed:

1602	CHVRCHWARDENS
MINISTER	WILLIAM GLOVER
THOMAS IONES	IHON WHITE

The wardrobe may be viewed by prior arrangement with the Vicar or a churchwarden.

Behind the vestry door there is a disused iron safe which it is thought may originally have been an iron chest purchased in 1814[24] for the storage of parish registers, and which was later built into the vestry wall when it was built in 1855-57.

THE NAVE

We now re-trace our steps into the North Aisle and from there move into the central part of the church, called The Nave - a term that comes from *navis*, the Latin word for 'ship', an early Christian symbol of the Church as a whole, though it may also have been suggested by the keel shape of the vaulting seen in many churches. The Nave is the oldest part of Geddington church, dating from around AD970 (possibly earlier), and roughly approximates to the Nave of the original Saxon stone church.

NORTH ARCADE

Positioning ourselves at the back of the Nave, near the Font, we turn to look eastwards into the main body of the church. On our left is an arcade of rounded Norman arches that were inserted when the North Aisle was built around 1170[25], although the only

Figure 12: Tenth Century window above the North Arcade.

Photo by M Hopkins

---

23   Markham (op. cit.) p 20. See also "*The History of Pews*": a paper by John Mason Neale read to the Cambridge Camden Society (Nov. 1841), which noted another pew then in the Nave inscribed TMMM (Thomas and Mary Maydwell) and dated 1604.

24   Recorded in Rev. Richard Dorrington's notes [source unknown, but probably the Churchwarden's accounts]

25   A.H. Thompson (op. cit.)

original Norman column remaining is the westernmost one abutting the tower arch, extensive repairs having been made to the remaining columns and arches in the period 1904-06. Strangely, there are only $2\frac{1}{2}$ arches. This may suggest that, at the time the North Aisle was added, it had been intended to demolish the eastern wall of the Nave in order to extend further eastwards, but that this idea was later abandoned.

Above the arches is the blocked up inner face of a late Saxon splayed window[26] (*Fig. 12*) whose narrower outer face we saw in the North Aisle (see above). In the 15th Century the north and south walls to the Nave and the Chancel were raised and large clerestory ('clear storey') windows in the Perpendicular style, each with plain glass only, were added to admit more light and increase the sense of grandeur.

SOUTH ARCADE

Turning to our right we see another arcade, this time of quatrefoil (four-leaved) piers and double-chamfered pointed arches in the Early English style. These date from about 1260[27], when the South Aisle was built. Forming three complete bays, this suggests that the position of the Nave's eastern (Chancel) wall was by then firmly accepted. We know from a contemporary newspaper report[28] that one of the supporting piers was rebuilt in the renovations of 1855-57, and another pier and the arches appear to have been repaired at that time also, or perhaps in the 1904-06 renovations.

PARISH CHEST

Positioned near the south door at the back of the Nave is a large ancient chest, certainly older than 1619, when it is mentioned in a church survey[29], although its exact age is unknown. Traditionally used for keeping parish registers, accounts, and other records, it was secured with 3 locks so that the Vicar and two churchwardens, each with separate keys, had to be present to open it.

The ancient records that were once held in the chest, including Vestry Meeting Minute Books, Constables'

records, Parish Registers of Baptisms, Weddings and Burials, Enclosure maps and various other diaries and parish records, are now held in the Northamptonshire County Archive and can be viewed by arrangement. Many of the Parish Registers have been digitised and are available online via family history websites.

Figure 13: The Font

THE FONT

In front of steps upto the modern servery at the base of the tower is the Font (*Fig. 13*), where infants are baptised with holy water and anointed with oil as part of a sacramental service in which they are received into the Christian family and their parents and godparents promise to raise them in the faith.

Octagonal in shape, Geddington's Font is lined with lead and sits on a cylindrical shaft on an octagonal base. The cover is of oak with a wrought-iron cross and a central ring on top. Believed to be of medieval origin, it is thought

---

26 Barnwell suggests that it was originally placed lower in the wall and was moved when the arcade was built. [See: *Churches Built for Priests? The Evolution of Parish Churches in Northamptonshire from the Gregorian Reform to the Fourth Lateran Council* by P S Barnwell pub. in *Ecclesiology Today*, January 2004, p12.]

27 A.H. Thompson (op. cit.)

28 *Northampton Mercury*, 7 Nov 1857, describing the extensive works completed in that year.

29 The *Church Survey* of 1619 (Vol. 3)

the Font was 'heavily re-worked'[30] during the changes of 1856-57. The word 'font' comes from the Latin word '*fons*' meaning 'spring'. Every medieval church had a font located near the main entrance in an area known as the 'baptistry' and this was the case at Geddington until it was moved to its present position in the 1960s. Fonts were originally large enough to allow the infant to be fully immersed, but in the Middle Ages it became the practice to baptise by partial immersion or pouring water over the head.

THE EAST WALL OF THE NAVE

Looking upwards above the tall arch that leads to the Chancel, we can see the scars in the stonework indicating the old Saxon roofline which, along with several other ancient features, was revealed when the plasterwork was removed by George Gilbert Scott as part of the major changes in the period 1855-57 (see the builder's estimate in *Appendix 6*).

MEDIEVAL ROOD SCREENS

Still looking upwards and turning to the right to where the Nave's southern wall joins its east wall, we see two oblong openings, one above the other. These were doorways (probably accessed by ladder) leading to the rood loft and beam that existed until their removal in 1558[31]. Geddington had both a 'Stooping Rood'[32] and a 'High Rood' above. We don't know exactly what the Geddington Rood looked like, but *Fig. 14* gives a general indication.

Medieval rood screens were often elaborately decorated,

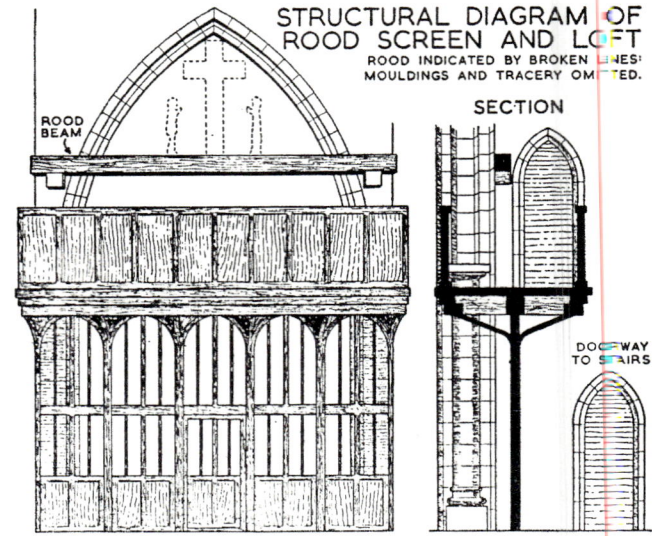

Figure 14: Typical arrangement of a medieval Rood Screen and Loft

and the figures were also sometimes clothed – a practice that goes back at least to the 11th Century (e.g. the Holy Face of Lucca in Italy). Some churches even had wardrobes of clothes and shoes: a bequest was made in 1517 to the coat that belonged to 'the Stooping Rood' at Geddington Church.[33]

The high rood beam probably had a second beam fixed parallel to, and in front of it, with planking between the two beams, which would have been accessed via the higher opening (now blocked up) that can still be seen. The High Rood would also have had a cross with the figures of the Virgin Mary and St. John the Evangelist surmounting it.

A rare example of a surviving English medieval rood

Figure 15: Medieval Rood Loft at St. Margaret's Church in Herefordshire

---

30   Markham (op. cit.)

31   The date of removal is given in the Notes of Rev. Richard Dorrington, former Vicar of Geddington (the source for this date is unknown, but it appears plausible).

32   E.g. Serjeantson & Longden (op. cit.), pp 226 and 326.

33   *'English Church Screens'* by Aymer Vallance (Batsford, 1936) pp 3-4

Figure 16: Painting by Edward Bradley of Anthony Freary's 1794 screen

screen can be found at the remote Herefordshire church of St. Margaret (*Fig. 15*). Originally it would no doubt have been more brightly-coloured as well as having figures of Christ crucified and saints.

The one element of Geddington's medieval rood screen that does survive is the lower part that now sits in an arch between the Lady Chapel and the Chancel.

LATE 18TH CENTURY ROOD

In 1794 a large screen was painted by Anthony Feary on the plasterwork above the Chancel arch, bearing the royal coat of arms and proclaiming The Apostles' Creed, the Lord's Prayer, and the Ten Commandments. It was removed in 1855, but not before a local artist, Edward Bradley, made a drawing of it (*Fig. 16*) that now hangs in the church. Its removal allowed the arch to be raised by 2 metres as part of George Gilbert Scott's major re-ordering[34], which also saw the removal of the 'Tresham Screen' to create an open view through to the Chancel and the High Altar. This change

was inspired by the *Oxford Movement*, that had begun in the 1830s and developed into Anglo-Catholicism. This open aspect lasted 51 years.

THE CHANCEL SCREEN

Designed by the distinguished architect Sydney Gambier-Parry and made of oak carved by Sam Abbot of Geddington from former roof timbers with wrought iron decorative elements, the present screen was installed in June 1908. The original design envisaged a cross mounted on top of the screen, but this was never carried out. Gambier-Parry was also the architect for the major renovations carried out between 1904 and 1906.

---

34   Copies of his re-ordering plan (Fig. 71) are held in the Northamptonshire County Records Office and in the Buccleuch Archive.

PART I: A TOUR OF THE CHURCH

THE PULPIT

To the north of the Chancel arch is the stone pulpit. Constructed in Caen stone, it was given in 1880 by the Rev. John Lucas Sutton Jnr., a former curate in the Parish. In 1908, to accommodate the new Chancel arch screen, the pulpit was moved from its original position within the Chancel arch to its current location on the north-western side. Previously plain panels were also pierced with carvings at this time. Pulpits had been made compulsory in English churches in 1603. An earlier and loftier timber pulpit dating from that period existed in roughly the same position as the present one until it was removed in 1855. It is depicted in Edward Bradley's drawing of the church 'in the early 19th Century' (see the front cover) that hangs in the church.

FRAMED PAINTING OF MARY WITH AN INFANT JESUS

This hangs to the right of the Chancel arch and was presented in 1934 by Hugh and Emily Patrick to commemorate the confirmation of their twin daughters, Mildred and Mabel. It can be seen in the picture of the church as it was in 1986 (*Fig. 18*).

SEATING

In the Saxon and Norman periods there was almost certainly no seating in the Nave. Some church walls had a stone ledge provided for the elderly and infirm (hence: 'the weakest go to the wall') but it is not known if that was the case in Geddington's original Saxon church. The first record of 'seating' at Geddington is in the Will of Henry German (Jarmon) dated 1486, which left money to provide new seating 'throughout the church', though we don't know what the seats were like. That they were 'new' seats suggests there was seating prior to this.

Geddington had 'box pews' at a very early date and certainly by 1601. These were enclosed structures with doors and were normally 'owned' by higher status families who paid for the privilege of this comfort and privacy. Geddington's box pews can be seen in Edward Bradley's painting (see the front cover). Behind the box pews were open-framed benches that most people describe as 'pews'.

All these old pews were swept away in 1855 by GG Scott's renovation scheme, which saw the introduction of rows of framed bench pews made of deal throughout the church, apart from the Chancel. Some of these pews remained in 1986 (*Fig. 18*).

Figure 17: The Mobile Altar

Modern chairs, almost all with small memorial plaques (see *Appendix 4*), form the great bulk of the present-day seating, although a few of the Victorian bench pews remain, one of which bears a brass plate on the reverse inscribed:

> *William George Harbourne*
> 24-6-1928 to 9-8-2006
> Sexton and Chorister
> He loved this Church.

MOBILE ALTAR

The elegant mobile altar (*Fig. 17*) normally sits at the east of the Nave in front of the Chancel arch and is used for most services. It was given in 2016 in memory of Canon Michael Baker by his widow, Margaret, with support from the *Friends of Geddington Church*. The brass plaque on the base reads:

> IN LOVING MEMORY OF
> CANON MICHAEL RH BAKER 1939-2012
>
> A GEDDINGTON LAD RETURNED HOME AND A FAITHFUL PRIEST OF THIS DIOCESE FOR 46 YEARS.
>
> THEN THEY TOLD WHAT HAD HAPPENED ON THE ROAD AND HOW HE HAD BEEN MADE KNOWN TO THEM IN THE BREAKING OF THE BREAD.
> LUKE 24:35

THE CHURCH IN 2000

On the west wall of the Nave and nearby against the Tower arch is a painting presented by Robert Horton to the then Churchwardens, Margaret Leaton and Ken Ryan, in January 2000 (this being during an Interregnum). It depicts the church as it was at the end of the 20th Century – very largely as it is today.

PAINTINGS BY EDWARD BRADLEY

Close by Robert Horton's modern view of the church are three paintings by Edward Bradley (1824-67), an important local artist who worked in the middle years of the 19th Century. He made several sketches and paintings of Geddington Church, both its exterior and interior, mostly dating from the 1830s and 1840s. The church was presented with three of his paintings from that time. Others are in private hands.

The first of Bradley's paintings was presented to the church by Rev. Ben Turton in 1908 and forms the front cover of this book. It is a view from the west of the Nave, showing the old high box pews, the canopied wooden pulpit, the Tresham screen in its original position with the painted Rood over, and the outline of the reredos in the distance. The Lady Chapel with the medieval screen within the arch surmounted by a mural depicting the tomb of Queen Elizabeth I can also be glimpsed through the south arcade.

The other two of Bradley's paintings depict in much greater detail the 1794-95 painted Rood (*Fig. 16*) and the mural of Elizabeth I's tomb (*Fig. 45*). They were both donated by Jim Harker in memory of his parents, James and Mildred Harker (1920-2006).

Figure 18: The Nave in 1986
Photo by M Hopkins

CLIFF PETTITT PLAQUE

Next to the northern jamb of the Tower arch is a wooden plaque commemorating a former parishioner:

Cliff Pettitt
He Loved the Lord and Served Him here.

LIST OF INCUMBENTS

Nearby is a framed list of the names of past Incumbents (Rectors, Vicars and Priests in Charge) which go back to 1222. See *Appendix 1* for further details.

FIRE BRIGADE PLAQUE

Finally, before we leave the Nave, high up in the roof above, the Geddington Volunteer Fire Brigade is celebrated with a plaque mounted on the roof timbers. Can you spot it?

THE CHANCEL

From the Nave we now move through Gambier-Parry's screen into the Chancel. *Chancel* is a term used to describe the holiest part of the church east of the Nave, and derives from the Latin '*cancelli*', meaning *gratings* or a *lattice* (a reference to the typical form of the screen separating the Chancel from the Nave). The need for separation arose in particular from the doctrine of transubstantiation (the belief that, in the Eucharist, water and wine become Christ's body and blood) laid down at the fourth Lateran Council of 1215. Clergy were required to ensure that the blessed sacrament was kept protected from irreverent access or abuse; and so, the area of the church used by the lay people was increasingly screened off from that used by the clergy.

This exclusivity sometimes led to the Chancel being called the *presbytery* ('presbyter' means 'priest'), although in practice the nobility and other persons of rank were often allowed to sit in the Chancel. This distinction was enforced through canon law, by which the construction and upkeep of the Chancel was the responsibility of the Rector, whilst the construction and upkeep of the Nave was the responsibility of the parish. After the Reformation, churches generally moved the altar (often then called the communion table) forward, typically to the front of the Chancel or into the Nave; and increasingly used lay choirs who were often placed in a gallery. The eastern end of deep Chancels in churches surviving from the Middle Ages often became little used, although at Geddington we know that an altar rail was installed in 1635[35], indicating that the High Altar was also re-instated in response to Archbishop Laud's instructions of 1633[36].

The High Altar, or at least the rail, appear to have survived into the mid-19th Century, when Anglo-Catholic influence saw a revival of interest in the Chancel as central to worship. At Geddington, the changes of 1855 included restoration of the medieval reredos behind the altar, the reconstruction of an inscription commemorating the Sanctuary's completion in 1369, and the re-tiling of both the Sanctuary and Choir areas. A decade or so later, the installation of a new organ north of the Choir enabled the choristers to sit near the organist. Different approaches to worship in the 20th Century again tended to push altars in larger churches forward, to be closer to the congregation, and this has happened to some degree at Geddington, where the priest normally presides at a mobile altar at the east of the Nave. The congregation may receive Holy Communion from there at smaller services, but for larger services they may receive at the altar rail in the Chancel. It is unusual, however (though not unknown), for the priest to preside from the High Altar – primarily because it is difficult for the congregation to see and hear from the Nave.

The Chancel at Geddington, as in many churches, has two parts:

The Sanctuary is the area behind the Altar Rail, where the High Altar is situated.

The Choir is the area in front of the Altar Rail, where the carved wooden Choir Stalls are found. In medieval times, this is where clergy would sit to chant Psalms and prayers during Masses; and where those of high rank might also be permitted to sit.

The existence of a long Chancel at Geddington is an indicator of its importance in the medieval period as this suggests there were sufficient numbers of clergy and high-status worshippers to warrant such provision.

EVIDENCE OF EARLIER CHANCELS

Roof scars on the eastern elevation of the wall above the Chancel arch bear witness to the existence of two earlier Chancel roof lines, the lower one of which was the original

Saxon Chancel, which would have been narrower than the present Chancel by approx. 1.5m overall[37]. This apart, there are no discernible signs of the original Chancel, which was probably significantly shorter than today, and we cannot say whether it had an apse (rounded) or a rectangular east end.

The higher roof scar marks the roof of the mid-13th Century Chancel and, associated with this, we can make out a line of stones forming a base for timber wall plates (on which an earlier roof structure would have sat) running around the Chancel immediately above the heads of the lower Clerestory windows, which themselves appear to have been part of such a Chancel. In 1863 the *Northampton Herald* reported that, during the re-ordering works of 1855-57, two Norman windows were uncovered in the Chancel that were said to have been blocked up as part of the late 14th Century alterations. This suggests that alterations were made to the old Saxon Chancel in the 12th Century. However, there is no obvious sign of these changes today – unless the Chancel's lower clerestory windows are regarded as being of the 12th Century. The 3 small Clerestory windows in the Chancel's south wall had been hidden, but were revealed in October 1875 when workmen took down the old Lady Chapel roof and reduced its pitch. They were un-blocked and ancient glass from elsewhere fitted in 1904-05[38] so that light could flow in again. One other feature in the north wall of the Chancel is what appears to be a blocked-up doorway partially concealed behind a Victorian radiator. Its age is unclear, although it seems likely that it was stopped up when the Clergy Vestry was built in 1855-57.

---

35   Recorded in a letter from Edmond Vialls (op. cit.)

36   *The Restoration of Altars in the 1630s* by Kenneth Fincham, pub. in *The Historical Journal* Vol. 44, No. 4 (Dec. 2001), pp. 919-940 [Cambridge University Press]

37   PJ Ellis (op. cit.). See also Barnwell (op. cit.)

38   *Geddington Monthly* Magazine, February 1905.

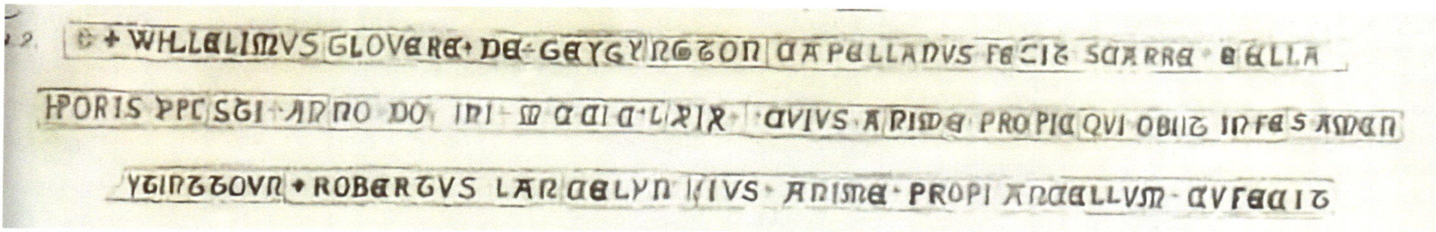

Figure 19: Drawing (c.1786) of the Latin inscriptions
(from Gough's Sepulchral Monuments in Great Britain, Vol. 2 p.249)

DATING THE PRESENT CHANCEL

There is some debate over when the Chancel we see today reached its present extent. Thompson (op. cit.) takes the view that *"from an examination of the outer masonry that the dimensions are those given to it by the 13th Century builders"*.[39] However, the dating of the Sanctuary area and the windows is problematic and has been inconclusively debated by experts, but two pieces of evidence shed some light:

(1) a transcript held in the Buccleuch Archive of an 18th Century translation of a Latin document in Lincoln Cathedral Archive dated 1358, in which the Bishop of Lincoln:

"…appropriated annexed united and granted the Parish Church of Geytingdon…….to the religious men the abbot and Convent of the monastery of Pippewell…" and ordained that "….the aforesaid religious men shall in the first place construct and build the Chancel of the same Church and the windows of the same competently…"

(2) Latin inscriptions in stones running around the foot of the Sanctuary wall and into the adjacent South (Lady) Chapel record the completion of work on the Chancel, one of which is explicitly dated 1369.

THE LATIN INSCRIPTIONS

The Latin text (in Lombardic script) that since 1857 has formed a stone skirting around the Sanctuary reads:

+ WILLELMVS · GLOVERE · DE · GEYTYNGTON · CAPELLANVS · FECIT · SCABELLA · EIVS · ARE · ET · PAVIMENTARE · ISTVM · CANCELLVM ; AD · hONOREM DEI · ET · BEATE · MARIE · Qvi · OBIIT · IN · FESTO · CORPORIS · ChRISTI · ANNO · DOMINI · M.CCC.LXIX · CVIVS · ANIME · PROPICIETVR · DEVS · AMEN

[*William Glover Chaplain of Geddington made this Scabella[40] and the raised pavement of this Chancel to the glory of God and the blessed Mary, and who died on the Feast of Corpus Christi[41] in the year of our Lord 1369, on whose soul may God look with favour. Amen*]

The text that runs along part of the south wall of the Choir and round into the the South Chapel (also in Lombardic script) reads:

+ ROBERTVS · LAVNCELYN · DE · GEYTINGTOVN · FECIT · ISTVM · CANCELLVM · CVIVS · ANIME · PROPICIETVR · DEVS · AMEN.

[*Robert Launcelyn of Geddington built this Chancel on whose soul may God look with favour. Amen*]

These inscriptions once formed the facings to steps in the Chancel and what is now the Lady Chapel. Bridges[42], who gathered his material in the early 18th Century[43], says: *"On the steps leading to the altar, many of the stones being transposed and some lost, is this imperfect inscription"*:

+ WILLELMVS GLOVERE DE GEYTYNTON CAPELLANVS FECIT SCAB...RELLA

....PORIS XPESTI ANNO DOMINI M·DC·CCLXIX[44] CVIVS ANIME PROPIC... QVI OB IIT · IN · FE... A..ME .[45]

---

39   Prof. A. H. Thompson, 1907 (op. cit.)

40   *Scabella* means 'footstool', but it is not clear to what that refers. The 3 sedilia are dated by Thompson (op. cit.) and others to the late 13th or early 14th Century. Perhaps it means the 3 steps on which the Latin inscription was originally carved; it may even refer to the Sanctuary itself as 'the footstool of Christ'.

41   *Corpus Christi* means 'Body of Christ' and the Feast Day celebrates the Real Presence of Christ in the Eucharist. It is held on the Thursday after Trinity Sunday, 60 days after Easter. The Feast didn't enter the official Church Calendar until 1317.

42   *The History & Antiquities of Northamptonshire*, Vol. 2, pp 310-11 by John Bridges (pub. Peter Whalley, 1791).

43   See also *Old English Churches* (1903) by George Clinch, and Markham (op.cit.)

44   This date (1869) is clearly an error in transcription.

45   Apart from 'WILLELIMVS' and the date, this wording is identical to that given by Vialls (op. cit.)

PART I: A TOUR OF THE CHURCH

"And also upon a step at the upper end of the south Chancel":

+ ROBERTVS · LAVNCELYN FECIT CAPEL-
LANVS.. GEYTYNTON.."

An illustrated record (*Fig. 19*) of the inscribed steps that dates from c1786 largely matches Bridges' record and is described as *"William Glover, and another broken inscription on the steps of Geddington Chancel"*.

There are clearly significant differences between these accounts, both in content and sequencing, from the current arrangement. Some current lettering contains traces of red pigmentation, whilst other stones appear to be of much cleaner and more recent cut. As the *Northampton Mercury* for 7 November 1857 put it:

"….some ingenuity appears to have been exercised in deciphering the inscription on the altar steps"

We know from a contemporary record that the task of reconstructing the ancient inscription was carried out by the father of one of Rev. Church's school pupils[46]; the work then being executed in stone around the Sanctuary.

THE SIGNIFICANCE OF THE INSCRIPTIONS

A leading expert, Nikolaus Pevsner[47] says that 1369 is 50 to 70 years too late stylistically for the inscription to relate to the building of the Chancel, but offers no clear alternative explanation other than possibly stylistic conservatism. However, it seems reasonable to infer that the 1369 inscription faithfully records the fulfillment of the obligation imposed on the monks by the 1358 Endowment. *If* the 1857 textual reconstruction is accurate, then we seem to have two events – first, the completion of the Chancel by Robert Launcelyn; and secondly the making by William Glover of *'this Scabella and the raised pavement of this Chancel'*.

The Launcelyn family were based in Newton and Great Oakley. There were two Robert Launcelyns (father and son) in the 12th Century, the younger one succeeding his father before 1121-22 and being confirmed in a grant of land at Pipewell in 1154-55[48]. If this is the Robert Launcelyn of our inscription, then this would indicate that there was an earlier, intermediate, rebuilding of the Chancel roughly contemporaneous with the construction of the North Aisle, which some sources[49] suggest may have happened.

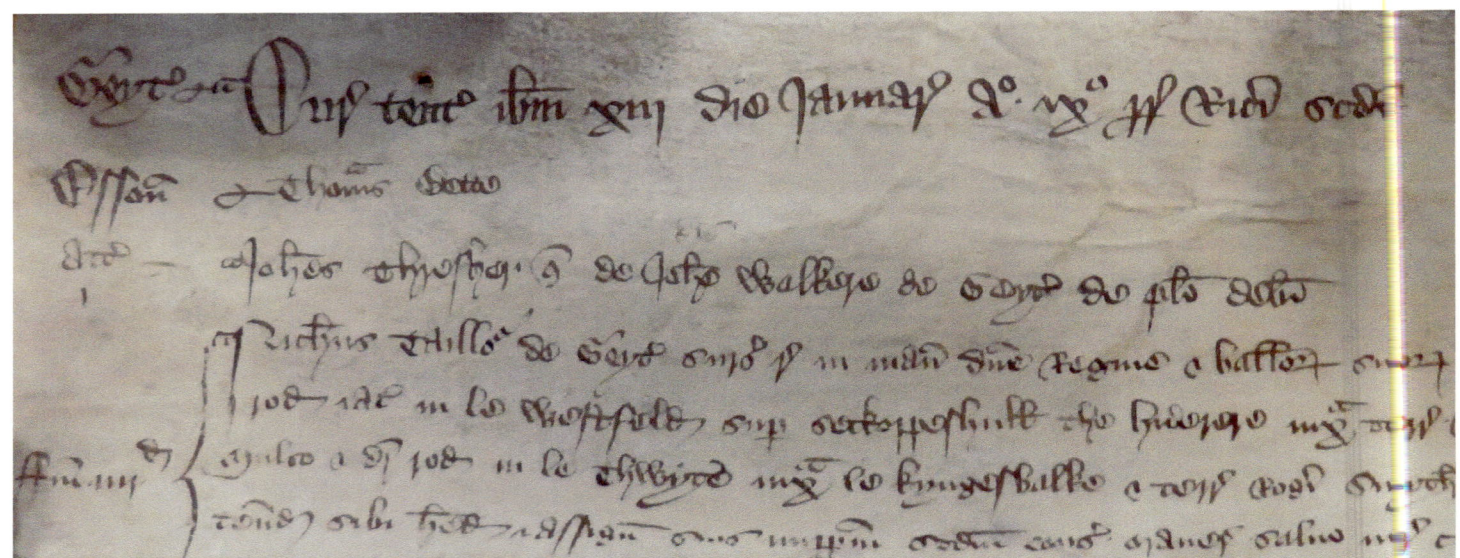

Figure 20: Extract from Geddington Manorial Court Rolls 13th January 1386
Photo: Edward Coulson

46   Correspondence between Rev. WMH Church and Walter, 5th Duke of Buccleuch 1855-57 [Buccleuch Archive], with thanks to Crispin Powell.

47   *Pevsner Architectural Guides* (Buildings of England Series) *Northamptonshire,* by Bruce Bailey, Nikolaus Pevsner & Bridget Cherry (2013)

48   *Domesday Descendants: A Prosopography of Persons Occurring in English Documents ; 1066 - 1166*, by Katharine S. B. Keats-Rohan [Boydell Press, 2002], with thanks to Vic Crouse for his research into the Launcelyns.

49   E.g. PJ Ellis (op. cit.) who references the discovery of the remains of two Norman windows in the Chancel reported in the *Northampton Herald* on 4th July 1873.

However, another Robert Launcelyn appears in the Geddington Manorial Court records[50] in the 1370s, being 'elected' a beadle in 1378; frequently appearing as a pledge provider; and a brewer of ale and *affeeror*[51]. Robert is also known to have held land in the common fields - again, he appears in numerous land transactions as the holder of selions (ridges) neighbouring those forming the subject matter of the transaction; and he was a miller too - he features several times being fined for charging excessive mill tolls. So, it is entirely possible that it was *this* Robert Launcelyn who paid for the building of this chancel during the years 1358-69. He certainly seems to have held a significant amount of land.

William Glover's name appears only once in these same Court Rolls. On 13th January 1378 we find: "*Nicholaus Comfort et Alicia uxoris eius venerunt in curiam & petunt se admissi ad medietati unius mesuagii post decessum Willelmi Glovere capellani cuius consanguine et hereditarie predicte Alicie est et sic admissi sunt et habent inde seisinam et fecerunt et dant de fine per ingressum prout patet in capite*", which roughly translates as: "Nicholas and Alice Comfort his wife come to the court and ask to be admitted to a half [share?] of a messuage after the death of William Glovere, chaplain, whose relation and heir is the aforesaid Alice and thus they are admitted and have seisin therein and make [fealty] and give as fine for entry as appears above[52]". The date and the identity with a deceased chaplain therefore make this very likely to be the William Glover of the church inscription.

If these identifications with the persons in the Court Rolls are correct, which seems very plausible, then we seem to have Robert Launcelyn building the Chancel and William Glover, Chaplain of the Church, carrying out the paving of the Sanctuary and making the 'Scabella'. Since the latter task would not have been carried out before the former then, given the requirements of the Bishop's 1358 Licence, it seems very probable that the Chancel was completed (or at least extended eastwards from a mid 13th Century Chancel)

in the period 1358 to 1369.

This is at odds with the view of Pevsner and others that the Sanctuary windows date from circa 1300, yet the evidence for a date in the 1360s is compelling. The conundrum posed by Pevsner might, however, be explained either by stylistic conservatism or by the monks having used earlier stone-working templates from Pipewell Abbey to form the windows in the Sanctuary for reasons of speed or economy.

This interpretation also suggests that the priestly effigy in the Lady Chapel – who was said[53] to be a '*Chaplain of this Church*' - commemorates this same William Glover. Since Pevsner dates the effigy to the 14th Century and gives the possibility of a link to the inscription, this certainly seems plausible.

That the inscription records William Glover as having died at the Feast of Corpus Christi[54] also suggests that a local legend of the priest dying whilst celebrating the Eucharist may have some substance to it [in the sense that *the Feast of Corpus Christi itself* celebrates the institution of the Eucharist].

50 *Geddington (Crown) Manorial Court Rolls 1377-1414* - Northamptonshire Record Office [NRA 23059 Montagu-Douglas-Scott]. Unfortunately, earlier records do not appear to be available. With grateful thanks to Edward Coulson for drawing the references to this Robert Launcelyn and William Glover to the author's attention.

51 An *affeeror* was a manorial official who assessed fines for transgressions of manorial customs and ordinances. Interestingly, Robert is mentioned in a land transaction on 25 September 1378 as the neighbour of a messuage (a dwelling with outbuildings assigned for the use of the occupiers) in Geddington which was acquired on that date by Henry Mulso, a relative of the John Mulsho commemorated in the North Aisle.

52 In fact in the margin of the original document.

53 *Unsigned letter to Charles Lamotte*, March 1736 [NRO Montagu Vol, 22 no.102], and reproduced as Letter L86 in *Estate Letters from the Time of John, 2nd Duke of Montagu* (pub. Northamptonshire Record Society, 2013).

54 The festival at which the 'real presence' of the body and blood of Christ, as manifest in the Eucharist, is celebrated.

PART I: A TOUR OF THE CHURCH

THE CHANCEL EAST WINDOW

The magnificent east window (*Fig. 21*) with 5 lights culminates in a large circle filled with trefoils without ogee arches. Dedicated on 17th December 1892[55], the window glass was designed by Ninian Comper[56]. Costing £340, it was paid for by public donations and replaced an earlier window by Clayton and Bell that formed part of George Gilbert Scott's mid-19th Century renovation.

The window glass illustrates *'the power of Divine Love shown in overcoming evil'*. In detail, the window depicts the following:

THE LEFT-HAND PANEL

This shows "𝕾𝖆𝖓𝖈𝖙𝖚[𝖘] 𝕻𝖊𝖙𝖗𝖚𝖘" (Saint Peter) holding the keys to heaven. Above him is the Old Testament Prophet, Isaiah; and below him is a winged man or angel, the emblem of St. Matthew. There are two pieces of Latin text:

"𝕯𝖎𝖈𝖎𝖙𝖊 𝖋𝖎𝖑𝖎𝖆𝖊 𝕾𝖎𝖔𝖓: 𝕰𝖈𝖈𝖊 𝕾𝖆𝖑𝖛𝖆𝖙𝖔𝖗 𝖙𝖚𝖚𝖘 𝖇𝖊𝖓𝖎𝖙". This means: *"Say to the daughters of Zion: Behold your Saviour is coming"* This comes from Matthew 21.5, which directly recalls the words in Isaiah 62.11.

"𝕽𝖊𝖈𝖔𝖗𝖉𝖆𝖙𝖚𝖘 𝖊𝖘𝖙 𝕻𝖊𝖙𝖗𝖚𝖘 𝖛𝖊𝖗𝖇𝖆 𝕵𝖊𝖘𝖚" which means: *"Peter remembered Jesus' words"*. This is a quotation from Matthew 26.75: *"And Peter remembered the saying of Jesus, 'Before the rooster crows, you will deny me three times.' And he went out and wept bitterly."*

These sayings are both about the fulfilment of prophesies: in the first case that the Saviour will come to save the Jews; and in the second, that the Saviour will be denied by his own people. And yet, God's love is so strong that a repentant Peter is entrusted with the keys to the gates of heaven – he is to become the first leader of the Church.

THE LEFT-CENTRE PANEL

This shows "𝕾 𝕸𝖆𝖗𝖎𝖆 𝕸𝖆𝖌𝖉𝖆𝖑𝖊𝖓𝖆" (St. Mary Magdalene) holding an ointment jar. Above her is the Old Testament prophet Zachariah, and below her is a lion, the emblem of St. Mark. Here there is a single Latin quotation:

"𝕰𝖝𝖘𝖚𝖑𝖙𝖆 𝖘𝖆𝖙𝖎𝖘 𝖋𝖎𝖑𝖎𝖆 𝕾𝖎𝖔𝖓, 𝕵𝖚𝖇𝖎𝖑𝖆. 𝕰𝖈𝖈𝖊 𝖗𝖊𝖝 𝖙𝖚𝖚𝖘 𝖇𝖊𝖓𝖎𝖊𝖙 " which means: *Rejoice greatly, daughter of Zion, Rejoice. Behold your king is coming"*. This comes from Zachariah 9.9: *"Rejoice greatly, Daughter Zion! Shout, Daughter Jerusalem! See, your king comes to you, righteous and victorious, lowly, and riding on a donkey, on a colt, the foal of a donkey."*

This is again about the fulfilment (this time in Mark 11) of a prophesy (in Zachariah 9.9) that the Saviour will come riding a donkey. The visual image of Mary Magdalene with a jar of ointment also links with two accounts in Mark's Gospel. First in Mark 14.3: *"While he was in Bethany, reclining at the table in the home of Simon the Leper, a woman came with an alabaster jar of very expensive perfume, made of pure nard. She broke the jar and poured the perfume on his head."* Though this does not mention Mary Magdalene by name, many commentators identify this woman with her, the point being that **she** recognises Jesus as the Saviour, even if others don't. Secondly in Mark 16.1, which says *"When the Sabbath was over, Mary Magdalene, Mary the mother of James, and Salome bought spices so that they might go to anoint Jesus' body."* Again, Mary is the first to recognise that Jesus has risen from the grave. Again, divine love triumphs.

THE CENTRAL PANEL

This depicts "𝕸𝖆𝖗𝖎𝖆 𝕸𝖆𝖙𝖊𝖗 𝕵𝖊𝖘𝖚", meaning *Mary Mother of Jesus*. She is holding the baby Jesus. Below them are Adam and Eve with apples and the letters 𝕬 and 𝕰 are shown in shields. The Latin script reads:

"𝕾𝖊𝖒𝖊 𝖒𝖚𝖑𝖎𝖊𝖗𝖎𝖘 𝖘𝖙𝖊𝖗𝖊𝖙 𝖈𝖆𝖕𝖚𝖙 𝖘𝖊𝖗𝖕𝖊𝖓𝖙𝖎𝖘", which means *The seed of the woman shall crush the head of the serpent*. This is a reference to Genesis 3.15 where Eve has been tempted by the serpent (who stands for Satan) to defy God and eat the fruit of the Tree of Life. God curses the serpent saying: *"And I will put enmity between you and the woman, and between your offspring and hers; he will crush your head, and you will strike his heel."*

Jesus is the ultimate seed (offspring) of Eve and although he is damaged by Satan (the serpent), his is the ultimate victory over evil and death itself (crushes the serpent's head).

55 *Geddington Parish Magazine*, January 1893 see Appendix 7.
56 Later Sir Ninian.

Figure 21: The Great East Window in the Chancel
Photo: Hirst Conservation Ltd.

Figure 22: Mary with the baby Jesus
Photo: John Barker, MRICS, CIOB

Figure 23: Adam & Eve
Photo: John Barker, MRICS, CIOB

Figure 24: St. George
Photo: John Barker, MRICS, CIOB

THE CENTRE-RIGHT PANEL

This shows "𝖘 𝕵𝖔𝖍𝖆𝖓𝖓𝖊𝖘 𝕭𝖆𝖕𝖙." (St. John the Baptist). Above him is the Old Testament prophet Micah; and below him is an ox, the emblem of St. Luke. The Latin text is simply:

"𝕰𝖝 𝖙𝖊" which is short for 'ex te mihi egredietur qui sit dominator in Israhel', meaning "*Out of thee shall he come forth unto me one who is to be the ruler in Israel*". This comes from Micah 5.2 which foretells that the Messiah will come from Bethlehem Ephratah (Bethlehem and its surrounding area), despite its tiny size. Chapter 2 of Luke's Gospel tells of how this prophesy is fulfilled with Jesus' birth in Bethlehem; and in Luke 3.16 John the Baptist, speaking of Jesus says: "*one who is more powerful than I will come, the straps of whose sandals I am not worthy to untie. He will baptise you with the Holy Spirit and fire.*" Soon after, in Luke 3.21-22, John baptises Jesus: "*….it came to pass that Jesus also was baptised; and while He prayed, the heaven was opened. And the Holy Spirit descended in bodily form like a dove upon Him, and a voice came from heaven which said, 'You are My beloved Son; in You I am well pleased.'*"

Once again, an Old Testament prophesy is fulfilled in the coming of Jesus, who will save the world from evil.

THE RIGHT-HAND PANEL

This panel shows "𝖘 𝕲𝖊𝖔𝖗𝖌𝖎𝖚𝖘" (St. George) (*Fig. 24*) who is killing the dragon. Above him is the Old Testament prophet Jeremiah, and below him is an eagle, the emblem of St. John. Each of these figures has a crowned initial in gold in the backcloth. The Latin text says;

"𝕰𝖈𝖈𝖊 𝖉𝖎𝖈𝖎𝖙 𝕯𝖔𝖒𝖎𝖓𝖚𝖘 𝖘𝖚𝖘𝖈𝖎𝖙𝖆𝖇𝖔 𝕯𝖆𝖛𝖎𝖉 𝖌𝖊𝖗𝖒𝖊𝖓 𝖎𝖚𝖘𝖙𝖚𝖒 𝖊𝖙 𝖘𝖆𝖕𝖎𝖊𝖓𝖘 𝖊𝖗𝖎𝖙 𝖊𝖙 𝖗𝖊𝖌𝖓𝖆𝖇𝖎𝖙 𝖗𝖊𝖝" which means: "*Behold says the Lord, I will raise up a seed of David, he will be just and wise and will reign as king.*" This refers to Jeremiah 23.5, which says: "*the days are coming, declares the Lord, when I will raise up for David a righteous Branch, a King who will reign wisely and do what is just and right in the land.*"

The legend of St. George slaying the dragon (snake) recalls the message of the window's central panel, that Jesus will crush the head of the snake (overcome evil). Not only will Christ overcome evil, but he will overcome death itself, for in John 6.40 we are told: "*For my Father's will is that everyone who looks to the Son and believes in him shall have eternal life, and I will raise them up at the last day.*" This is Jesus' ultimate triumph, the greatest victory of all. Love truly has overcome all evil.

ABOVE THE 5 PANELS

Above the outer 4 panels and 'supporting' the circle above, are two sets of trefoils that depict the Angel Gabriel announcing to Mary that she is to bear the Son of God (an event known as 'the Annunciation'). Underneath these two trefoils are the monograms 𝕸 and 𝕴𝕳𝕾 (see below for meanings), with two roses between them.

In the circle above these 5 panels, we see trefoils of red and blue-clad angels carrying the text "**Dans gloriam Deo**", which means "*Give glory to God*". These angels alternate with the two monograms :

> **𝕴𝕳𝕾**, which is an abbreviation of *Iesus Hominum Salvator* – meaning *Jesus Saviour of Mankind*;
>
> 𝕸 (for *Maria*) in gold on red background.

These monograms take us back to the central panel: Jesus, the blessed fruit of Mary's womb, was ordained *from the very beginning* to save mankind by overcoming the evil that had been let loose in the world when Adam and Eve first tasted the forbidden fruit. And so, we are called upon to give glory to God for giving us his only Son to save us from the evil that we do.

THE EMBLEMS OF THE FOUR EVANGELISTS

We have seen that the figures of the four Gospel writers, Matthew, Mark, Luke, and John each have their own emblems beneath them in this window. These are spoken of in Ezekiel 1.10 and 10.14 and in Revelations 4.7 and were widely used in the medieval period, so their introduction by Comper (and earlier by Scott with his tiling of the Sanctuary) very much reflected 'High Anglican' theology.

Seen as representing the highest forms of various types of animals, each king in their environments, a winged man signifies Matthew, representing Jesus' Incarnation, and so His human nature, adopted because Matthew's gospel starts with Joseph's genealogy from Abraham. A winged lion stands for Mark, a figure of courage and monarchy. The lion also represents Jesus' resurrection (because lions were believed to sleep with open eyes, a comparison with Christ in the tomb), and Christ as king. A winged ox represents Luke. A figure of sacrifice, service, and strength, the ox represents Jesus's sacrifice in His Crucifixion and also Mary's obedience. Luke's Gospel begins with the duties of God's faithful servant Zechariah in the temple. An eagle is John's emblem. A figure of the sky, it represents Jesus's Ascension and Christ's divine nature. John's gospel starts with an overview of Christ's eternal nature ('*In the beginning was the Word…*').

THE REREDOS

The word *reredos* is ultimately derived from the Latin words *arere*, meaning 'behind' and *dorsum*, meaning 'back' which, via Norman French and Middle English emerged as *areredos* in the 14th Century – later shortened to *reredos*. In medieval churches the high altar was placed against the east wall, with the reredos literally behind its back.

Sitting immediately below the East Window, the stonework of the 14th Century[57] stone Reredos (*Fig. 25*) has a frieze

Figure 25: The Reredos after completion of conservation work in 2023

Photo: Hirst Conservation Ltd.

---

57   Thompson (op. cit.), p. 155. See also Francis Bond, *The Chancel of English Churches*, OUP (1916), page 80, who gives it a 14th Century date. Prof. David Stocker, on a visit to the church, dated it to approx. 1350-1370.

PART I: A TOUR OF THE CHURCH

of quatrefoils, above which are thirteen arched niches, the central one of which is twice as wide as the others, all topped with a crenellated cornice. It is 4.72m wide and 1.28m high. Markham[58] says that the niches once contained statues of Christ and His twelve Apostles.

In 1888[59], Sir Ninian Comper inserted 13 exquisitely painted zinc panels into these niches and created elaborate decorations on the stonework. These reredos panels depict the following:

The central panel shows the Crucifixion of Christ with St. Mary Magdalene kneeling and the cross inscribed 'I:N:R:I', which stands for *Iesus Nazarenus, Rex Iudaeorum*, meaning 'Jesus of Nazareth, King of the Jews' – the inscription given in John's Gospel Ch.19 v.19. Beneath the Cross is a skull, representing Jesus' victory over Death in the Resurrection. A follower and supporter of Jesus, Mary Magdalene probably came from Magdala on the Sea of Galilee and was present at Jesus' Crucifixion and burial and at the Resurrection, for which she is known as 'apostle to the apostles'. She has been the Patron Saint of Geddington Church since the 16th Century.

To the left are:

- **St. Thaddeus**, holding a club in his left hand. Commonly called 'Jude Thaddeus' to distinguish him from Judas Iscariot, he is sometimes identified as the brother of Jesus, but more commonly as the brother of James the Less. He is also closely associated with St. Simon, with whom he was said to have been martyred in Beirut in AD65. He is usually depicted holding a club.

- **St. Jacobus:A** [James, the son of Alphaeus: also known as 'James the Lesser'] holding a book in his right hand. There is much uncertainty over his identity: some think he was the son of Jesus' aunt, Mary of Clopas; a few think James, brother of Jesus; and even possibly the brother of St. Matthew. He is often also depicted holding a fuller's club. His martyrdom is said to have been at the hands of Herod Agrippa (Acts 12.1-2), but there is a tradition he was crucified in Egypt.

- **St. Matthaeus**, holding a halberd in his left hand. Originally a tax collector, 'Matthew the Apostle' has often been identified as the writer of Matthew's Gospel, although many scholars dispute this. He preached first in Judea and then in Ethiopia where, according to

tradition, he was martyred at the hands of King Hirtacus.

- **St. Jacobus:Z**, [James, the son of Zebedee: also known as 'James the Great'] holding a staff in his left hand and wearing a pilgrim's hat with the pilgrim's symbol of a scallop shell. His mother, Salome, was a sister of Jesus' mother, Mary. One of the first disciples, together with his brother John and with Peter, he was close to Jesus; and he was the first to be martyred at the hands of Herod Agrippa in Jerusalem. The patron saint of Spain, his relics are held at Santiago de Compostella, one of the great pilgrimage sites.

- **Stus. Petrus**, [St. Peter, also called Simon Peter] holding a key in his right hand (symbolising the keys to Heaven) and an open book (the Gospels) in his left hand. The founder of the Church in Antioch, he is venerated as the first Bishop of Rome, and the first Pope. Two letters in the Bible (1 Peter and 2 Peter) are traditionally attributed to him, though modern scholars discount this. He was crucified in Rome under the Emperor Nero, and St. Peter's basilica in Vatican City bears his name.

- **Beata Maria**, [the Blessed Mary, mother of Jesus] with her arms crossed. Usually portrayed wearing 'Marian blue', St. Mary the Virgin – the mother of God - i generally regarded as the greatest of all the Saints. She is especially venerated in the Catholic tradition, in which she carries the title of 'Blessed'. She is also recognised as the greatest among women in Islam. Countless churches are named in her honour.

To the right are:

- **S. Johannes**, [St. John] holding a closed book in both hands. The brother of James, son of Zebedee, John the Apostle was the youngest apostle and is usually identified as 'the disciple whom Jesus loved' and as John the Evangelist, writer of John's Gospel, three letters in the Bible and the Book of Revelation. He was the only apostle to die naturally: it is believed this was in Ephesus in modern-day Turkey at some time after AD 98.

- **S. Andreas**, [St. Andrew] leaning against a cross saltire, holding an open book with both hands. A fisherman, he was the first to follow Jesus, bringing his brother Simon Peter with him. He is said to have preached from Byzantium (later Constantinople) along the Black Sea and up the River Dnieper to Kiev and on to Novgorod,

58   Markham (op, cit.), p.10

59   This dating is confirmed by a letter from William Bucknall (Comper's business partner) written in February 1892 referring to the reredos work having been carried out four years earlier. [Northamptonshire County Record Office].

Figure 26: The Reredos during conservation work, showing traces of Sir GG Scott's 1857 scheme.
Photo: Hirst Conservation Ltd.

becoming a patron Saint of Ukraine, Russia, and Romania. Tradition said he was crucified in AD 60 on a saltire cross at Patras in Greece, deeming himself unworthy of the cross of Christ. Relics of Andrew came with St. Augustine to Britain and thence to Scotland, which adopted him as patron too.

- **S. Phillipus**, (St. Phillip] holding a staff in his right hand. Said to have come, like Peter and Andrew, from Bethsaida, Phillip the Apostle had strong connections with Greek communities and features prominently in John's Gospel. Sent with his sister Mariamne and Bartholomew to preach in Greece, Phrygia, and Syria, he was martyred at Hieropolis in modern-day Turkey having upset the king by converting his wife. Crucified upside-down with Bartholomew, he continued to preach, persuading the crowd to release Bartholomew but, refusing release for himself, he died. Relics of Philip are held in Rome, and the possible site of his tomb in Hieropolis was discovered in 2011.

- **S. Bartholoaeus**, [St. Bartholomew the Apostle] holding a knife in his right hand and a closed book in his left. After Christ's death Bartholomew went to India, where he left a copy of Matthew's Gospel, later returning to preach alongside St. Jude Thaddeus in Armenia, where both are patron saints. Accounts of his martyrdom vary, either being crucified upside-down at Hieropolos or beheaded near Baku in modern Azerbaijan.

- **S. Thomas**, [St. Thomas, also called *Didymus*, meaning 'twin', or 'Doubting Thomas'] holding a scroll in his right hand and a staff in his left. Tradition says he preached the Gospels in India, travelling to the far south. Many churches in India and the Middle East claim Thomas as founder, including at St. Thomas' Mount, Chennai where he was reportedly martyred with a spear in AD72. His relics were said to have been taken back to Edessa.

- **Stus Simon**, [St. Simon the Apostle, sometimes called 'The Zealot' to distinguish him from Simon Peter] holding an open book in his right hand and a cross-cut saw with his left. Little is known of him after Jesus' death, but he is said to have travelled to Persia with Jude Thaddeus, where he was martyred by being cut in half with a saw. However, another account says he died peacefully at Edessa.

When Comper's zinc panels were removed for conservation work in 2023, traces of George Gilbert Scott's 1857 scheme (*Fig. 26*) were revealed along with some even earlier bright-blue paintwork which analysis found to contain French Ultramarine / synthetic ultramarine, indicating that this layer must be post-1826[60].

Although there were no signs of statues, the niches behind had a few remnants of gold *fleurs de lys* on a blue background and the names of saints inscribed in gothic lettering[61], the following being decipherable (from left to right):

St. Judas – St. Thomas – St. Bartholomew – St. Matthias – St. ? – St. ? –

the central panel inscribed 'INRI' and St. Maria Magdalena

St. ? – St. ? – St. Phillipus – St. ? – St. Johannus – St. Simon

---

60 *Final Treatment Report* by Mackenzie Higgins of Hirst Conservation Ltd. (Jan. 2024) p.33
61 The fragile lettering very easily fell/peeled off and is now stored in a separate archive box in the parish chest.

Figure 27: Ancient heads beneath the Reredos
Photos: Hirst Conservation Ltd.

Below the Reredos on each side are two ancient grotesque figures (*Fig. 27*) serving as corbel-stones: one appears to be a jester, and the other is what appears to be a monkey. During conservation work in 2023, they were found to be decorated with a deep red ochre. Their origins and significance are unknown, but one possibility is that they came from the former royal palace.

The reredos dates from the period c1350 to c1370, but on close inspection it does not appear to have been constructed specifically for this window opening and may have been inserted at an unknown time after the east window was built[62]. If this is the case, it raises the question of its origin.

Louis Francis Salzman[63] calculated that, in the Middle Ages, it was not generally economic to cart stone further than 12 miles by road as, above that distance, the cost of transport exceeded the value of the stone. The most obvious possibility is therefore that the reredos was originally made for one of the royal chapels that are known to have existed within the adjacent palace, and later removed to the church. Its high quality, both in original design and in execution mean it would have been very expensive to create, which supports the possibility of a royal provenance. However, the date of the reredos makes it unlikely, though not impossible, that either Edward III or his mother Queen Isabella of France (who held the manor between 1333 and 1357) would have commissioned it at some point before the Black Death of 1348-49. We know the palace was in

ruins by 1374[64], so the time window available to this possibility is a narrow one.

A second possibility is that it was brought to Geddington from Pipewell Abbey at or soon after its suppression in 1538 – it is certainly close enough to have been feasible. Sir George Tresham, who was granted the advowson of Geddington Church after the Dissolution, is believed to have taken possession of other features from the abbey. It is not certain that he shared the Catholicism of the senior branch of the Tresham family at Rushton Hall, but he would nevertheless probably have been interested to preserve this holy item from the Abbey, as would the monks, who had a very close association with Geddington. However, Pipewell was a Cistercian Abbey, and the Rule of St. Bernard that governed the Order required absolute simplicity in ornament and decoration, though this was by no means always observed, especially in the later medieval period. The Abbey was also facing financial troubles by the 14th Century, so creating this expensive artwork would have been a further drain on their resources. So, although Pipewell remains a good possibility, there must also be a degree of scepticism about it.

CHANCEL AUMBREY

To the left of the reredos, a 14th Century Aumbrey (*Fig. 28*) is set into the east wall. This is where the 'reserved sacrament' (consecrated bread and wine set aside for administering the sacraments to e.g. sick or dying people) was kept. It was later fitted with a stone shelf and served as a credence table for the High Altar. The bracket-head above it has a metal ring near the figure's left

Figure 28: The Aumbrey during conservation work in 2023
Photo: Hirst Conservation Ltd.

62   Prof. David Stocker of Leeds University concurs with this view following an inspection of the reredos.

63   *Building in England down to 1550* by LF Salzman (OUP 1952) Ch. VII p 119

64   *History of the King's Works*, Vols. I & II, p944 (Pub. Dept. of the Environment, HMSO 1977); The *Calendar of Inquisitions* for 1374 and the *Writ of the Privy Seal to the Sheriff to Inquire* concerning this (17 May 1374).

ear, which may have been used to hang a perpetual lamp signifying the presence of the blessed sacrament within the aumbrey below. The outer surfaces of the aumbrey were decorated by Ninian Comper at the same time as his work on the reredos (1888).

It will be noted that the shape and mouldings of the face of the Aumbrey exactly match the central niche of the Reredos, indicating that the same mould was used for both, and that therefore both are contemporaneous. If the reredos was indeed re-located from elsewhere, then so was the Aumbrey.

Figure 29: Medieval bracket-head, believed to represent St. Mary the Virgin
(note traces of medieval colour)

HEADS & STATUES BESIDE THE WINDOW

On each side of the east window are projecting medieval stone bracket-heads (still with traces of the original medieval paintwork), each surmounted by a 20th Century plaster cast statue.

The ancient head to the right is believed to represent Mary, mother of Jesus. The floral garland she wears (*Fig. 29*) comprises rosettes that closely resemble those seen in the frieze of the reredos, suggesting a common 14th Century origin. Each May, it was traditional to crown a statue of Mary, Queen of Heaven with roses (usually followed by a parade) and this may be the origin of the tradition, still followed each year by Geddington CofE Primary School, of crowning the 'May Queen'. The dedication plaque on the statue above this head reads:

AMDG James Bell 1943 – 1964.

James Bell, the son of James and Kath Bell of Newton Road, Geddington, died in a tragic accident on 5th Dec. 1964. Sadly, both his mother and brother Robert were also killed in separate accidents in later years. 'AMDG' is short for *Ad maiorem Dei gloriam* [to the greater glory of God]. This is also the motto of the Society of Jesus (the Jesuits).

The bracket-head to the left of the window may represent St. John (or perhaps St. Andrew as Patron?), though no identification is certain. A dedication plaque at the foot of the statue above the head says:

To the Glory of God and in memory of
RS – AES – MES 1935.

It is believed these initials refer to Robert Sykes, who

died in 1917 aged 87, and his wife Mary Elizabeth Sykes (née Sheffield) who died in 1924 aged 84. 'AES' probably refers to Mary's mother Ann Sheffield (nee Banks, d. 1888), and the statue was probably donated by Elizabeth Ann (their daughter) who died in 1949. All were lifelong residents of Geddington and are buried in the churchyard.

Markham (op. cit., p.11) says that ancient statues once stood on these bracket-heads but disappeared well before 1899. Markham also says that two inscriptions (lost when the plasterwork was removed from the walls in 1855-57) had been painted on the walls above the brackets:

AVE MARIA GRATIA PLENA DOMINVS TE CVM BENEDICTA TV IN MVLIERIBVS

[Hail Mary, full of grace, the Lord is with thee;
Blessed art thou among women]; and

ECCE ANCILLA DOMINI FIAT MIHI SECVNDVM VERBVM TVVM

[Behold the handmaiden of the Lord;
be it unto me according to thy word].
These refer to *The Annunciation of Mary* in Luke 1.38.

THE HIGH ALTAR

In the early church, the altar came to symbolise Christ's tomb, and where the sacrament of the Eucharist takes place. Over time, it became ornamented with a cross and candles set upon a cloth (representing the shroud that covered Christ's body), and eventually an altarpiece (a work of art set behind and above the altar and depicting themes associated with Christ's passion) which became known as a reredos.

In the medieval period, the High Altar would have stood hard up against the east wall, as the officiating priest would then have prepared and consecrated the bread and wine facing eastwards. Today, whenever the High Altar is used to celebrate Holy Communion, the priest does so facing the congregation. The original Altar would have been removed after the Reformation and in all probability a 'communion table' positioned at the western end of the Chancel replaced it until 1635, when the Altar and altar rail were re-instated[65]. Standing approx. 1 metre forward from the reredos, the large stone Altar slab we see today is believed to originate in the 1855-57 alterations[66]. Supported by timber framing, it is 3.2m long and extends across almost the entire width of the Reredos.

MARBLE FLOOR TILES

The black and white chequered marble floor tiling surrounding the Altar was laid by Sir Ninian Comper as part of his renovation works in 1888-92 and are the same as those he later used in Westminster Abbey. Prior to this, the Sanctuary had been laid with encaustic tiles in 1855-57, including 5 large ones - the central one with the Sacred 'Chi-Ro' Monogram and the other four with the winged emblems of the four Evangelists (see the section on the East Window).

THE CHANCEL SOUTH WINDOW

The glass of the window in the south wall of the Sanctuary (*Fig. 30*) was made by Clayton and Bell and was given in 1860 by members of the family of Rev. James Hogg, who was the Vicar of Geddington between 1814 and 1844, and who is also commemorated in the Parish Church of Ss. Peter & Paul, Kettering, as he was Headmaster of the Grammar School.

The window is inscribed:

To . live . is . Christ . and . to .die .is . gain

and consists of three lights each with figures illustrating Faith, Hope, and Charity.

The first light shows St. Stephen bearing a palm in his left hand and a scroll in his right with the words: + 𝔖𝔱𝔞𝔫𝔡 . 𝔣𝔞𝔰𝔱 . 𝔦𝔫 . 𝔱𝔥𝔢 . 𝔣𝔞𝔦𝔱𝔥 and underneath the words:- 𝔅𝔢 . 𝔱𝔥𝔬𝔲 . 𝔣𝔞𝔦𝔱𝔥𝔣𝔲𝔩 . 𝔲𝔫𝔱𝔬 . 𝔡𝔢𝔞𝔱𝔥

The centre light shows St. Paul carrying a sword in his right hand and a scroll in his left with the words:- 𝔥𝔬𝔭𝔢 . 𝔱𝔬 . 𝔱𝔥𝔢 . 𝔢𝔫𝔡. and below: 𝔚𝔥𝔦𝔠𝔥 . 𝔥𝔬𝔭𝔢 . 𝔴𝔢 . 𝔥𝔞𝔳𝔢 . 𝔞𝔰 . 𝔞𝔫 . 𝔞𝔫𝔠𝔥𝔬𝔯 . 𝔬𝔣 . 𝔱𝔥𝔢 . 𝔖𝔬𝔲𝔩

The third light shows St. John carrying a closed book in his left hand and a scroll in his right with the words:- + 𝔣𝔬𝔩𝔩𝔬𝔴 𝔞𝔣𝔱𝔢𝔯 ℭ𝔥𝔞𝔯𝔦𝔱𝔶 and below: 𝔥𝔢 . 𝔱𝔥𝔞𝔱 . 𝔩𝔬𝔳𝔢𝔱𝔥 . 𝔥𝔦𝔰 . 𝔟𝔯𝔬𝔱𝔥𝔢𝔯 . 𝔞𝔟𝔦𝔡𝔢𝔱𝔥 . 𝔦𝔫 . 𝔱𝔥𝔢 . 𝔩𝔦𝔤𝔥𝔱

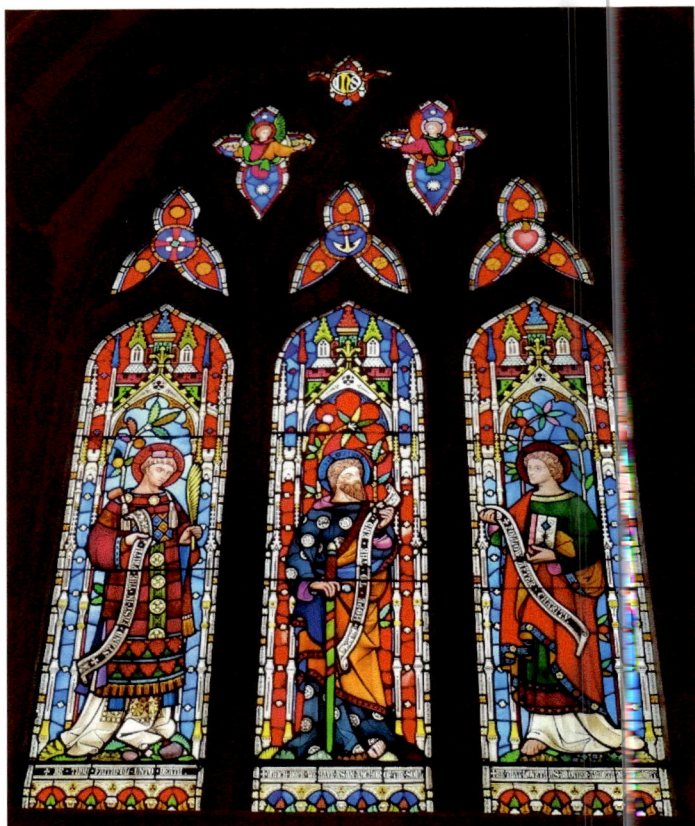

Figure 30: The South Window in the Chancel Sanctuary

In the tracery above are the Cross, Anchor and Heart – the emblems of Faith, Hope and Charity – and two angels with immortal crowns and the Christogram (𝔍𝔥𝔖) above. Until 1904 there was also an inscription painted above the window moulding:-

+ 𝔑𝔬𝔴 + 𝔞𝔟𝔦𝔡𝔢𝔱𝔥 + 𝔣𝔞𝔦𝔱𝔥, + 𝔥𝔬𝔭𝔢 + 𝔞𝔫𝔡 ℭ𝔥𝔞𝔯𝔦𝔱𝔶 – i . ℭ𝔬𝔯. . 13 . 13 +

THE CHANCEL NORTH WINDOW

Made by Clayton and Bell, this two-light window (*Fig. 31*) in the north wall of the Sanctuary represents the Crucifixion - in *type* and *antitype*. Christians believe that Old Testament events, persons or statements [*types*] either prefigured, or were fulfilled, or were superseded by, events (or if not by events then by aspects of Christ or by his revelation) [any or all such events etc. being *antitypes*] described in the New Testament.

The left light shows Moses with the stinging serpents and a brazen serpent on a cross, and Elias representing the

---

65 Letter dated Nov. 1809 from Edmond Vialls (op. cit.) says the altar rail door was dated 1635 – two years after Archbishop Laud instructed that altars be returned to their pre-Reformation positions.

66 A photograph taken before Comper's window was installed (1892) shows an altar of the same size. [reproduced in *Geddington as it Was: the Social History of a Rural Community*, by Monica Rayne (1991)]. Markham's 1899 Plan also shows an Altar of similar size. On the other hand, GG Scott's 1852 Layout Plan (*Fig. 71*) shows the altar set hard against the east wall, so either this was not carried out or the position may have changed at some point between 1857 and 1899.

Law and the Prophets.

The **right light** shows St. Paul and St. Peter, Apostles to the Gentiles and Jews respectively. The *type* is Moses lifting up the serpent, and the *antitype* is Christ on the Cross attended by angels and flanked by the Virgin Mary and St. John, with the text: "*Holy, Holy, Holy*".

Above Moses are the Old Testament prophets Isaiah, Jeremiah, Ezekiel and Daniel; whilst above Christ are the four Evangelists: Matthew, Mark, Luke, and John.

Above the four Prophets is a woman blindfolded representing Judaism - the crown falling from her head, the Tables of the Law in her right hand, and the sceptre broken in her left.

Above the Evangelists is a woman representing Christianity, crowned, bearing a sceptre in her right hand and the Gospel in her left. This denotes the passing of authority from the Jewish to the Christian Church.

At the apex is the *Agnus Dei* [Lamb of God].

THE SEDILIA & PISCINA

Beneath the South Window three Sedilia (seats where officiating clergy sat at times during the Mass) are set into small arches within the south wall of the Sanctuary. Set within a smaller arch immediately left of the Sedilia is a *Piscina* - a basin within which the chalice and patten would be washed after the Mass.

Above the Sedilia and Piscina are five mutilated stone heads (*Fig. 32*), probably damaged after the Reformation. Set within the easternmost of the 3 sedilia is a brass plaque that reads:

To the glory of God

and in loving memory of

Revd James Hogg Vicar of this Parish

Who died 25th Novr 1844, aged 70 years; also of

Mary his wife who died 24th May 1851 aged 68 years;

And of William Edward their eldest son

Who died 26th December 1856, aged 47 years.

The window above this record was dedicated AD 1860

By the members of this family

To . live . is . Christ . and . to . die . is . gain.

Figure 31: The North Window in the Chancel Sanctuary

Figure 32: a stone head
above the Sedilia

TRACES OF MEDIEVAL PAINTWORK

Close inspection of the stonework round the Sanctuary reveals traces of medieval paint (mostly a red ochre colour around windows, on some of the carved stone faces and even within some lettering of the Latin inscription on the Sanctuary skirting[67]) that has survived the various changes of the past 500 years.

THE ALTAR RAIL

The rail separating the Sanctuary from the Choir came from St. Mary's Church, New Road, Peterborough[68], which was de-consecrated in 1989 and demolished to make way for a redevelopment; the sale of land paid for the building of a new church.

There was an earlier Altar Rail, the door of which bore the date 1635. As this was still present in 1809[69] and can also be glimpsed in Edward Bradley's painting of the church in the early 19th Century (see the front cover), it seems almost certain that it remained until the 1855-57 re-ordering by GG Scott.

A MEDIEVAL SQUINT

Not far above the right-hand end of the Altar rail, a convex recess has been cut into the stonework. This is believed to be a 'squint', probably of medieval origin, whose purpose was to enable someone sitting in the adjacent screened-off chapel to observe the priest elevating the bread – a key moment in the Mass, because this is the point at which (for Catholics and many Anglo-Catholics) the bread and wine become Christ's body and blood.

THE CHOIR

Taking roughly two-thirds of the area of the Chancel, this is the area where, in the medieval period, clergy would offer chants and prayers as the officiating priest said or sang the Mass. As the Middle Ages progressed, they were increasingly joined by persons of high status. Following the major renovations of 1904-06, Sydney Gambier-Parry's new Chancel screen was installed in 1908 and it was four years later that the present Choir Stalls, designed by Ninian Comper[70] and crafted from old roof timbers[71], were installed. The red and black encaustic Minton floor tiles in the Choir were installed as part of the 1855 re-ordering. The carvings (1906) on the cornices of the Chancel roof were the work of Charles Frith[72], the brother of the famous artist, William Powell Frith.

CHOIR WAR MEMORIAL

On the north wall of the Choir is a memorial commemorating Choir members who fell in the Great War (*Fig. 33*).

In the form of an alabaster tablet within a framing of Ketton stone, it was designed by Talbot Brown of Wellingborough, who also designed the war memorial in the churchyard.

Nearby, the Royal British Legion banner is carried from a wall bracket.

Figure 33: The Choir War Memorial Tablet.
Photo: M Hopkins

---

67   The lettering with such colouring is very probably part of the 1369 original (e.g. the letters MCCCLIX themselves), whilst the clearer-cut lettering without colouring probably dates from the 1857 interpolations.

68   Information courtesy of Bryony Dorrington, widow of the late Rev. Richard Dorrington.

69   A letter dated Nov. 1809 from Edmond Vialls (op. cit.) states: *"On the Door of the Altar Rails is the date 1635".*

70   *'Sir Ninian Comper; An Introduction to his Life and Work with Complete Gazetteer'*: A Symondson & S A Bucknall (2006).

71   See *Kettering Guardian*, 3 July 1908.

72   See *Kettering Guardian*, 11 May 1906.

CLERESTORY WINDOWS

There are two levels of Clerestory windows in the Choir. At the lower level are five small, recessed windows (2 in the north wall and 3 on the southern side) that might pre-date the 13th Century enlargement of the Chancel and construction of the Lady Chapel and South Aisle. Previously hidden by timbers and plasterwork, the three windows in the south wall above the arches came to light in 1875, when they were discovered by workman taking down the old roof from part of the South Aisle. The larger upper clerestory windows in both the Chancel and the Nave date from the 15th Century.

FLOOR MEMORIALS

The Chancel contains three stone floor monuments, which are listed below.

A blue slate slab which reads:

Anna The second wife of

Thomas Maydwell Esq. and daughter of

-----kwood [*presumed Lockwood*], Esq. --pril, 1731

A blue slate slab inscribed:

Elizabeth, ye daughter of Thomas Maydwell

Esq. and Anna his wife dyed 2d Jany 1725

A third blue slate slab inscribed:

Thomas the son **of Thomas Maydwell**

Esqr. and Anna his wife dyed 7th July 1717

According to Markham (op. cit.) the following slabs were located in the Chancel in 1899, but they no longer are, so presumably they were removed in the changes of 1904-06, or perhaps when the Choir Stalls were installed in 1912 -

A plain freestone slab:

The Revd. Henry **Boulton.**

A second plain freestone slab:

Here lies the body of iohn noon

who died (August the) 3rd 1723 Aged 38 years.

A third plain freestone slab:

....e body of **Mr Christian Actonwid**

Who departed this Life

The 21st of July 1698 Aged 83

THOMAS CHANNON BRASS

Also commemorated on the west wall of the Choir is a former Choir-Master, Thomas Channon, who was born in Ottery St. Mary in Devon in 1829 and lived in West Street as the lodger of local farmers, the Dainty family, throughout his 37 years in Geddington. He was buried in the churchyard. The brass plaque reads:

This brass is placed here by former pupils.

In grateful memory of Thomas Channon

37 years School Master and Choir Master In this

Parish

Who fell asleep July 22 1886 aged 57 years.

There remaineth therefore a rest

To the people of GOD.

Mounted on stone ledges on either side of the Lady Chapel Altar are two brightly-decorated statues that were the gifts in 2017 of Jasmine and Thomas, the children of the then Priest-in-Charge, Fr. Rob Parker McGee and his wife Sarah. One is a figure of Jesus; and the other is of the Virgin Mary.

A PRIESTLY STONE EFFIGY

On the floor to the left of the Altar is the stone effigy (*Fig. 35*) of a recumbent priest. Thompson (op. cit.) dates it to the 13th Century, whilst Pevsner (op. cit.) gives the 14th Century, possibly linked to the 1369 inscription. For reasons discussed earlier (see section on *The Significance of the Inscriptions*), it seems quite possible that the effigy dates from c1369-70 and commemorates William Glover, Chaplain, who died at the Feast of Corpus Christi, 1369.

Lying west to east, he has a tonsure and long neck, a chalice in his right hand, a Missal in his left, and a paten (for the bread) under his right arm. He is vested for Mass, with a chasuble over his alb. Next to his head is a worn-down cherub. The stone shows signs of having been trimmed in the past, and a piece appears to have been lost from the eastern end.

The artist Peter Tillemans drew the effigy in 1719 (*Fig. 36*)[77], showing a well-defined face, upper body, and angel. A note on the back of this drawing (though not in Tillemans' hand) says it lay in the "*N Isle at Ye upper end under the N Wall*". The rough saw-marks on the southern side of the stone suggest it was attached to a wall, and so not now in its original position. The upper end of the effigy has been badly worn – thought to be the result of weathering in the late 18th and early 19th centuries. A letter dated 1809[78] placed it in 'the South Chancel' and described it as "*a stone figure in a kind of armour, but much mutilated*".

Sir Henry Dryden also recorded this monument in 1843 (*Fig. 37*)[79]. By this time, the lowermost part of the effigy seems to have been lost, and the facial features and cherub appear less distinct. By 1899, a drawing by Christopher Markham shows it much as we see today, with the eyes only just discernible.

Figure 35: 14th Century memorial effigy of a priest

The antiquarian John Bridges[80], who had commissioned Tillemans and gathered his material at about the same time (c1719), said: "*Adjacent to* [the Robert Launcelyn inscription on the Chapel step] *is the portrait in stone of a person with a chalice in his right hand; supposed by the tradition of the place to have been a priest who died as he was administering the sacrament. But the cup is added only to shew that he was in priest's orders. And had therefore the power of administering the eucharist.*"

77   Reproduced in *Northamptonshire in the Early Eighteenth Century: The Drawings of Peter Tillemans and Others*, pub. Northamptonshire Record Society (1996), Ed. Bruce Bailey.

78   Letter from Edmond Vialls dated 17 Nov. 1809 (op. cit.)

79   The drawing by Sir Henry Dryden is held in Northamptonshire Central Library: DR/25/120/001

80   *The History & Antiquities of Northamptonshire*, Vol. 2, pp 310-11 (op. cit.). This brought together Bridges' notes gathered in the years 1718-2.. See the earlier section (above) on *The Significance of the Inscriptions* for a discussion of the tradition that the priest died during the celebration of the Eucharist.

Figure 36: Drawing of priestly effigy by Peter Tillemans (1719)
©*British Library Board.*
Ackn.: Northants Record Society

Figure 37: Drawing of priestly effigy by
Sir Henry Dryden (1843)
© *Northamptonshire Central Library: DR/25/120/001*

A letter[81] dated c1736 in the Buccleuch Archive says that:

> *"a stone may be seen in the Chancel of Geddington Church with a figure of a man with a cup in his hand and round the stone 'Hujus ecclesiae capellanus.'"* [Chaplain of this Church].

No trace of that inscription can be seen today, though it is conceivable that it may be hidden by the base of the adjacent timber screen. This letter also says that local people believed the priest died while celebrating Mass, and other sources also report this belief.

ROBERT LAUNCELYN INSCRIPTION

Along the skirting of the Choir and turning into the face of the step of the Lady Chapel's Sanctuary there is an inscription that reads:

+ ROBERTVS · LAVNCELYN · DE · GEY-
TINGTOVN · FECIT · ISTVM · CANCEL-
LVM · CVIVS · ANIME · PROPICIETVR ·
DEVS · AMEN

[Robert Launcelyn of Geddington built this Chancel on whose soul may God look with favour. Amen].

The earlier section on *The Chancel* considers Robert Launcelyn, the significance of the inscriptions, the building of the Chancel and the identity of the person commemorated by the effigy.

THE CHAPEL AUMBREY

Set in the wall behind a curtain to the left of the Altar is an Aumbrey, where sanctified bread and wine is kept for later use. The original late 14th Century opening[82] has been stopped up and a smaller locked cabinet inserted, which is still used today. Some (but not all) Christians believe in 'transubstantiation' - that is that the bread and wine are transformed into Christ's body and blood during the Eucharist - and so will bow or genuflect (bend the knee) towards the Aumbrey, above which a perpetual light symbolises the continuing presence of Christ in the sanctified bread and wine inside.

THE ARCADE

The chapel is separated from the Chancel by an arcade of two double-chamfered arches of late 13th Century design, similar to, but slightly later than, those of the South Aisle, although the western arch is an 1857 re-build.

CHRIST CRUCIFIED

Occupying a recess formed by the blocking-up of a 15th Century window[83], a large cross bearing Christ crucified dominates the chapel's south wall. This is a focus for people to venerate, pray quietly or meditate – especially on Maundy Thursday and Good Friday or when commemorating lost loved ones on All Saints Day; and perhaps also to light a candle[84] at the nearby votive stand, signifying prayers offered for a loved one.

---

81   Unsigned letter to Charles Lamotte, March 1736 [NRO Montagu Vol, 22 no.102], and reproduced as Letter L86 in *Estate Letters from the Time of John, 2nd Duke of Montagu* (pub. Northamptonshire Record Society, 2013). This account closely mirrors Bridges', which suggests the author may have had access to Bridges' notes.

82   A.H. Thompson, 1907 (op. cit.) p. 156.

83   A print of the church made in 1845 (Fig.70) by Edward Bradley shows this window already blocked up.

84   For insurance reasons normally candles are only available when the church is attended

PART I: A TOUR OF THE CHURCH

SAXON WORK

There are indications that the Saxon church may have had a south transcept or perhaps a *porticus* occupying the western part of the chapel. A vertical joint with 'long and short' stonework typical of Saxon corner-stones can be seen on the external face of the south wall, and there is a pad-stone (used to support a roof beam) and a roof scar above the central pillar of the arcade on the chapel's north side, that may evidence an earlier structure.

SOUTH WALL STONEWORK

The internal stonework of the south wall of the chapel is complex, showing signs of several alterations down the centuries. The chapel once had two 14th Century windows, but little remains of either.

Of the eastern one the only trace is its eastern jamb in the form of a V-shaped groove a few centimetres deep and wide and about 80cm high, wedged between the western jamb of the lancet window and the eastern jamb of the blocked-up window.

The second one is partly covered by the large Maydwell memorial, with just a small section of the eastern jamb visible between the Maydwell monument and the brass to Louise Wetherall below, and with two voussoirs and a defaced section of hood-moulding visible to the right of the Maydwell monument. *Fig. 38* illustrates the position of the western 14th Century window.

THE PATRICK WINDOW

The glass in this lancet window (*Fig. 39*) in the south-east corner of the Chapel dates from 1921 and is by Arthur Louis Moore (1849-1939) of Russell Square in London.

It depicts St. Paul holding a sword and a book. The dedication reads:

> To the Glory of God and in
> loving memory of
> Harry Arthur Patrick
> who passed to higher service
> Jan 20th 1920
> after returning from India and
> Egypt.

Below this window there was once a small door (blocked up in 1855) that gave separate entry for priests and the private sponsors of the Chapel.

Figure 39: The 'Patrick Window' in the Lady Chapel

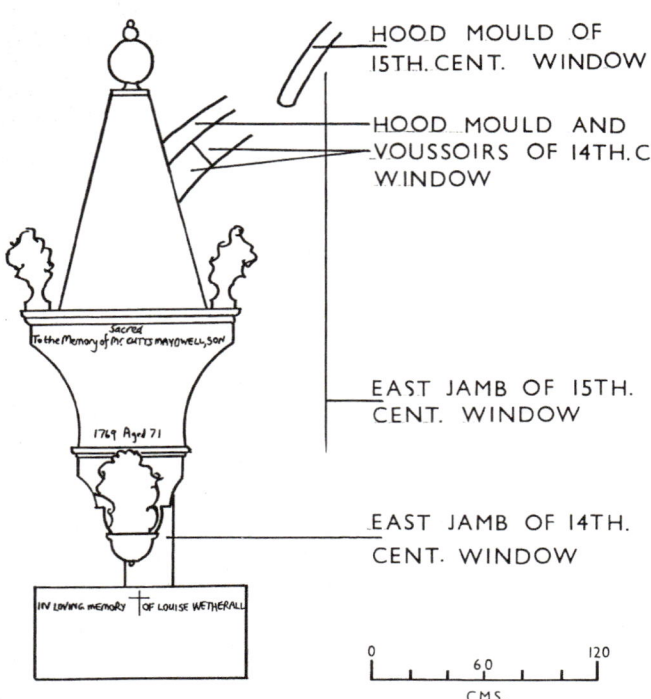

Figure 38: Relationship of stonework features in the south wall of the Lady Chapel

drawing by PJ Ellis (1986)

Labels in figure:
HOOD MOULD OF 15TH. CENT. WINDOW
HOOD MOULD AND VOUSSOIRS OF 14TH.C. WINDOW
EAST JAMB OF 15TH. CENT. WINDOW
EAST JAMB OF 14TH. CENT. WINDOW
CMS.

ANCIENT & MODERN SCREENS

Separating the Lady Chapel from the Choir, and framed by arches, are two wooden screens, each about 2.4 metres high. Best viewed from the Lady Chapel, the more westerly of these screens (*Fig. 40*) retains its central door and is the original medieval Chancel screen which is believed to date from the 14th or possibly the 13th Century. It was probably moved to the arch between the South Aisle and Lady Chapel in about 1618, when the Tresham screen replaced it in the Chancel arch. From there, it is thought to have been stored in the tower from 1855-56 and moved to its present position in 1906-07. Its companion screen to the east is a replica dating from 1907 and made by Samuel Townley and George Freeman of Geddington[85].

---

85   The replica screen was installed 'just before Easter' 1907. *Geddington Monthly Magazine* April 1907. See also Monica Rayne (op. cit.) page 15.

Figure 40: the medieval Chancel screen (now in the Lady Chapel)

A WINDOW MADE IN GEDDINGTON

The glass in the 15th Century window (*Fig. 41*) next to the Tresham Screen is the work of Joseph Freestone (1848-1929), who lived at 1-3 West Street in Geddington.

Joseph was a talented man who, as well as being an artist in stained glass, was a member of the Royal Academy. He is buried in the churchyard with his nephew, Conrad William Henry Groves.

The window's centre light shows Christ seated, speaking to Mary Magdalene, and in the background three men are feasting at a table.

The left-hand light shows Christ driving the money-changers from the Temple.

The right-hand light depicts Christ standing by the seashore with three apostles.

The window's inscription reads:

𝕿o the glory of God and in memory of 𝕰.𝕽 and 𝕷.𝕸.𝕾 1882

[identities currently unknown].

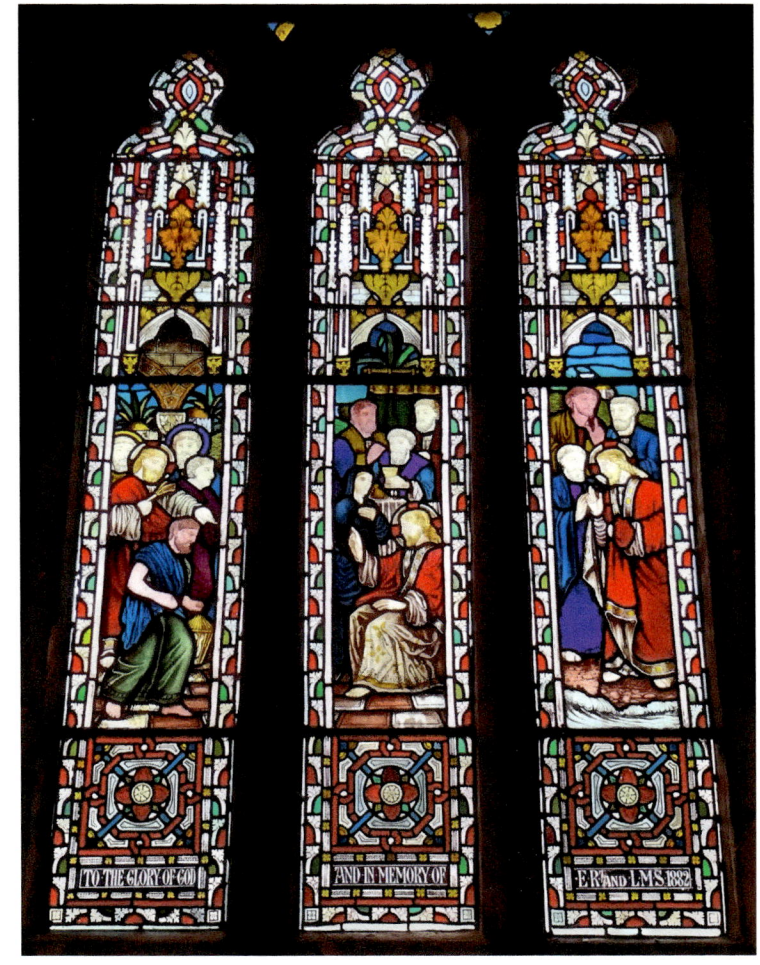

Figure 41: Joseph Freestone's window in the Lady Chapel

Figure 42: The Jarmon Brass (1486)

THE JARMON BRASS

Situated in the floor just in front of the step is a small brass (*Fig. 42*) of two figures with hands clasped in prayer, with an inscription band at their feet, reading:

> Hic jacent Henricus Jarmon et Anna Uƒ eius
> qˉuor acabus ppicietur deus. Amen.
> [*Here lies Henry Jarmon and Anna his wife may*
> *they be received with favour by God. Amen*].

The brass is the work of a Coventry workshop run by a mason and marbler named Robert Crosse[86]. The Will of Henry German (Jarmon) is dated 1486[87], so the brass must have been made in that year or shortly afterwards. This memorial was moved from its original position in the North Aisle in 1906.

It is also clear that its current stone slab is not the original as its layout differs from the Coventry norm of leaving a gap between figures and foot inscription. We do not know if the original work included children or other features. The middle portion of Anna's figure has gone and that of Henry's has had to be refixed. He has a knife in his girdle, and a rosary hangs from his waist.[88]

The figures are typical of Crosse's work, with smiling rather than solemn faces. Henry wears a hood with a long streamer over his left shoulder, a fashion also shown on other Coventry brasses and some from London workshops at this period, although more usually shown hanging on the right shoulder.

The plant below Henry's feet with its three-leaf clovers (the Tresham arms?) is also typical.. The elongated lower bodies reflect the way that human figures were depicted before the Renaissance.

THE MAYDWELL BRASSES

Also in front of the chapel step are two floor brasses commemorating members of the Maydwell family. First (*Fig. 43*) is a Memorial plaque to Thomas Maydwell (d 1624 & his wife Maria (d 1628). In 1588 this same Thomas Maydwell contributed £25 against the Spanish invasion. There was once a pew[89] in this chapel bearing the inscription "TM. MM.1604", presumably also for Thomas and Maria.

The second brass is a rectangular inscription plaque with a decoratively carved border, let into a stone slab. The inscription on brass reads:

> Mrs Anna Maydwell Daughter of Thomas Maydwell
> Esqre and Anna his wife.
> Died November 2. 1767, in the 80th Year of her age.

Still legible on the stone slab are the words: "Elizabe Aged In the"

OTHER FLOOR MONUMENTS

There are three further stone slabs set into the floor of the Lady Chapel. The first is found next to the chapel sanctuary step, and is inscribed:

> here lyeth the body of John Goodman Esqr.
> who dyed Jvne 21 1668. aged   yeares.

The other two slabs commemorate members of the Maydwell family, and read:

> Here lyeth ye body of Mar^g Maydwell
> who dyed ye 22th of July 1682

and, at the west end of the chapel:

> Thomas Maydwell Esq. dyed 30 Novr. 1720

---

86   See online article (Oct. 2021) by Jon Bayliss for the Monumental Brass Society: https://www.mbs-brasses.co.uk/index-of-brasses/henry-anne-jarmon

87   Serjeantson & Longden (op. cit.)

88   Male rosaries of this period were generally straight, as shown here (information courtesy of Kelcey Wilson-Lee, President, Monumental Brass Soc.). See also a footnote on p210 of *A Manual of Costume as Illustrated by Monumental Brasses by Herbert Druitt* [pub. de la Mare Press, 1906]

89   Recorded in a letter from Edmond Vialls dated 17 Nov. 1809 (op. cit.)

Figure 43: Brass commemorating Thomas and Maria Maydwell

Translation:

Here lies Thomas Maydwell of noble birth

and Maria his wife, daughter of the noble William Brackenbury

which said Thomas died on the sixth day of December 1624

and the aforesaid Maria who died on the third day of January

in the year of Our Lord 1628

SOUTH WALL MONUMENTS

In the centre of the south wall are two wall monuments, the largest being an in the shape of an ornamental urn and inscribed:

Sacred to the Memory of Mr. Cutts Maydwell, son of Thomas Maydwell, Esqʳ.

& Anna, sister of Richᵈ· Lockwood, Esqʳ· of Dews Hall, Essex.

He liv'd Twenty years in Turkey, and then settled at the seat of his Ancestors

in this Town; where he Dyed June ye 24 1769, Aged 71.

Beneath this is a brass plaque inscribed:

In loving memory + of Louisa Wetherall

who fell asleep at Geddington Priory Novʳ· 18ᵗʰ 1881. Aged 76.

Blessed are the pure in heart for they shall see God. Matt. V. viii.

BOOK OF REMEMBRANCE

A Book of Remembrance records past parishioners and their deceased loved ones and sits within a display case bearing a brass plaque inscribed:

Kindly donated by
THE FRIENDS OF GEDDINGTON CHURCH
From funds raised within the local community
October 2016

The Book was the gift of Phyllis Lockwood in memory of her husband, Charles.

The Lady Chapel St Mary Magdalene Church, Geddington.

Figure 44: The Tresham Screen and South Aisle circa 1939
Reproduced from Geddington.net

THE SOUTH AISLE

We now move through the wooden screen into the mid-13th Century South Aisle, and turn around to face eastwards to get a good view of the Tresham Screen.

THE TRESHAM SCREEN

The arch between the South Aisle and the Lady Chapel is occupied by a particularly fine and rare carved screen (*Fig. 44*) given by Maurice Tresham, that Pevsner describes as a 'piece of early Gothic revival'. It bears the Tresham arms and the inscription:

1618

LAVS DEO

M ♣ T

[Translation: *1618 – Praise the Lord – MT*].

A further inscription (from Psalm 26, verse 8) around the outer margin reads:

𝔓𝔰𝔞𝔩 ; 𝔵𝔵𝔳𝔦. – 𝔏𝔬𝔯𝔡 𝔍 𝔥𝔞𝔳𝔢 𝔩𝔬𝔳𝔢𝔡 𝔱𝔥𝔢 𝔟𝔢𝔞𝔲𝔱𝔦𝔢 𝔬𝔣 𝔗𝔥𝔶 𝔥𝔬𝔲𝔰𝔢 ; 𝔞𝔫𝔡 𝔱𝔥𝔢 𝔭𝔩𝔞𝔠𝔢 𝔴𝔥𝔢𝔯𝔢 𝔗𝔥𝔦𝔫𝔢 𝔥𝔬𝔫𝔬𝔲𝔯 𝔡𝔴𝔢𝔩𝔩𝔢𝔱𝔥. 𝔙𝔢𝔯. 𝔳𝔦𝔦𝔦.

And over the central arch of the screen (taken from Psalm 115 verse 3):

𝔔𝔲𝔦𝔡 𝔯𝔢𝔱𝔯𝔦𝔟𝔲𝔞𝔪 𝔡𝔬𝔪𝔦𝔫𝔲𝔰 [the Lord will render as He will].

The screen was a thank-offering by Maurice Tresham for the birth of a son (also Maurice, born in 1618), and followed the gift of a bell in 1616 (see the section on THE BELLS). Many of the Tresham family were Catholics, though it is not clear whether Maurice shared their faith. This gift was ostensibly a sign of fealty to the post-Reformation church and a proclamation of status but, if Maurice did secretly hold to Rome, the screen's inscriptions are intriguing. In this case we might speculate that they conveyed covert recusancy (refusal to accept the authority of the Church of England): it was certainly the case that other members of the Tresham family used cleverly-disguised architectural and textual devices to signal their Catholic faith[90].

Thus, the passage from Psalm 26 may suggest that honour truly lay with the 'old religion'. The reference to Psalm 115 might hint not only that the Lord will render justice to those who have broken with Rome, but might also be a play on '*Quid retribuam domino….*' in the traditional Latin Mass: "*What shall I render to the Lord, for all the things he hath rendered unto me? I will take the chalice of salvation; and I will call upon the name of the Lord. Praising I will call upon the Lord: and I shall be saved from my enemies*". These words, spoken by the priest, are considered suitable for use on occasions of special thanksgiving, such as the birth of a child – but also when seeking relief from the Persecutors of the Church.

90　See *Building the Badge of God: Architectural Representations of Persecution and Coexistence in Post-Reformation England* by Susan M. Cogan, from *Archiv für Reformationsgeschichte* (Reformation History Archive), 2016.

Figure 45: Painting by Edward Bradley
of the Cenotaph of Queen Elizabeth I

and sat upon it, was a painted cenotaph of Queen Elizabeth I laid out on a canopied altar tomb (*Fig. 45*). Although in good condition, it was demolished as part of the renovation works in 1855-57.

However, a drawing of this mural was made by Edward Bradley prior to its destruction and is now displayed in the church. It can also be glimpsed in another of Bradley's drawings (see the cover photo) showing the church as it was in the first half of the 19th Century.

The text in capitals that can be seen in the background of the mural says:

"TVMVLVS ELIZABETHÆ REGINÆ ANGLIA"

[The tomb of Queen Elizabeth of England],

and in the central arch:

"SEMPER EADEM"

[Always the same – the wording on her personal coat of arms].

Bradley has annotated his drawing: *"The Tomb of Queen Elizabeth painted in distemper, formerly in the Chancel of Geddington Church, removed by the Rev. M. Church when Vicar."*

The screen originally sat within the Chancel arch - the carver having faithfully reproduced the tracery of the east window, though with additional scroll-work infilling. It was moved to its present location in 1906, having previously been stored in the Vestry[91] following its removal from the Chancel arch in 1855-57.

THE FORMER PAINTED CENOTAPH

It is believed that, in the period between c1618 and 1855, the arch linking the South Aisle and the Lady Chapel held the old medieval screen that had been removed from the Chancel arch to make way for the Tresham screen. Above,

TWO WINDOWS FROM MELLS

On each side of the South Door are two late-19th Century windows made in the laboratory of the Rev. J.S.H. Horner of Mells Rectory, near Frome in Somerset.

The first (western) one (*Fig. 46*) was the gift of parishioners and comprises three lights representing: (a) The Nativity; (b)

Figure 46: Window by Rev. Horner of Mells in the South Aisle - the gift of parishioners

Figure 47: Window by Rev. Horner of Mells in the South Aisle - the gift of Rev. WMH Church

---

91   Markham (op. cit.) p19.

the Salutation of Saints Mary and Elizabeth (The Visitation); and (c) The Annunciation.

The second (southern) one (*Fig. 47*) was the gift of a former Vicar, the Rev. W.M.H Church, in which the middle light depicts the Adoration of the Magi, and below which are two brass plaques also given by Rev. Church to commemorate his daughter and son. They are inscribed:

𝕳arriet 𝕰lizabeth 𝕮hurch	𝕭asil 𝕮hurch
Aged 41 years	Born at Geddington, 19th Oct. 1849
"Safe Home"	Died at Melbourne, 30th Jan. 1881
19 Oct. 1892	"It is the Lord: let Him do what seemeth to Him good".

MEMORIAL TO REV. HENRY BOULTON

Immediately to the left of the south door, a memorial mounted on the wall reads:

In memory of The Reverend Henry Boulton,
Vicar of Sibsey in the County of Lincoln,
Eldest son of Henry Boulton Esq. of Geddington House
and of Moulton in the County of Lincoln,
who died July 13th 1825, Aged 38 years.

Rev. Henry Boulton was staying with his father at Geddington when he died. His father, a barrister, had no fewer than 5 wives, four of whom pre-deceased him, including Henry Jnr.'s mother Susannah Foster (1761-88). Susanah had two other children. Both outlived their brother. Rev. Henry Boulton was also commemorated by a stone slab in the Chancel[92], but this is no longer visible.

MEMORIAL TO REV. THOMAS CORNWELL

Beneath the Boulton memorial is a brass plaque dedicated to a former vicar, Rev. Thomas Cornwell, whose extensive notes formed the basis of an important history of Geddington and its church by Christopher Markham (1899). It is inscribed:

to the glory of God
in affectionate memory of
Thomas C Brand Cornwell M.A.
twenty four years vicar of this parish
he entered into rest July 21st 1893 +
this brass is placed by his former parishioners and friends +

the souls of the righteous are in the hands of God +

Thomas Charles Brand Cornwell was curate of Stanwick (1851-53) and then at Geddington before serving as Vicar here from 1856 to 1885. He then served as Rector of Scaldwell until his death in 1893. With his wife Frances Richardson Gascoyen, he had at least ten children, the youngest of whom, Brand, became a vicar too. Thomas died in Cambridge and is buried there in Mill Road Cemetery. His widow Frances died in Somerset in 1898 and was buried in Chew Magna.

MEMORIAL TO REV. JAMES HOGG

Further east, between the two windows in the south wall is a stone plaque, which reads:

Sacred To the Memory of The Revd. James Hogg
Fourteen years Curate, And Thirty years
Vicar of this Parish.
He departed this life November 25th 1844 Aged 70 years.
Conjugal and Filial Love has raised this Tablet as a
memorial of an affectionate Husband, a Reverand Father,
and a Faithful Minister of Christ.

"God forbid that I should glory, save in the Cross of our
Lord Jesus Christ. Gal. vi. Xiv.[93]

In addition to being Vicar of Geddington, James Hogg was Master of Kettering Grammar School, and lived in Gold Street, Kettering. He was evidently a much-loved man

SAXON TRACES

Formation of the southern arcade obliterated the Saxon arcading on the southern elevation of the Nave save for one small section remaining at the eastern end of that wall[94]. There is also some 'long and short' stonework set within the end of the aisle's north-eastern end indicating the south-east corner of the Saxon Nave. But other evidence of the church's Saxon origins came to light in 1990 when a number of burials were discovered and dated to between the 10th and 12th centuries as the floor of the South Aisle was being renewed.

---

92   Markham (op.cit.)

93   Gal. vi. Xiv is a reference to St. Paul's letter to the Galatians, chapter 6, verse 14.

94   Uncovered when plaster was removed during the restoration works in 1905 (*Kettering Guardian* 13 October 1905). The newspaper article seems to imply that the arcading in the North Aisle had been known about for some time past.

THE ALLAWAY WINDOW

To the left of these plaques we find another window (*Fig. 48*), which is dedicated:

TO THE MEMORY OF
EDWARD MICHAEL ALLAWAY
DIED 25TH JULY 1992 AGED 66 YEARS
AND HIS MOTHER CONSTANCE ADA
DIED 21ST MARCH 1977 AGED 81 YEARS

The left-hand light depicts Samuel; the centre one gives the Dedication; and the right-hand one shows David holding a crook, a sling and a harp. The outer two lights were part of a triptych designed and made in 1925 by Hubert Blandford of Exeter for the Rowe Family Congregational Church, Exeter. When that church was demolished in 1976, the glass was rescued and donated to the Stained Glass Repository (now Museum) at Ely in Cambridgeshire.

In 1999, with the aid of the late Ken Ryan, Churchwarden, the two panels were obtained and then adapted by Peter Saunders of Northampton. The central panel was added to fit the window tracery - the original backgrounds being removed and replaced with clear glass. The window was installed in October 2001. The original central light from Exeter (depicting the newly-risen Christ with Mary Magdalene) is now in St. John's Church, Orsumoghu, Nigeria.

Figure 48: The 'Allaway Window' in the South Aisle

WALL RECESSES

A curious feature of the south wall is that it has a couple of recesses cut into the stonework. These were once used to house bowls or stoups containing holy water with which people would make the sign of the cross, first on entering the church, and secondly when about to enter the Lady Chapel. It is said[95] that the recess near the south door was at one time used by gentlemen to deposit their top hats on entry to the church!

PART I: A TOUR OF THE CHURCH

THE TOWER ARCH

Before completing our tour of the inside of the church, we should note the Tower Arch and the area beyond it.

It has been said[96] that the peculiar and dissimilar finishing of the capitals to the Tower arch suggests it was by William Howard, who built the tower at Fotheringhay, and if so, it would mean the arch is later than the Tower. *Fig. 49* shows the Tower arch in 1986, before the servery and ringing floor were built. Joseph Freestone's West Window can be seen in this picture. The modern (2022) curtains that draw across the face of the ringing floor and across the servery below were gifts of the *Friends of Geddington Church*.

THE WEST DOOR

The west door is located at the foot of the Tower. By tradition, the west door of a church forms the main entrance at the furthest point from the altar, although the door at Geddington is very rarely opened these days, the South Door forming the normal entrance.

MODERN SERVERY

A modern (2004) servery now occupies the tower's ground level. The timber facings were formed from an old pew.

THE TOWER

Dating from the late 14th Century (though perhaps springing from the base of a 12th Century tower[97]) and heightened in the 15th Century, the tower comprises 4 stages with clasping buttresses, two pairs of two-light bell-openings with transom, a quatrefoil frieze, castellated parapet, and a recessed spire with three tiers of lucarnes in alternating directions. The stonework was extensively repaired in 1904-06, and to a more limited extent in 1954-55.

There is no public access to the Tower beyond the ground floor servery. Arrangements may be made in special cases to view the ringing floor, but access beyond that is not possible for health and safety reasons. The following section is for the reader interested to know what lies within the Tower.

Figure 49: The Tower Arch as it was in 1986.
Photo: M Hopkins

THE CLOCK

The clock mechanism is dated 1766 and is a rare example of a turret clock by Thomas Bailey of Stanion, who is better-known as a maker of longcase clocks. The dial was renewed in 1897[98] and restored in 1994.

THE RINGING FLOOR

The timber bell-ringing floor above the Servery was constructed in 1994 by P.S. Clipstone, builders of Geddington, who were based at Lyons Yard in Wood Street. It may echo an 18th Century musicians' gallery[99] that it is believed was removed in 1855 and the front screen came from the pews at the church of St. Peter, Little Oakley, which had been de-consecrated and converted to a monument restoration centre by the Orton Trust, but which is now a private dwelling. A small brass plaque featuring images of fire and of sheaves of wheat records that:

THIS BELLRINGERS FLOOR
Was erected to the memory of
MATTHEW JAMES HARKER
1921 – 1984
By his many friends in the village of Geddington
and his fellow members of
The Geddington Volunteer Fire Brigade, 1994

---

96   *Northampton Mercury* (8 June 1867). Also by Markham (op. cit.) p 8.

97   Description cited in **Historic England** List Entry Number: 1052076 (see **Appendix 5**)

98   *Kettering Guardian* (26 October 1897). The new clock face was supplied by Gillett & Johnson of Croydon and fitted by Mr. Patrick.

99   *"At a vestry…holden this 29th day of August 1816"* it was *"resolved that an alteration shall be made in the gallery for the accommodation of the singers."* [from Rev. Richard Dorrington's notes, assumed to be from the Vestry Minutes at the County Record Office]. However, this gallery may have been the one described in Vialls' 1809 letter (op. cit.) which was in the North Aisle.

TOWER WEST WINDOW

The two-light window in the west wall of the ringing floor was made by Joseph Freestone of Geddington. The left-hand light represents Christ's baptism by St. John the Baptist in the River Jordan, and is inscribed:

"He that believeth, and is baptised shall be saved"

The right-hand light represents Jesus receiving little children with the inscription:

"Suffer the little children to come unto me, and forbid them not".

Above all this are shown the Ark, Dove, and the Holy Spirit.

THE BELLS

There is a peal of six bells in the Tower.

The oldest bell dates from 1550 and was cast by Leicester bellfounder Robert Newcombe. It has a diameter of 34 inches (863mm) and is inscribed:

S. THOMAS

between the symbols of a scarab and a *fleur de lys*.

The next oldest is from the Watts family foundry in Leicester and dates from 1580, which probably makes the founder Francis Watts. Again 34 inches in diameter, it is inscribed:

A B C D E F   G H I K L M   N O P Q R S

together with a shield bearing three bells, then two and one [the symbol of the Watts foundry].

The third bell (tenor) has a diameter of 40 inches (1016mm). It was cast by Hugh Watts (Jnr.) in the family foundry at Leicester, and is inscribed:

ser robert Dallington
gabe me to geddington
aged 69 1630

together with the Watts' crest of a shield bearing three bells, then two and one.

Next is a 36 inch (914mm) bell cast by Thomas Eayre I of Kettering. It is inscribed:

Omnia fiant ad gloriam dei Gloria deo soli:
anno . domini. 1732.

[*Let all be done for the glory of God. Glory to God alone in the year of our Lord 1732*]

The fifth bell is a treble, cast by Taylors of Loughborough in 1835. With a diameter of 24 inches (610mm) it is inscribed:

✸ w. dainty & w : branson churchwardens
✸ w. & j. taylor founders 1835
on the rim is: j. cadley agent
and on the waist the stamp of a cow.

It seems that this fifth bell replaced an earlier one, for there is a record[100] of a bell dated 1616 bearing the inscription:

In honorem sanctae trinitatis Mauricus Tresham
Dedicavit.
[*Maurice Tresham Dedicated this in honour of the Holy Trinity.*]

Finally, the most recent, is another 24-inch treble which was hung at the same time as a new steel bell frame was installed in 2004. It is inscribed simply:

Whitechapel 2004.

MEMORIAL TO WILLIAM MOORE

On the wall of the bell-ringing floor is a memorial to William Moore, who had rung every Christmas at Geddington in an unbroken sequence of 50 years dating back to 1858[101]. Made by Samuel Abbot and unveiled by the Vicar in September 1910, the inscription reads:

This tablet was erected to commemorate the jubilee of
William Moore,
who has rung on these bells for 50 years without omission
on Christmas Eve.
In honour of this splendid record, a peal of doubles, 5040
changes in seven methods,
was rung on Monday December 28th 1908,
in two hours and fifty seven minutes by the following:
George Black, treble;
Arthur Robinson 2;
Walter Robinson 3;
Matthias Hobbs 4;
Frederick J Tite, Tenor.
Conducted by Matthias Hobbs.
Rev. B Turton vicar. CBW Brook, John Abbot,
Churchwardens. S Abbot

Figure 50: The tenor bell given by Sir Robert Dallington in 1630

---

100   Letter dated Nov. 1809 from Edmond Vialls (op. cit.)
101   Mr. Moore had also rung to celebrate the Golden Wedding anniversary of the Duke and Duchess of Buccleuch on 20th November 1909.

PART I: A TOUR OF THE CHURCH

WOODEN PLAQUE COMMEMORATING THE 700TH ANNIVERSARY OF QUEEN ELEANOR

Beneath the Coat of Arms of the King of England and the personal Arms of Eleanor and Edward I is inscribed:

Saturday 1st December 1990

A PEAL of 5040 Doubles

15 extents each of Grandsire

& Reverse Canterbury & 12

Extents of Plain Bob (2hrs 47mins.)

Julie E. Green — treble

Elizabeth A. Betts — 2nd

Kenneth P. Jackson — 3rd

Robert J Jackson — 4th

David Kingman (cond.) — tenor

tenor . 11 cwts. 3qrs. 17 lbs.

1st peal . 1st of doubles

1st peal of doubles as conductor

Rung to commemorate Queen Eleanor (died 1290)

Wife of King Edward 1st of England

Vicar: Rev. R.B. Dorrington: Churchwardens: P.W.

Rogers H.G. Stafford

RICHARD BEST BRASS

This brass wall monument was, until the late 20th Century, on the west wall of the Nave by the Tower arch, but is now on the north wall of the ringing chamber. It reads:

If who lies here thov do enqvire

Reade and so have thy desire

Richard Best his name and free

O th' Haberdasher's Companye

The priviledg of Merchants : He

Did claim with ye like libertye

The years that here he passed ore

Wanted bvt one of fovrscore.

Fovrty years he abroad did toyle

The rest he spent in his owne soyle

Free from wedlock care or strife

He wedded was to single life.

To have more spoke he did deserve

Bvt 'twas his will yt this shovld serve

He dyed ye 26 of Aprill 1629.

MARGARET TRESHAM BRASS

Also mounted on a wooden plaque on the north wall of the ringing chamber is a brass that once graced St. Faith's Church, Newton. It comprises three brasses: First, the Tresham coat of arms, underneath which is a brass engraving of Margaret Tresham, from whose mouth the Christogram 'IHS' is issuing. Below that is the following inscription:

HEARE LIETH INTERRED THE BODIE
OF MARGARET TRESHAM LATE WIFE
OF MVARICE TRESHAM OF NEWTON
AND DAUGHTER OF FRAVNCIS TAN
FIELD OF GAYTON IN THE COVNTIE
OF NORTHAMPTON ESQVIRES. WHO
YIELDED UP HER SOVLE INTO THE HAN
DES OF THE ALMIGHTIE GOD. THE
26 OF SEPTEMBER ANO 1604 . ÆTAT:SVÆ.66

['ÆTAT:SVÆ.66' = 'in the 66th year of her age']

In the early church 'IHS' was a contraction of the Greek ΙΗΣΟΥΣ, meaning 'Jesus'; but in the later medieval period became Latinised as 'IHS' which was then taken to stand for *Iesus Hominum Salvator*, meaning 'Jesus Saviour of Mankind', and was used to signify deep devotion and as an appeal for Christ's help. It is common in Catholic and 'High Anglican' usage, so its use in 1604 for a member of the Tresham family, many of whom were recusants, might also be a sign of devotion to the Catholic faith, though this is pure speculation.

This motif can also be seen in gold lettering on the blue frontal hanging from the pulpit in Bradley's painting (see the front cover) and in stone on the War Memorial. Together with other indications, such as the retention of the 1635 High Altar and rail, these suggest that 'high church' leanings long persisted at Geddington. Older parishioners attest to this being the case through to the end of the 20th Century.

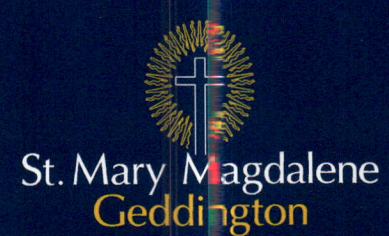

St. Mary Magdalene
Geddington

The churchyard is large and divided into sections by paths. In the Plan (*Fig. 51*), the sections are designated A to H. The older stones are mainly found to the south of the church, whilst the newer sections extend back some distance to the north side of the church and the newest section of all (H) is to the east.

The churchyard was extended to the north of the church in 1857 and again in 1907[102], on the second occasion to enclose land given by the Duke of Buccleuch, when substantial quantities of artefacts associated with the former royal palace were unearthed.

A further increase in capacity was made in 1970 when an elevated section (H) was constructed. Although the churchyard is still open for burials, space is now very limited. The churchyard is regularly visited by villagers with many well-tended graves. There are ancient rights of way through the churchyard.

There are several substantial yew trees within the churchyard, and three large lime trees. All are subject to Tree Preservation Orders. There has been little opportunity for rare flora or fauna to become established beyond significant growths of lichen on stonework. No special scientific or ecological designation attaches to the site.

The churchyard is maintained by a small team of volunteers, and members of the village's Volunteer Fire Brigade periodically undertake heavier maintenance work and clearance. An open area in the south-western section alongside approach paths is also used for church fetes.

THE WAR MEMORIAL

A war memorial cross (Grade II Listed[103]) was erected to the south west of the church in 1921 and, together with memorial plaques in the wall of the church forms the focus for Remembrance in the village. The memorial comprises a c9m high floriated Latin cross with '𝕴𝕳𝕾' in a shield at the top. The cross-head is set on an hexagonal pillar which rises from a square plinth set on a two-stepped octagonal base.

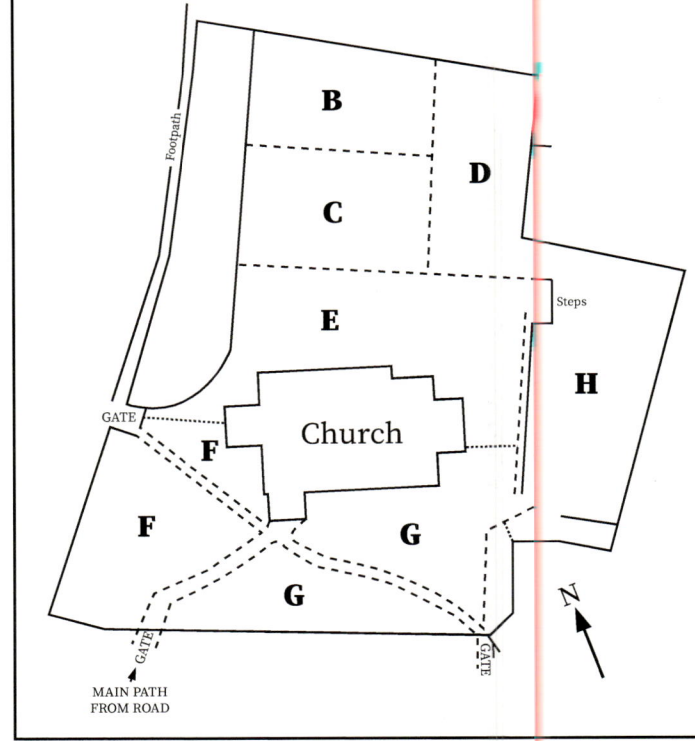

Figure 51: Plan of the Churchyard

On the plinth is inscribed:

1914 – 1918

IN UNDYING MEMORY OF
THE MEN OF GEDDINGTON
WHO IN THE GREAT WAR
GAVE THEIR LIVES FOR US

The following inscription has been added below, to the top step of the base:

ALSO
1939-1945

Nearby, on the outer west wall of the south aisle of the church are three tablets bearing names and additional inscriptions, including those from Newton. On 20 November 1918 a public meeting was held and a memorial committee, chaired by Rev. Turton, was elected. The committee reported its proposals in January 1920 for a memorial

---

102   The extension was consecrated by the Bishop of Peterborough in August 1908. (*Kettering Leader*, 28 August 1908)

103   *Historic England* List entry Number: 1425141. First listed: 10-Mar-2015. (see *Appendix 5*)

Figure 52: War Memorial Service of Dedication (28 July 1921)
Photo from Geddington.net

cross, and the necessary funds raised by public subscription. The cross and separate wall tablet were designed by Mr. Talbot Brown of architects Talbot Brown & Fisher Ltd., Wellingborough for a fee of £20.[104]

Built by Mr. Patrick of Geddington, construction took a month and, on 28 July 1921, the memorial was unveiled (Fig. 52) by Major Wetherall of Northampton. Seventy years later, all 170 of those who served in the Great War were commemorated in book form[105]. In 2018 those who died were remembered with special commemorations; and a *National Lottery Heritage Fund* grant enabled the village school to mount an extensive educational programme about the War for their pupils and parents.

WAR GRAVES

The Commonwealth War Graves Commission commemorates all those who fell in these conflicts and there are four graves in Geddington churchyard maintained by the Commission. There are also seven men buried or commemorated elsewhere who are additionally commemorated here on memorials erected by their families.

Although not commemorated by the CWGC, there are seven men who died of war-related causes in the years following the Great War and are buried in the churchyard. Full details of these graves are given in *Appendix 2*.

---

104 Minutes of the War Memorial Committee, 29 July 1920.
105 *Geddington, A Village at War*, by Melvyn Hopkins (1989) – ISBN 978-0951502907

PART II: THE CHURCHYARD

NOTABLE TOMBSTONES

SAMUEL LEE

Approx. 10m south of the church is the tomb of Samuel Lee, whose generosity to the people of Geddington is recorded on his tombstone:

> Here lieth interred the body of Mr. SAMUEL LEE
> who died March the 3rd, 1708. He was Ranger of
> Geddington Chase to His Grace the Duke of Montague
> and bequeathed to the Post of Geddington the profits of a
> Piece of land lying in Cranford St. John[106]

The Samuel Lee Charity is still active today and continues to help local residents facing difficulties.

OTHER CHEST TOMBS

Two similar tomb chests nearby (which form part of the same Grade II listing) are no longer legible, although it is thought one commemorates a member of the Maydwell family; whilst another almost illegible Grade II listed tomb nearby is that of Samuel Rowlatt who died in 1710.

To the North-West of the church, another Grade II Listed chest tomb sits approx. 15m from the west end of the church. Early to mid 18th Century in date, this tomb is also illegible.

L^T. JOHN HAMES R.N.

Next to the latter chest tomb is a small brass plaque set into a flat stone, commemorating John Hames, a naval officer from Geddington. The Parish Registers record that he was born on 2nd September 1782 and baptised in the church on 16th May 1785. He married Mary Cox on 14th February 1811 and was buried on 6th April 1813. The plaque reads:

> LIEU^T JOHN HAMES R N
> DIED April Ye 1st 1813 Aged 31 Years

Figure 53: Tomb of Samuel Lee

TRESHAM FAMILY REMAINS

The remains of Isobel Tresham and other family members removed from under the floor of Newton church when this was de-consecrated were re-buried in 2000 following investigations by Leicester University. A small, discreet tablet marks their grave.

FORMER INCUMBENTS

Several former vicars are buried in the churchyard, although the location of many of their graves is unknown. Those interred here include: John Barton (1719); Samuel Quincy (1777); and Wilfred Opie (1950). Buried at Newton were Isaac Bassett (1721); and Francis Groleau (1716).

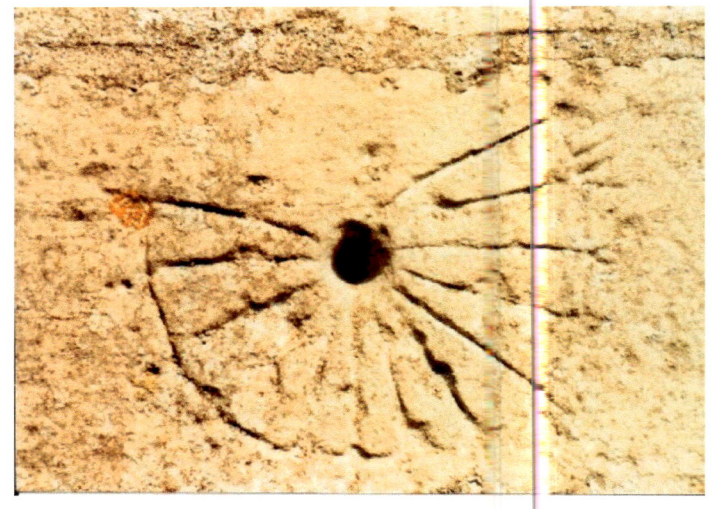
Figure 54: Early sundial on the south wall.
Photo: M Hopkins

---

106 The inscription must have been written sometime later because it specifies that he left the *"profits of a piece of land lying in Cranford St. John"*. The purchase of the land would have been made by the Trustees at some time after 1710 when the will was proved.

FEATURES IN THE CHURCH STONEWORK

EARLY SUNDIALS

On the central buttress of the external wall of the South Aisle, is an interesting early sundial of uncertain date (*Fig. 54*), the central hole of which is about 97cm above the ground. Markham (op. cit.) suggests it was of Saxon date and moved to this position from an earlier location, though a later date seems more plausible.

Measuring about 19cm across, the markings are divided in a very unusual way. There is no trace of a gnomon, suggesting that a finger or a stick would have been used to cast a shadow. It may have been used by priests to tell the times for Mass. There are three further such sundials on the next buttress to the west. One is well-delineated, the others less distinct.

CROSS MARKINGS

Nearby are some very faintly-scratched crosses. There is no evidence that these were 'pilgrim crosses' and it may be that they were etched to swear debts, or perhaps bargains struck at Geddington's medieval charter market[107].

A SAXON FEATURE

Also nearby, close to the junction of the South Aisle and Lady Chapel, the remaining external 'long and short' stone quoins that form a clear vertical joint in the wall are strongly suggestive of an earlier structure of Saxon origin, perhaps a *Transcept* or a *Porticus*. A *Porticus* originated in Roman architecture and was usually a small room, often forming extensions to the north and south, giving the church a cruciform plan. They functioned as chapels, small transepts, or burial-places. Other internal features add weight to the view that a Saxon structure once occupied an area to the south of the Chancel.

107 Charter dated 1248 [Curia Regis Rolls, quoted in
     Geddington : A Diary of a Village by M Hopkins (op.cit.)]

Part III: A History of the Church

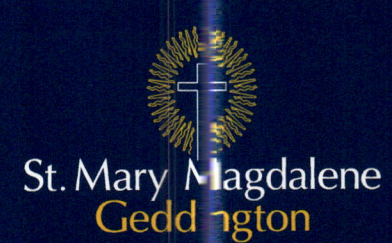

St. Mary Magdalene
Geddington

BEGINNINGS: THE SAXON CHURCH 950 – 1066

Experts tell us that the original stone Geddington Church dates from sometime between AD 850 and 970. The later date seems more likely since the parish system only became established in the 10th Century, before which most clergy were grouped in cathedrals and their offshoot minster churches. This was also a very turbulent time in English history. There had been Danish raids during the 840s and 850s, and between 865 and 875 the 'Great Heathen Army' led by 'Ivar the Boneless' had overrun all the English kingdoms except Wessex.

Over the following decades, Alfred the Great and his descendants gradually drove the Danes back, but for lengthy periods Geddington was surrounded by Danish-held towns, including Kettering (Cytringan), Northampton, Leicester and Stamford, and it was not until 942 that English control was firmly re-established over the area. By 955, Alfred's grandson Eadred ruled over a united England, and a revival of Christian worship spread rapidly through the Nene valley and beyond in the second half of the 10th Century.

The English church had for some time been organised into dioceses (*Fig. 55*), each governed by a bishop who, although selected by the Archbishop of Canterbury (in consultation with the King), ultimately derived authority from the Pope in Rome as head of the Catholic Church. At this time, Geddington was part of the Dorchester Diocese.

FOUNDATIONS - THE PARISH SYSTEM

We don't know exactly how the original stone church came to be built in Geddington, but we do know that it was dedicated to St. Andrew – a name that it bore for more than 500 years. Until the mid-10th Century, the locations of cathedrals and 'minster' churches were themselves closely linked to patterns of royal and aristocratic land tenure. As the royal

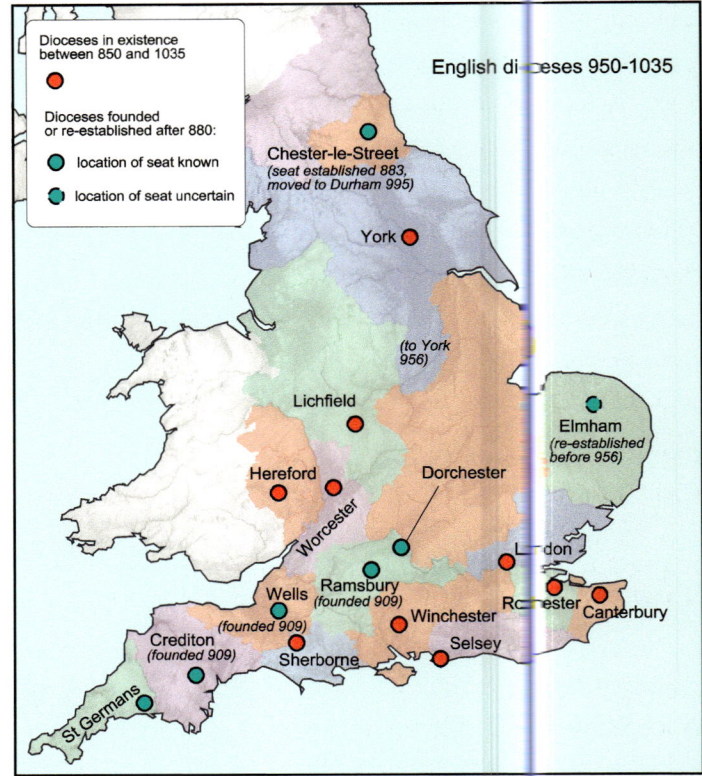

Figure 55: English Dioceses in the late Saxon period
By Hel-hama - Own work, CC BY-SA 3.0
https://commons.wikimedia.org/w/index.php?cu..=20001502

estates tended to be formed into smaller units in the late Saxon period, so too did their associated minster *parochiae* (which often centred on royal *tuns*), frequently with coterminous boundaries[108]. Geddington may initially have been a 'dependent' church within the care of St. Andrew's Brigstock, only becoming a separate parish at some point in the late Saxon or early Norman period.

Geddington was one of the principal manors of Edward the Confessor, who married Edith in 1045; and it was possessed by Edith until the Conquest. During the late Saxon period the crown increasingly enforced the payment of tithes – compulsory levies on arable production in support of the church. This greatly increased the resources available to support clergy and the church's charitable works, but it also incentivised local landowners (the King being no

---

108 E.g. as shown in *"The fragmentation of the minster parochiae of south-east Shropshire"* by Jane Croom (1988) [from *Minsters & Parish Churches: the Local Church in Transition, 950-1200*, Ed. John Blair, pub. Oxford University Committee for Archaeology]. See also *"The administrative organisation of Northamptonshire in the Saxon period"* by Glenn Foard in *Anglo-Saxon Studies in Archaeology and History*, pub. University of Oxford (1985).

exception) to found churches so as to retain tithe income within their estates rather than see it go elsewhere.

THE SAXON CHURCH BUILDING

Figure 56: The Nave of St. Lawrence, Bradford-on-Avon

Geddington's Saxon origins can be traced in the stonework of today's church. The Nave we see today occupies roughly the same 'footprint' as the original Saxon Nave: confirmed by the exposure of Saxon foundations when major structural and floor repairs were undertaken in 1990. At Geddington we have excellent examples of ornamental Saxon triangle-headed tracery or 'arcading' in the North Aisle which suggests a fairly prestigious church. Both faces of a splayed window pierced in this wall can also be seen and these features, together with the roof scars high on the east wall of the Nave and the relatively small Nave with 'long-and-short' quoins (corner-stones) visible at the north east and south-east corners of the Nave, are all strongly diagnostic of a Saxon church.

We do not know whether the Saxon Chancel took the round-ended form of an apse or was rectangular in shape, but the steeply-pitched roof-line is still visible in the lower of two scars on the eastern face of the wall dividing the Chancel from the Nave. The original roofing material would probably have been thatch, although Collyweston slates (like those seen on the porch today) may have been used,

either from the outset or later on. There are also tantalising hints of a Saxon structure in the external stonework of the south wall, where there is a vertical full-height straight joint that is dressed on its eastern side with 'long and short' quoin-stones; also for the full height. The orientation of this feature means there must have been a structure here before the south aisle was built in the mid-13th Century. Internally too, there are several pad-stones (used normally to support roof beams or rafters) whose locations suggest a lower roofline of a much older building on the south side of the Chancel, and which also sit in line with what is thought may have been the position of the east wall of the original Saxon Chancel. All this is suggestive of either a Saxon *porticus*, a side-chapel or the southern wing of a cruciform (cross-shaped plan) church. Unfortunately, this must remain conjecture because the Lady Chapel has been so much modified throughout the church's history that virtually nothing remains of the early period other than these small, intriguing details.

The Saxon church's walls were rather thinner than today and would have been very plain, with few window openings. Although different in some details, the pictures of St. Lawrence's Church at Bradford-on-Avon in Oxfordshire, and of Escomb Church in County Durham (*Figs. 56-58*) give an impression of how the original Geddington Church might have looked and felt before the major changes of the 12th and 13th centuries.

There may also have been a Saxon tower, either between the Nave and Chancel as part of a 'cruciform' (cross-shaped) arrangement or - perhaps more likely - echoing the arrangement at the 'mother' church of St. Andrew at Brigstock - at the west end of the Nave.

Figure 58: Escombe Church in Co. Durham

Figure 57: The exterior of St. Lawrence Church, Bradford-on-Avon

THE NORMAN CHURCH 1066 - 1200

The Norman Conquest brought fundamental changes to English life, including that of the church. There was a reorganisation of dioceses and nearly all of the Saxon bishops were replaced by appointees of King William I. From 1085 Geddington became part of a new Diocese of Lincoln and remained so until the Reformation. At the time of the Domesday Book (1086) Geddington was a small settlement with a recorded population (which excluded those of lower status) of nine households, of whom 5 were freemen (*socmen*) and 4 were smallholders (*cottagers*). It had two ploughlands (*curucates*) and 2 men's plough teams. As had been the case pre-conquest, the lands at Geddington were owned partly (one **hide** – about 120 acres) by the King's manor of Brigstock and partly (one **virgate** – roughly 30 acres) by the Abbey of Bury St. Edmonds in Suffolk.

Until this time, the western church was heavily decentralised, which meant the Pope held comparatively little power outside of his position as Bishop of Rome. But, in the decades immediately after the Conquest, a series of reforms began a process whereby the church (as God's representative) both insisted on celibacy among the clergy and increasingly asserted its separation from, and spiritual authority over, secular authorities. Before the reforms, local bishops were granted land by secular rulers ('lay investiture'). A ban on this practice was a key part of the reforms, along with an insistence that lords of manors should not receive any part of the tithes levied for the support of the church – achieved by the lord donating land and property into a '**glebe**' whose revenues accrued to the church.

Having incurred great expense in building the church and parsonage and having suffered a loss of income, however, lords of the manor insisted on the right to select the parish priest. Equally, the bishop, from whom religious authority flowed, in turn demanded the right to confirm the appointment. This was part of a wider European 'investiture' controversy[109] between kings and the church over the right to appoint bishops and abbots. From this developed the right of patronage or '**advowson**' – the right of a lord to present a nominee to the diocesan bishop for appointment as the parish priest. This **right of presentation** is still very widespread today: in Geddington the right belongs to the church's patron, the Duke of Buccleuch.

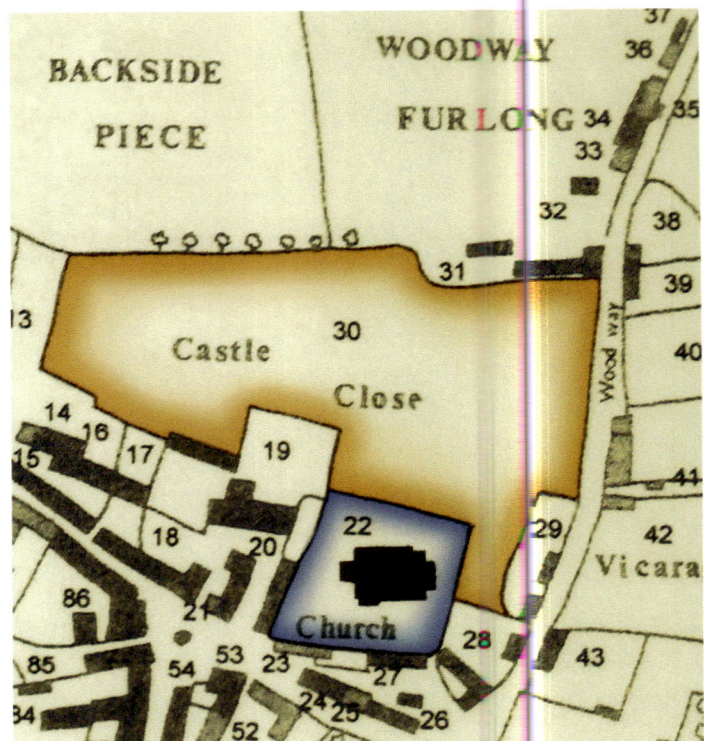

Figure 59: The site of Geddington Palace (map of 1770)

A NEW ROYAL RESIDENCE

In 1129, things in Geddington began to change in a big way. Henry I's accounts for that year show £7 being made *'in the making of the king's house at Geytinton'*.

Its location on the Stamford to Oxford road, the proximity of Rockingham Castle and the surrounding Rockingham Forest meant the royal love of hunting had given Geddington a new importance.

Built a little way north of the church in an area later known as 'Castle Close' (**Fig. 59**), this 'house' was initially a hunting lodge, but eventually became an important residence, evidenced by documentary and archaeological sources, including parch-marks seen in aerial photographs.

By the late 12th Century, the royal residence must have been quite substantial, for it was capable of hosting the Great Council of the King, which was twice summoned to meet at Geddington, first in 1177 and then (following the news that Jerusalem had fallen), on 11 February 1188, to levy a tax for a crusade that never took place

> *"Henry, king of England, having returned to England after the feast of the Purification of the Blessed Virgin Mary [2 February] called together all the chief persons of the whole of England*

---

109 One aspect of the tension between church and state concerned whether bishops owed their primary allegiance to the Pope or to the King (and indeed which Pope, as there were two in the late 11th Century). The Council of Rockingham (1095) attempted to resolve this dispute within England. The Council was attended by St. Anselm, Archbishop of Canterbury, and one intriguing speculation is whether he paused at Geddington Church on his way back to Canterbury.

including Baldwin, archbishop of Canterbury, and all the bishops and abbots, and other chief men of his kingdom at Geddington. And after he had explained his wishes to them, Baldwin, archbishop of Canterbury, and John [of Oxford], bishop of Norwich, assumed the Cross of the Lord at Bristol"[110].

Stukeley (op. cit., p67) says *"…at Dene Thorpe is a stone whereon is cut this old inscription: HERE IS THE PARLIAMENT STEERES. The Duke of Montagu says that there was a Parliament held formerly in Geddington, and this stone probably came from thence."* This sounds rather unlikely.

Richard I ('Lionheart') received William, King of Scotland, at Geddington and spent the Good Friday of 1194 with him here. It seems very possible that they would have worshipped together in the church on this most holy of days. His brother John, who became King in 1199, was a regular visitor to Geddington: as chronicled in Vic Crouse's book *The Magna Carta King in Geddington and the Rockingham Forest*.

During the reign of Henry III, the palace became a more commodious and richly-appointed place[111]. Some archaeological evidence of this emerged when preparing the ground for the churchyard extension in 1907, when *"several running feet of the palace foundations, varying from two feet six inches upwards in the thickness"* were unearthed[112]. The finds also included smelted iron pieces, perhaps evidence of the four royal furnaces in the time of Henry III, and these probably helped supply munitions for use in the siege of Rockingham Castle (1220)[113].

The King's interest in Geddington extended beyond his palace for, on 28 November 1248 Henry III decreed that:

> *"every week at his manor at Geytinton, a market shall be held every Wednesday, and that in the same place every year a public festival shall be held and shall last for three days, namely on the day before, on the day and the day following the Blessed Mary Magdalene".* [114]

This would have been at about the same time that the bridge was built across the River Ise. Indeed, the market and the various improvements to the palace may have provided the impetus for building the bridge. Geddington was clearly a place favoured by Plantagenet royalty, and especially in the second half of the 13th Century, as both Henry III and his son Edward I were regular visitors. Yet, as we shall see, within little more than a century, this palace was a ruin.

NORMAN ALTERATIONS

The first major post-conquest change to Geddington Church was the construction of a new North Aisle around the year 1170. This involved removing much of the solid wall construction of the Saxon Nave's north wall, with extensive propping by skilled Norman engineers and masons, using techniques superior to those of the Saxon epoch. Fortunately, much of the thinner high-level Saxon walls, and the NE and SE quoins remain intact. It is possible that the original Saxon Chancel may have been enlarged at this time also, although this is not certain.

The Saxon south wall, which would have included the main southern entrance, remained intact at this time, although all traces of a Saxon doorway have long since disappeared under later changes. The arcade separating the North Aisle from the Nave was built with the rounded 'Romanesque' arches typical of the Norman period. There was clearly a link with the nearby Royal palace – the external door in the north wall still being called the 'King's Door' to this day, though the Norman door was probably a metre or so lower than today. We can imagine every English King from Henry I to Edward I, along with Queens and other magnates of the realm decked in their fine robes processing into the church for Mass.

---

110 *Annales Cestrienses Chronicle of the Abbey of S. Werburg, At Chester*, ed. Richard Copley Christie (London, 1887) p 38
see https://www.british-history.ac.uk/lancs-ches-record-soc/vol14/pp36-49

111 E.g. *The Calendar of Liberate Rolls 1251-60*, 24 describes private chapels for the King and Queen being painted green with spangled gold, and including a Chancel in the King's Chapel – see *The Archaeology of the Medieval English Monarchy*, by John Steane (1994)

112 *Kettering Leader* 7 June 1907. In addition a stone mortar, glazed pottery shards (some ornamented), and bones (thought to be of wolves) were found.

113 *The History and Antiquities of Northamptonshire*, by the Revd. Thomas James (1864) p 22.

114 (i.e. 21-23 July each year) Henry III : *Curia Regis Rolls*, 1247–51

PART III: A HISTORY OF THE CHURCH

THE HIGH MEDIEVAL CHURCH 1200 - 1357

In 1222, King Henry III[115] presented Nicholas de Breaute to Hugh of Wells, the Bishop of Lincoln, to become Rector of Geddington, the first known holder of this office, indicating that Geddington had become a parish in its own right by this time. A rector held his position for life or until he surrendered it, and he was legally responsible for the upkeep of the Chancel – being entitled to the glebe income to enable him to do this. In this period rectors often employed chaplains (clergy without a right of income directly from tithes) to carry out their priestly obligations.

Both the King and Queen would also have had their own private chaplains for their chapels at Geddington Palace: in 1247 the King authorised a chapel for the Queen to be built, and in 1248 he authorised the construction of a *fair and suitable chapel at the King's manor of Geytinton'* and payment of 50 shillings yearly to his chaplains *'celebrating divine service in his chapels'* here and elsewhere[116]. Despite the 12th Century changes, however, the church would still have been a recognisably Saxon church; but this all changed in the mid-13th Century, when there was a much bigger transformation in the size and character of the building.

Following the church reforms of the 12th and early 13th Century, the church's influence was growing rapidly. With greater income from tithes, the church was able to support more clergy and, with generous patrons and benefactors, was able to embark on more ambitious building works in an age when new, more elegant, and adventurous building techniques were being applied across Europe. In the Early English Gothic style, rounded arches gave way to lighter, pointed arches in windows, doorways, and arcades. The key features are pointed arches, lancet windows (tall and narrow with a pointed arch at the top) and clustered shafts of tall, narrow piers replacing the massive, rounded ones of the Norman style. This was also a time when Henry III was having a substantial amount of work done to the adjacent royal palace, and this energetic approach was no doubt reflected in the life of the church.

MID-13TH CENTURY CHANGES

And so, we find that the South Aisle, south doorway, and Lady Chapel are all mid-13th Century work. The pointed arches and slender columns are typical of the period, although the external stonework suggests that the Lady Chapel was at least in part formed from an earlier Saxon structure. However, no windows of this period survive in the South Aisle, nor in the rest of the church, apart from a few traces in the Lady Chapel.

The Chancel also underwent a complete re-modelling in the mid-13th Century, with all traces of the Saxon Chancel being lost, apart from the lower roof scar on the west wall. This new Chancel may have extended eastwards only as far as the present Sanctuary step, although most experts (e.g. Pevsner and Thompson) think that, by around 1300 or soon after, the east wall of the Chancel – including the great East Window and the two other windows in the Sanctuary - had been established in its present position. However, as discussed earlier (*The Chancel: the Significance of the Inscriptions*), there is good reason to think that the Chancel was not completed until the 1360s. Nevertheless, the arches that pierce both north and south walls of the Chancel are all early or mid-13th Century in date, as are probably the splayed lower clerestory windows in the same walls.

These 13th Century alterations also involved the opening up of a larger Chancel arch, similar in height and width to the arch between the South Aisle and Lady Chapel. It is also conceivable that the original timber screen with central doorway that now separates the Choir from the Lady Chapel was installed in the (then) new Chancel arch as part of this mid-13th Century re-ordering, though it is more likely of the 14th Century.

Geddington's bridge across the River Ise dates from this period too, and all of this activity clearly indicates the growing prestige and importance of Geddington, derived no doubt from its close royal associations. Interestingly, the Rector from 1245 to 1282, and who must have been instrumental in many of these changes, was Guydo de Palmere who, alone of all the incumbents of Geddington, was a sub-deacon rather than an ordained priest – an example of the laxity that had crept into church governance and which Bishop Grosseteste of Lincoln fought strenuously to eliminate.

---

115 As Henry was only 15 at this time, the presentation may well have been exercised by Hubert de Burgh, who was then Chief Justiciar and effectively the young king's Regent.

116 *Calendar of Liberate Rolls* 15 July 1247, 20 July 1248, and 8 August 1248

QUEEN ELEANOR OF CASTILE AND THE CROSS

The last monarch to stay at Geddington was Edward I, who was a frequent visitor as he travelled around his kingdom. But it was his Queen, Eleanor of Castile, who has left the most lasting impression on Geddington. Eleanor was born in Burgos, daughter of Ferdinand III of Castile and Joan, Countess of Ponthieu and was a highly intelligent and cultured woman, though she was not fluent in English, and spoke mostly French. She married Henry III's heir, Edward at the monastery of Las Huelgas in Burgos in 1254 and subsequently gave birth to 17 children, of whom only 6 survived into adulthood: one son, later to become King Edward II, and 5 daughters.

After a difficult time during the 2nd Barons' War, when she and Edward were held captive, she joined the 8th Crusade with her husband in 1271 – where she gave birth to Joan of Acre, and where Edward survived an assassination attempt[117] - returning to England in 1272 on news of Henry III's death, stopping only to give birth to Alphonso in Gascony. Edward and Eleanor were crowned together in August 1274.

The available evidence indicates that they were devoted to each other, and the couple were rarely apart - she accompanied him on military campaigns in Wales, giving birth to their son Edward in 1284 at the partially-constructed Caernarfon Castle. She was a patron of the Dominican Friars, popularised the use of tapestries and carpets, promoted the use of fine tableware and utensils and was influential in the development of garden design on royal estates. She also gave significant sums to charities.

Eleanor died at Harby, near Lincoln on the evening of 28th November 1290, aged 49 and after 36 years of marriage. Her embalmed body was borne in great state from Lincoln to Westminster Abbey, led by Edward and a large cortege of mourners. On their way, they stopped at Geddington for one or two nights[118] sometime between the 6th and 8th December. It seems likely that Eleanor's body lay in the

Figure 60: Effigy of Queen Eleanor in Westminster Abbey

Church whilst here, for the King and Queen's private chapels in the palace would probably have been too small.

Eleanor's viscera were buried in Lincoln Cathedral, where the original stone chest survives, although her effigy was destroyed in the 17th Century (replaced with a copy in the 19th Century). Her heart was buried in Blackfriars Priory in London, along with her son Alphonso. It was reportedly highly elaborate, including wall paintings and a beautiful metal statue under a carved stone canopy. Sadly, it was destroyed in the 16th Century.

Eleanor's funeral took place in Westminster Abbey on 17th December 1290. Her tomb consists of a marble chest with carved mouldings and shields (originally painted) of the arms of England, Castile, and Ponthieu. On top is a magnificent gilt-bronze effigy (*Fig. 60*) by the great 13th Century sculptor William Torel.

After her death Edward endowed each church that had sheltered Eleanor's body with lands[119] to pay for a perpetual commemoration; a commitment that in Geddington is remembered each December with a Mass.

Following the French example of crosses marking Louis IX's funeral procession, the King also commanded that:

"in everie town and place where the corps rested by the waie the King caused a cross of cunning workmanship to be erected in remembrance of her; and in the same was a picture of her engraven"[120].

These crosses were built at Lincoln, Grantham, Stamford, Geddington, Hardingstone, Stony Stratford, Woburn, Dunstable, St. Albans, Waltham, Westcheap, and Charing. Only 3 original crosses survive, the best-preserved being that at Geddington[121].

---

117 It was said that Eleanor sucked the poison from Edward's arm which had been stabbed by a poisoned dagger. This is questionable.

118 "It is possible more than one night was spent at Geddington. After Stamford the pace at which the Cortége had been travelling was reduced. An extra night was spent either at Stamford, Geddington or Northampton. The two last, offering royal residences are more likely". [from *Eleanor of Castile* by Jean Powrie, p. 108].

119 However, in 1547 the King seized any lands left to the incumbent with the specific charge of saying such masses, including those at Geddington [*Victoria County History of Northamptonshire Vol. II* (op.cit.) p.36]

120 *The Chronicles of England, Scotlande and Irelande* by Raphael Holinshed (1577). Quoted in 'Queen Eleanor's Crosses' by Walter Lovell [Archaeological Journal, 49:1, 17-43 (1892)] - see http://dx.doi.org/10.1080/00665983.1892.10852513

121 The other 2 surviving crosses being at Waltham Cross and Hardingstone.

PART III: A HISTORY OF THE CHURCH

Completed in 1294 or 1295, the Geddington Cross (*Fig. 61*) is triangular in form (perhaps representing the Holy Trinity), rising in stages from a stepped base to an ornate pinnacle. The lower two stages are beautifully embellished, and these give way to a third stage with canopied statues, below the hexagonal pinnacle. There was originally a cross topping the pinnacle, but this has disappeared – possibly during the Civil War or the Commonwealth period; and in the 18th Century a sundial was mounted about half-way up facing the bridge, though it was removed by the end of that century.

At the base of the cross on the south-west side is a conduit house, built in 1769, making this the only British example of a public water supply incorporated into a royal memorial.

A MEDIEVAL MURDER MYSTERY

In 1292 a drama of another kind must have occurred for, on the 30th January that year, the churchyard was re-consecrated because *'blood had been shed therein'*.[122] This suggests a murder took place, though we know nothing more beyond this tantalising hint.

THE EARLY 14TH CENTURY

Relatively little is known of the church during the 60 years following Eleanor's death, but we do know that Edward I never returned to Geddington and that in less than a century the royal palace had become a ruin. Although the Crown retained its interest in Geddington Woods until 1629, the close association that there had been under the earlier Plantagenet monarchs ended with Eleanor's death. In 1324 Edward II (who had been granted the manor of Geddington by his father in 1299[123]) learned that:

"*the manor of Godynton…is wasted for lack of good keeping and the houses whereof are in great part broken and fallen down*"[124]

and on his accession in 1327, Edward III granted the manor, together with the town, castle, and forest of Rockingham, to his mother, Isobel of France, for life. In 1333 she was also granted the advowson of Geddington, which she held until she surrendered it on 31st January 1357. We also know nothing directly of how badly the Black Death of 1348-49 affected the parish, but it was probably just as bad as elsewhere: in August 1348 alone thirty-six Northamptonshire clergy had to be replaced as a result of the epidemic (the normal monthly figure was four). Whatever the exact effects, the plague probably contributed materially to the final decline of the palace and village, for by 1374 none of the palace buildings remained fully standing and the village's weekly market was worthless because *'nobody comes there'*.[125]

By this time, stone was probably being taken from the palace buildings, and in 1394 we find that Richard II's Queen, Anne of Bohemia was quoted[126] as giving permission for the King's tenants in Geddington to take stone from the former manor house for the repair of their houses. Moreover, similar permission was granted to *'notre bien ame lankyn Mulso pour reparacion de ses mesons en Newton pres notre ville'*[127].

It is therefore hardly surprising that, by Camden's time the Palace had almost disappeared, although he notes *'the gatehouse was repaired in 1610 and still stands'*. In 1742, Stukeley found the ground uneven and many foundations still visible[128].

Figure 61: The Eleanor Cross, Geddington

122 *Northamptonshire & Rutland Clergy from 1500* by Rev. Henry Isham Longden. See also Markham (op. cit.)

123 *Eleanor of Castile* by Jean Powrie, p. 103 [pub. Brewin (1990) ISBN 0947331 79 2]

124 *Calendar of Fine Rolls* 22 Nov. 1324

125 Writ of the Privy Seal to the Sheriff to Inquire Concerning a Petition of the King's poor tenants of the manor of Geytyngton (17 May 1374) - quoted in *Geddington: Diary of a Village* [Ed. ML Hopkins, 1986]

126 Letter from Anne of Bohemia to Thomas West, Bailiff of Northampton, quoted in the *Geddington (Crown) Manorial Court Rolls* (op. cit.), 8 May 1394. With thanks to Edward Coulson for drawing this to the author's attention.

127 Norman French, translates as: *'our good friend Jenkyn Mulso for the repair of his houses in Newton next to our town'*. [Jenkyr or Jenkin was a diminutive of 'John' – emphasising the close relationship that John Mulsho enjoyed with Richard II].

128 The quote by Camden is from Powrie (op. cit.) p. 103. See also *The family memoirs of the Rev. William Stukeley, M.D. and the Antiquarian and other Correspondence of William Stukeley*, Roger & Samuel Gale, etc. Vol. III, 1887

PART III: A HISTORY OF THE CHURCH

THE MONKS' CHURCH 1357 -1538

THE BISHOP'S LICENCE

Following the death of the Rector, William de Walcote, and with the palace buildings probably increasingly ruinous, Queen Isobel surrendered the advowson on 31st January 1357. The Crown granted the right of presentation to the Abbott of Pipewell Abbey who, on the 1st February 1357, presented the first Vicar of Geddington, William Freman, to Bishop Glynwell of Lincoln. The Bishop granted his licence to the Abbot in 1358.

PIPEWELL ABBEY

Pipewell was a Cistercian abbey lying between Wilbarston and Rushton. Founded in 1143, it was never large in size, with fewer than 20 monks in 1365, and its principal income came from an estate in Warwickshire and from the woods of the surrounding Rockingham Forest. Bishop Gynwell's 1358 licence stated that the abbey was in great poverty, owing to various causes, including damage to crops by wild beasts, some disastrous fires, and the sudden flooding of its fishponds.

COMPLETING THE CHANCEL

It is not entirely clear how much of the Chancel we see today was built at this time but, despite some scholarly doubts that date its Sanctuary windows to c1300, the 1358 Endowment points strongly to some significant works being of this later time, including to windows. Whatever the exact scope of the work carried out, however, the monks clearly set about their commission with energy, for an inscription in the Chancel records the death in 1369 of William Glover, who it says was responsible for work carried out at this time.

Within two or three decades of this achievement, the present tower was also completed, perhaps replacing an earlier tower. During the following (15th) Century there were further substantial building works, including all the upper clerestory windows in the Chancel and Nave, and a new rood loft (c1450), with the stonework of the windows in the North and South Aisles also belonging to this period.

The walls at this time were covered with plaster and decorated with Biblical scenes. These would have been whitewashed over at some point after the Reformation[129], and lost entirely when the plaster was removed in 1905; although traces of red ochre paint are still visible on stonework around windows and other features in the Sanctuary. A faded impression of how Geddington Church might have looked in the late medieval period can be gathered from surviving medieval wall paintings (*Fig. 62*) at the nearby St. Mary's Church in Raunds.

FINANCIAL TROUBLES

In the early 15th Century, there were four chapels dependent on the revenues of the Rector of Geddington Church (the Abbot of Pipewell). However, in 1441 we find this arrangement creating difficulties and the Pope writes:

"To the Abbot and convent of the Cistercian monastery of Pypwell in the diocese of Lincoln. Grant at their recent petition – containing that the vicarage of the parish church of Geydyngton near their monastery are united and appropriated four chapels, distant from the monastery about two miles of those parts, one in each of the towns (ville) of Little Newton, Great Ocle, Great Newton and Barforde[130], and that the perpetual vicar [the Abbot] is bound to keep at his expense a secular priest in the chapel of Little Newton and one in that of Great Ocle, and one in each of the others, which have cure [the care of souls], in order to celebrate mass and other divine offices daily and administer the sacraments to the parishioners in the said towns; and adding that the fruits etc. of the said vicarage are so much diminished that the said vicar cannot keep the said priests, and that in consequence the burden of doing so falls entirely on the abbot and convent, to whom the said parish church is united and whose many other burdens are daily increasing – that they and their successors may appoint monks of the monastery to celebrate the said masses etc. in the said parish church and chapels."

A little later, in 1450, the problem was eased when Great Newton chapel (dedicated to St. Leonard[131]) was

---

129 Although in 1619 the **Church Survey** of that year said the Chancel wall lacked whitening.

130 Barford was a small, now deserted, village near Rothwell and its church, on a ridge to the south of the River Ise, was dedicated to St. Martin. According to Bridges (op. cit.) the church was complete in 1625 but by c1720 was completely destroyed. See **The Lost Churches of Northamptonshire** by Stephen Swailes (2023)

131 Serjeantson & Longden (op. cit.) p 371

Figure 62: Medieval wall paintings at St Mary's Church in Raunds, Northamptonshire
Photo: Michael Garlick

demolished to provide material for the repair of the chapel at Little Newton.

A HIRED KILLER SEEKS SANCTUARY

A measure of the Church's power in the medieval period was the existence of its own courts to which people could appeal for judgement. Even today, Church courts have jurisdiction over certain matters relating to the conduct of clergy and churchwardens. A similar example of Church power was the right of sanctuary, under which a fugitive from the King's justice who took refuge in a church or churchyard was protected from immediate arrest. The following story is based on an account in *Sanctuary Seekers in England, 1394-1557* by Dr Shannon McSheffrey.[132]

On 25 April 1446, three men of Geddington – two yeomen and a labourer – lay in wait to attack one William Shirwode. According to the indictment, the two yeomen attacked Shirwode with swords drawn, and the labourer, William Campyon, with a pitchfork. It was Campyon who struck the fatal blow, hitting Shirwode on the back of the skull with the pitchfork, killing him instantly.

The killing was allegedly ordered by Thomas Mulsho of Geddington, son and heir of the MP for Northamptonshire, Thomas Mulsho (Snr), and the grandson of John Mulsho, whose monument can be seen in the North Aisle. Thomas was charged as accessory; we might guess the two yeomen were his household retainers and Campyon a thug-for-hire. Following the attack, the yeomen fled and were eventually outlawed, whilst Campyon sought sanctuary at the parish church in Geddington.

Campyon then invoked a legal process under which an accused person, having obtained sanctuary, would formally confess to the crime (or alleged crime) and surrender to the church authorities. He then formally "abjured the realm", which entailed agreeing to leave the country as a condition of avoiding prosecution. It was effectively self-imposed exile. This process was overseen by a coroner and coroner's jury - we still have the names of the jurors in this case. Campyon would have sworn an oath to leave the country directly, by the shortest route, and not to return without the King's permission. He would probably have

132 Dr. McSheffrey quotes the original sources as: TNA, KB 9/252/2, m. 20; KB 29/78, m. 31d; KB 27/746, rex m 19. With thanks to Anthony Lawton for unearthing this nugget of information.

been assigned a specific port of departure and given a limited amount of time to reach it, wearing a distinctive garment as a sign of his status. He would have been required to board the first available ship and, if no ship was available, to wade into the water daily as a sign of his intention to leave.

Fleeing was not really an option for Thomas Mulsho, whose income and status depended on his landed property in Geddington and Newton. It is recorded that he pleaded not guilty, put himself "on the country" (i.e. asked for a jury trial by his peers), and was bailed. Although we don't have the trial verdict and no pardon survives, the most common trial outcome in such cases was acquittal. Thomas Mulsho died in 1460, leaving his estates to his daughter Anne, and her husband, Henry Tresham – thus beginning a period in which the Treshams became the pre-eminent family in the area.

Another Northamptonshire case quoted[133] in Dr. McSheffrey's book shows that kingly mercy was also a feature of medieval justice. It concerns Newton Bromswold near Higham Ferrers:

On 24 October 1433, a husbandman of Newton, John Marchall, took sanctuary and abjured for the theft of a sheep. Six years later, in 1439, he petitioned the king to pardon his felony and erase his abjuration. As the petition notes, Marchall *besought the king's mercy* with *tears and sighs,* as he had *the greatest horror of his ill deeds, intending to avoid all such in future.*

The young King Henry VI magnanimously granted the pardon, persuaded by Marchall's contrition, connecting (as did other kings) his power to forgive crimes with God's redemption of sin. Henry's determination to be merciful and to see his kingly role as tightly connected to Christian forgiveness was a very important factor in the development of sanctuary in both practical and ideological terms in the later medieval period.

England outlawed sanctuary in 1623, a few decades after the Catholic church restricted the crimes to which sanctuary could apply. The memory of churches as places of refuge still persists however, even today, when occasionally a church will shelter a refugee facing deportation, for example.

MEDIEVAL BEQUESTS TO THE CHURCH

The making of bequests to the church in people's Wills was very common and cast light on the everyday religious practices of the time; and also upon the features of the church building itself on the threshold of the Reformation. One such Will was made in 1504 by William Downhall, esq. and proved after his death in 1505[134]. It read:

"In the name of the high Trynitie fader son and holy gost, amen. 28 Nov. 1504, I William Downhall Esquier, of our lorde godds visitacion weyke seeke and feeble in body, my body to be buried in the chapell of Seynt John Baptiste in the church of Geydyngton. To the mother church of Lincoln vjs viijd [6 shillings and 8 pence] It. to my mortuary my best horse. To the high alter vj. viijd. To the Abbot of Pipwell the parson of the sacd church of Gedyngton vj viijd. It. A new vestment of Gedyngton price of iiij or v Marks."

His Will also made bequests to his wife and son. The then Vicar, Richard Foster, was one of the witnesses. Other gifts and bequests to Geddington St. Andrew in this period included:

HIGH ALTAR: *"To the hye aulter a hyve full of beys and waxe"*: Robert Malarye, 1529.

HIGH ROOD: *"To the hy rode lyght xijd"* : Richard Thorne, 1515; *"To ye edefyynge of ye heye rode lofte of Geydynton vj wethurs"* : J. Comford, 1517 *"To the makyng of the hye rood vjs. viijd"* : Agnes Canford, 1532; *"I bequethe to the use of the churen the oulde rode loffte the which remaneth nowe in the church there"*: T. Freman, 1536.

STOOPING ROOD: *"To the stopyng the rode 2 xijd"*: Richard Thorne, 1515; *"To ye stowpyng rods cotte (coat) ij wethyrs"* : J. Comford, 1517. *"I gyve to the stowpyng roode xijd"*: W. Colfex, c. 1528.

SEPULCHRE: *"To the sepulture ij wether schepe"*: Rich. Thorne, 1515; *"To ye sepulker lyght jd"*: J. Comford, 1517; *"To the sepulchre iiij wether"*: Nicholas Veyssacorley, 1528; *"I bequethe to the use of the church the oolde sepulcher there"*: T. Freman, 1536.

TORCHES: *"To the torchys viijd"* : W. Colfex, c. 1528.

133 The source given is: CPR 1436-41, 275-76

134 This, and the other bequests listed here are taken from Serjeantson & Longden (op. cit.). See also pp 226-30 and 263. 'William Downhall of Geddington' was Lord of the Manor of Hanborough, Oxfordshire at the time of his death [P.R.O., PROB 11/14, f. 284]

VESTMENTS: "*I bequethe to the church a vestament price xxvjs. viijd*" : T. Freman, 1536

SEATS: "*Item volo quod de bonis meis fiant nova sedilia per totam ecclesiam de Gedyngton secundum formam quam carpentarius cepit facienda*" [Also I will that of my goods new seats be made throughout the whole church of Gedyngton according to the pattern which the carpenter took to make them"] : Henry German [Jarmon], 1486.

PULPIT: "*To be buried in the churche . . . afore the pulpitt*" : W. Colfex, c. 1528.

CROSSES: "*To the foyte* [foot] *of the grete crosse in the* [towne] *of Gedyngton xijd. Item to the crosse well xijd.1 to the mendyng of the new cross iijs. iiijd. and to the . . . . aghe crosse vjs. viijd*" : W. Colfex, c. 1528.

PILGRIMAGE: "*Also that Henry my son have my colte to performe my pilgrymage, yt is to saye to our Lady of Walsynghen &* [our Lady] *of Northampton.*"W. Colfex, 1528

SPECIAL MASSES: "*My wife shall cause to be said* χ [ten] *masses at Scala Coely*" : Nicholas Veyssacorley, 1528. [The Latin *Scala Coeli* means 'stairway to heaven'. This is probably a reference to the church of *Santa Maria Scala Coeli* in Rome].

NOTES: (a) a *wether* or *wethur* is a castrated sheep or goat; (b) a 'j' is the same as an 'i'; (c) the monies given are in shillings and pence. Thus '*vjs. viijd*' means 'six shillings and 8 pence'.

Apart from noting the piety of many folk and that gifts in kind were commonplace, we see from the Will of Agnes Canford (1532) that the parishioners of Geddington had provided a new high rood, and apparently sold the old one, for in 1536, T. Freman leaves to the parish the old rood loft which remained in the church at that date. We also see from J. Comford's 1517 Will that the Rood had one or more figures who were clothed with an actual coat (Christ's loincloth would have been permanent).

We can only speculate how the Geddington 'High' and 'Stooping' Roods once appeared, but the example from France in Fig. 63 gives an impression of the often brightly-decorated and intricate nature of medieval rood lofts.

The death of Henry VIII brought the militantly Protestant Edward VI to the throne, and a law of 1547 decreed that all images were to be removed from rood screens and lofts, although at Geddington, the rood screen itself remained

Figure 63: a 15th Century rood loft (Jubé) in the chapel of St. Fiacre, Le Faoet Morbihan, France
Photo by Zairon, via Wikimedia Commons

until 1558[135] when it was removed on the accession of Elizabeth I following the death of the Catholic Queen Mary.

Several bequests mention a sepulchre. An Easter Sepulchre was essential to every English medieval church. Often it was a recess in the north wall of the sanctuary, but more commonly (as at Geddington) it was a small wooden chest into which a *pyx* (generally a small cylindrical box kept on the altar) containing consecrated bread was placed on Maundy Thursday or Good Friday, together with a crucifix. Candles and incense were burned and the sepulchre constantly watched until dawn on Easter day, when the pyx was taken out and replaced upon the altar. A wooden sepulchre sometimes needed to be repaired or replaced – as we see from the will of T. Freman.

It seems reasonably certain that the 'Henry German' who left money for new seating throughout the church in 1486 was none other than Henry Jarmon, who together with his wife, Anna, is commemorated by a brass floor monument, originally located in the North Aisle, but (since 1906) now found in the Lady Chapel. The location of the Chapel of St. John the Baptist, in which William Downhall asked to be buried in 1504, is uncertain but may well have been the north chapel that later became the 'Maydwell Chapel', which in turn fell into dereliction.

Pilgrimage, the saying of masses for the dead, high altars, rood lofts, incense, and the wearing of elaborate vestments were all part of the weave of religious life in the early 16th Century, as they had been for centuries. The folk who left these bequests could not have imagined the turmoil into which their church and the lives of their descendants were about to be plunged.

The last Vicar of Geddington to be presented by the Abbot of Pipewell was Henricus Bisshopp, who was invested on 12 February 1510. Vicar for the next 30 years, he survived the suppression of Pipewell Abbey and, by the time of his death in 1545, the English church no longer received its spiritual leadership from Rome, but from the King, and Pipewell Abbey was fast becoming a ruin.

REFORMATION & REVOLUTION 1538 – 1660

Once the advowson of St. Andrew's, Geddington had been granted to George Tresham of Newton and Edward Twynho in 1538, it was to John Chamber, the Bishop of the recently-created Diocese of Peterborough, to whom George would have presented Richardus Freman as the new Vicar in November 1545. Most of the Tresham family remained loyal to Rome, but George may not have been, so we can but guess his thoughts as he presented the new Vicar, who also had to navigate these turbulent times. From a distance of nearly five centuries it is hard to over-estimate the tremendous shock caused throughout society by the severing of ties with the church of Rome. The struggles it set in train ebbed and flowed for at least another 200 years, and is arguably still detectable in social attitudes even today.

Despite Henry VIII's rejection of Papal authority, he had largely retained the liturgy and practice of the Catholic church. However, his successor, the strongly protestant Edward VI (1547-1553), enforced many changes, including the new church liturgy in the *Book of Common Prayer*. He was succeeded by the militantly Catholic Queen Mary (1553-1558), who re-introduced the Latin Mass and the 'old ways'; only for her successor, Elizabeth I, not only to re-assert the protestant reformation of the church, but who also made failure to accept the authority of the Crown over the English Church punishable by fines, imprisonment and even death.

Geddington church, its clergy and congregation would have been profoundly affected by all this. Nevertheless, during Elizabeth's reign, although the removal of the rood loft and the high altar, the whitening of at least some walls[136] and the replacement of stained glass with plain glass would have created a more austere feeling, the building itself would have remained largely as it had been before the Reformation: it was in worship that fundamental changes occurred. Services were conducted in English, rather than Latin; much greater emphasis was placed on scripture as a source of authority; seeking mediation with Christ through his mother Mary was actively discouraged; and the *Book of Common Prayer* (BCP) ensured uniform use of the new liturgy. Despite the upheaval, strict social distinctions of rank remained. Private, boxed-in seating for the higher status members of the congregation were becoming the norm,

---

135   According to the notes made by Rev. Richard Dorington (source unknown).

136   In 1619 the Chancel wall still lacked whitening (*Church Survey 1619*, Vol. 3).

and pieces of some of the earliest such pews in England now form part of a vestment cupboard in the church Vestry.

A PURITAN MINISTER IN GEDDINGTON

Distinctions of rank may have remained, but the 17th Century was no less turbulent than the previous one. By this time, Puritan beliefs were commonplace, as seen in the actions of Thomas Jones, Vicar of Geddington between 1601 and 1607. Following Elizabeth I's death in 1603, Puritan ministers collected signatures for a petition, known as the 'Millenary Petition' because it was said to be signed by 1,000 Puritan ministers. The Petition was careful not to challenge royal supremacy over the Church of England, but called for a number of church reforms to remove ceremonies perceived as 'popish', among which was the use of the sign of the cross in baptism, which Puritans saw as superstitious. In March 1605 it was alleged that Rev. Jones "*hath omitted the sign of the cross in Baptism*". He admitted the offence but pleaded that he had taken it to be something left to his discretion[137].

'SMELLING' OF PURITANISM

This dislike of 'popish' practices was shared by the 1st Lord Montagu of Boughton. When King James I visited Boughton in 1604 he said the family 'smelt' of Puritanism and in 1605, with other gentlemen of Northamptonshire, Lord Montagu presented a petition to the King in favour of those ministers in the county who refused 'subscription' to official church doctrines. The petitioners were warned that their combination "*in a cause against which the king had shewed his mislike … was little less than treason*." Montagu was for the time deprived of his lieutenancy and justiceship of the peace in the county, but was later re-instated, becoming one of the key founders of what is known today as 'Guy Fawkes Night' through his sponsorship, in Parliament, of the *Observance of the 5th November Act,* 1605.

THE NEWTON REBELLION

There were economic as well as religious changes causing massive social upheaval. One reminder of this is at nearby Newton, where a plaque (Fig. 64) by the old church tells of the Newton Rebellion of 1607 – the last time that agricultural workers rebelled against the gentry. The culmination of wider disturbances across the Midlands, this was a

Figure 64: The Newton Rebellion (1607) - commemorative stone at St. Faith's, Newton (since replaced)

protest against the inclosure of common land at 'The Brand' near Little Oakley by Thomas Tresham, a cousin of the more famous Sir Thomas Tresham of Rushton (whose son Francis was implicated in the Gunpowder Plot and who died in the Tower of London in 1605).

The protesters, some of whom were from Geddington, were led by John Reynolds, known as 'Captain Pouch', a tinker from Desborough. He claimed authority from the King and from God to destroy inclosures and proclaimed the contents of his pouch would protect the rebels.

On 8 June, over 1,000 protesters gathered at Newton and the King ordered his county lieutenants to suppress the rebellion. The local militia, led by Lord Edward Montagu, refused to take part and so Thomas Tresham led his own men, ordering the protestors to disperse. When they refused, the King's proclamation was read twice, but to no effect. Eventually, Tresham and his men charged, and over 40 peasants were killed. Those captured were imprisoned in St. Faith's Church, and the ringleaders were later tried and hung and quartered. The miraculous contents of Captain Pouch's pouch turned out to be a piece of mouldy green cheese!

PART III: A HISTORY OF THE CHURCH

Although principally about economic grievances (the loss of rights to graze and gather wood from common land), there was also a religious edge to the protests, because Thomas Tresham was a recusant (a Catholic who refused to submit to the King's authority over the church), and was widely disliked locally, largely for his rapacity, but also partly for his religious beliefs. However, the experience traumatised Edward Montagu and caused his subsequent opposition to enclosure. His successors shared this antipathy, which meant the land around Geddington wasn't enclosed until the early 19th Century. The rebellion cast a long shadow.

THE KING JAMES BIBLE

The 'King James Bible' was published in 1611, the first widely available English translation authorised for public use and still much-loved for its wonderfully-crafted language even today. In the same year, one of the earliest volumes held by the parish[138] was published: a collection of sermons by John Jewel (Bishop of Salisbury from 1559 to 1571) refuting Catholic doctrines. It was ordered that copies of this book should be displayed in all churches, and Geddington's copy still has the chain once used to secure it to a lectern – tangible evidence of the insecurity felt by the new protestant order as the 'old religion' was ruthlessly suppressed.

MAURICE TRESHAM'S THANK-OFFERING

One of the glories of Geddington Church dates from this period too: a carved wooden screen given by Maurice Tresham in 1618 as a thank-offering for his wife, Muriel, giving birth to a son in that year. Displacing the medieval screen, the handsome new screen filled the Chancel arch. In making such a conspicuous gift to the established church, Maurice may also have been seeking to underscore his loyalty, given the wider family's association only 13 years earlier with the 'Gunpowder Plot' to blow up Parliament, and the use by the plotters of a summerhouse at Newton Hall (*Fig. 65*).

All this suggests that Maurice Tresham did not share the recusancy of his more prominent relatives, but we cannot be sure, as the quotations inscribed on the screen have

Figure 65: The Gunpowder Plot House, Newton Hall
Picture courtesy of Jim Harker [Gentleman's Magazine, Feb. 1783]

a certain ambiguity (see the section on THE TRESHAM SCREEN). Maurice Tresham died in 1646 and was buried with his wife Muriel in the Chancel of Geddington church[139].

A CHURCH FOUND WANTING

The Church Survey of 1619 (Vol. 3) noted several deficiencies, however, including that:

> *"the Chancell wall wants whyteninge And A pte of ye Chancel unpaved"*;

> *"The East end of the North ally altogether within out of repare"*; [140]

> *"The chest hath but 2 locks[141]"*;

> *"The common cup and the flagon not kept with the churchwarden and not showen he beinge not at home"*;

> and *"the East end of the churchyard fenced with A ded hedge"*.

THE ENGLISH CIVIL WAR

One of the factors leading to the Civil War was a growing fear that King Charles I had Catholic sympathies. In 1633 Archbishop Laud imposed requirements that altars should be moved back to their medieval position at the east end of the Chancel and enclosed with a communion rail. Although Laud's edict was never fully enforced, it raised alarm

---

138 It is recorded at the end of this book that, on 10th April 1669, Samuel Lee paid the sum of six shillings to *"Redeme this Booke oute of ye Kings hands"*. Another entry in 1653 is signed by Basill Sargent and others, perhaps when removing it from the church.

139 The large stone ledgers marking their graves were re-located to the North Aisle in 1855-57, and in 1974 were stood up against the north wall.

140 A clear indication that the Maydwell Chapel was already in a very dilapidated state. By 1719, a drawing by Peter Tillemans [*North Prospect of Geddington Church* (1719) – *Fig. 67*] shows it was no longer standing.

141 It was usual for parish chests to have 3 locks, whose keys were held by the Vicar and 2 churchwardens, all of whom needed to be present to open the chest.

among Puritans, and the order was rescinded by Parliament in 1641. The edict was clearly observed at Geddington, however, for a new altar rail was installed in 1635[142], which lasted until it was removed in GG Scott's changes of 1855-57.

During the Civil War, Geddington was often close to the boundary between royalist and parliamentary control and, although the faces of several of the church's carved stone images appear to have been defaced by having their noses cut, both the church and the Eleanor Cross appear to have survived the war more or less intact.

In the Civil War, choosing sides was inevitably fraught with danger. Thomas Tresham of Geddington took the King's side against Parliament and was only pardoned in 1647 on payment of a fine of £150[143]. And just 3 years later, a Warrant was issued to Colonel Brookes to "*apprehend Edward Tresham at Geddington. He being lately come from abroad about some dangerous business.*"[144] By this time, however, the Tresham family's star was waning, and the Montagu family of Boughton House were increasingly pre-eminent in the area.

THE COMMONWEALTH AND THE END OF TRESHAM FAMILY INFLUENCE

News of the execution of King Charles I in 1649 must have been received with shock and astonishment in Geddington but, despite this dramatic turn of events, we know very little about how the advent of The Commonwealth under Oliver Cromwell affected Geddington or its church. It appears to have had no lasting impact, however, except that the Tresham family connection with Geddington and Newton ended.

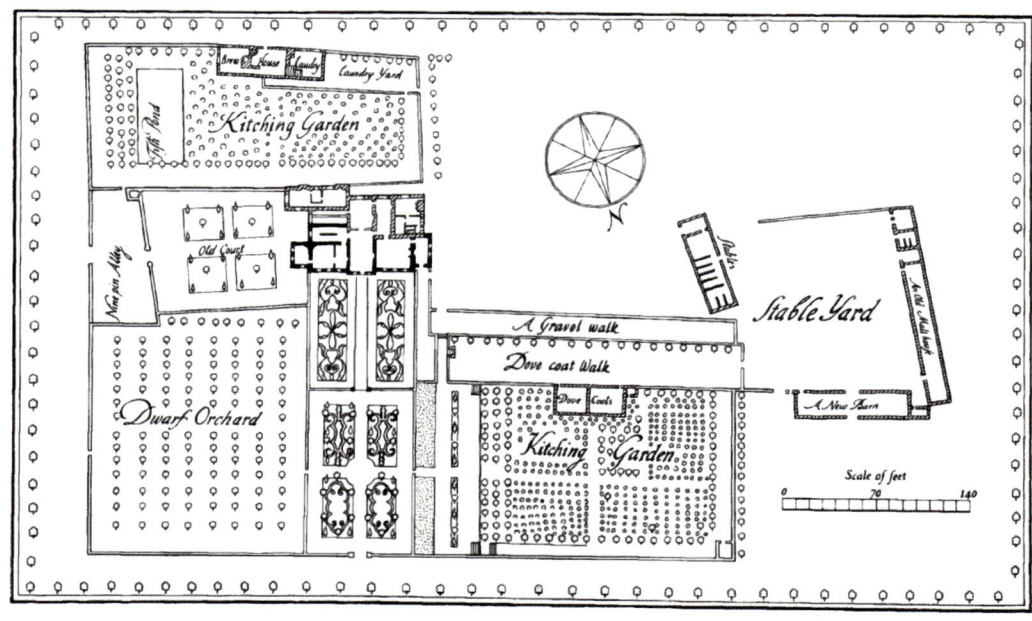

Figure 66: Newton Hall and garden (based on a plan of c 1715)[145]

In about 1660 the Treshams' estate at Newton passed to Sir John Langham who enlarged the house. Some years later it was sold to Sir Caesar Child and in 1713 it was bought by Benjamin Bathurst whose widow, Frances, sold it in 1715 to the 2nd Duke of Montagu, whose descendants have been Patrons of Geddington Church to this day.

Newton Hall appears to have been still standing in about 1720, for Bridges recorded it as being built of brick and stone[146]. The house was, however, demolished soon afterwards and the garden abandoned. By 1740 a terrier of Newton (NRO) states that the 'Hall Gardens' were being leased to one William Wheelwright, apparently a farmer living at Great Newton. In the late 19th Century it was said that flowers from the garden could still be found in the surrounding fields[147].

THE DALLINGTON CHARITY

The monasteries of the medieval period had often been important charitable institutions. So too were the 'Guilds' that were associated with most parish churches which, as well as supporting their church, also acted as friendly societies for their members when trouble struck. Monastic dissolution left a void that increased pauperism and left many

---

142 The date on the door of the altar rail was noted by Edmond Vialls in his letter of 1809 (op. cit.)

143 *House of Commons Journal* Volume 5: 23 December 1647 Pages 397-401

144 *Calendar of State Papers* (21st December 1650)

145 From: *An Inventory of the Historical Monuments in the County of Northamptonshire,* Volume 2, Archaeological Sites in Central Northamptonshire. Originally published by Her Majesty's Stationery Office, London, 1979. Reproduced by British History Online.

146 J. Bridges (op. cit.) pp. 322–3

147 *Northants. N. and Q.*, 2 (1886), No. 216; from British History Online. See https://www.british-history.ac.uk/rchme/northants/vol2/pp112-116

communities and churches short of resources. Individual philanthropy was therefore very welcome, although it often came with a very hard edge.

One such example was Sir Robert Dallington (1561-1636), who was said to have been born a poor lad in Geddington and left to make his fortune, which he did, becoming secretary to Francis, Earl of Rutland, Gentleman of the Bedchamber to Charles I, and later Master of Charterhouse. On his death in 1636 he left £300 (worth about £40,000 in 2024) for the benefit of 24 aged inhabitants of Geddington. The money was later used to buy just over 30 acres of land at Highway Close and Deepdale Close, Loddington, which the still-extant charity holds to this day. In his lifetime, he had also built the village school (then to the north-west of the church[148]) and paid for a bell in the church tower.

Recipients of the Charity were each to receive a weekly loaf of bread subject to their attending church and complying with other rules, which were both harsh and exclusive. 'Deserving' persons were to be selected by the trustees, '*and then to draw lots till they have* [the bread]'. There were three basic requirements for eligibility:

a. 'the honest number of twenty four shall not contain any who has made himself poor by idleness, drunkenness or disorder';

b. recipients must be either born in Geddington '*or have dwelt in the town in good behaviour at least fourteen years before*'. (thereby excluding many servants, apprentices, and young married couples).

c. 'if any have consumed their estates by giving away their estates to their children or by buying or building houses they shall not be partakers of this charity'. (thus re-inforcing the obligation on children to maintain their elderly parents).

Beyond these basic eligibility criteria was a system of penalties and forfeitures. Recipients of the dole might have their loaf indefinitely withheld if they allowed '*married folk . . . strangers or children*' into their houses, or if they '*let part of their houses whereby the poor are increased and the town overcharged*'. One week's provision would be forfeited by any of the twenty-four '*found begging, either at home or abroad*', by any heard '*lying, scolding or slandering*', and by

any failing to attend church on Sunday morning. A whole month's entitlement would be withheld if any of the twenty-four or their families indulged in hedge-breaking, fence and gate-smashing or unauthorised gleaning, a provision whose severity explicitly reflects the immediacy of memories of the 1607 Newton Rebellion. Concern to prevent young people staying at home (where they would have to be supported from the poor rates) and to force them to find work was explicit: any of the twenty-four could be (permanently) '*displaced and another put in their room*' if they '*kept more children at home than is needful for their use*'.

The Charity's rules are still displayed in the church porch, and a triangular buffet or shelf was used for the storage of the bread which, until the Covid pandemic of 2020, continued to be distributed to designated persons.

RESTORATION & CONSOLIDATION 1660 - 1845

The Restoration of the monarchy in 1660 was welcomed by most people, tired of constant conflict, and although religious controversy remained (not least with fears of a return to Catholicism under James II, followed by the 'Glorious Revolution' of 1688 that saw James' staunchly protestant daughter Mary and her husband William of Orange jointly take the throne) church life evolved over the following two centuries into a more settled and confident pattern, the Jacobite rebellions of 1715 and 1745 being the last serious stirrings of the old conflict. Indeed, it was concern over the growth of protestant non-conformism after the Civil War that increasingly pre-occupied the Church of England, the Monarch and Parliament.

NON-CONFORMITY & THE 'GREAT EJECTION'

The 1662 *Act of Uniformity* prescribed that any minister who refused to conform to the *Book of Common Prayer* by St. Bartholomew's Day (24 August) 1662 should be ejected from the Church of England. Thomas Elborowe[149], who was newly-installed in Geddington in 1662, initially refused to conform and was ejected from the vicarage as part of the 'Great Ejection', in which over 2,000 priests were deprived of their livings. He conformed shortly after however, and remained Vicar until his death in 1675.

---

148 The ruins of that school building can be seen in Tillemans' 1719 drawing (*Fig. 67*): *North Prospect of Geddington Church*

149 Longden's *Northamptonshire & Rutland Clergy* (op. cit.) gives his name as 'Robert'.

Another instance of dissent appeared in a letter from the Bishop of Peterborough to Lord Montagu[150] dated 18 March 1667 in which the Bishop writes that:

"he has just received a complaint that during the last fort-night two very factious un-licensed preachers preached at Geddington, viz Parkins and Winter, which Winter he has had particular order from the Archbishop of Canterbury to apprehend, and requesting Lord Montagu, if he can find them, to send them to gaol".

Lord Montagu, clearly reluctant to get involved, responded that he was neither the church's patron nor lord of the Manor, but that he believed Winter to be dead and Perkins to be living in Rutland.

Whilst the **Act of Uniformity** suppressed controversy within the Church of England, it resulted in growing frag-mentation of the Christian family and created an abiding concept of 'non-conformity' that has lasted into the pres-ent day. The famous nonconformist Vincent Alsop lived in Geddington for some time and he applied for a licence to preach in his own house here in 1672[151].

The 2nd Duke however, was well known for his toleration of religious diversity[152], as were his successors, which meant it was possible to establish a Quaker Meeting House in 1729 on Grafton Road (now a private dwelling). Non-conformists were refused burial in the churchyard, and so a burial ground was established at the rear of the meeting house, where human bones were discovered when the house was extended in the 1950s. A Wesleyan Chapel also existed for a time in Queen Street, and in 1875 the United Reform Church eventually established a chapel, also in Queen Street.

These tensions shaped lives, for 'dissenters' were denied entry to universities, the holding of public office, and various other restrictions. The Maydwells of Geddington Priory were an important Geddington family, several of whose members are commemorated in the church. John Maydwell however, (b. 1609) became Rector of Kettering in 1661, but was ejected from his living on 24th August in the following year:

"He was a firm unflinching man When Nonconformity began;

He left the church in sixty two, A noble thing for him to do."

THE IMPORTANCE OF GLEBE LAND

The importance of the Vicar having sources of income to enable him to maintain the Chancel emerges in an account of the receipt of £200 from 'Queen Anne's Bounty' – some-thing which the 2nd Duke of Montagu was instrumental in securing. The money was used in 1724 to purchase 40 acres of land known as 'Collier's ffreehold' at Raunds, which was conveyed to the Rev. Francis Groleau and his successors, Vicars of Geddington[153] – so becoming part of Geddington's 'glebe lands', which in 1700 also included an acre of land in each of Debdale and Ham Fields in Geddington. This was certainly needed, as the accounts reveal that £47 and 12 shillings (about £13,800 today) was spent on repairing the Chancel of the church in 1753.

Queen Anne's Bounty was a scheme established in 1704 to allow poorer clergy to buy land to supplement their incomes. It was funded from payments of 'first-fruits' (first year income from new clergy) and 'tenths' (annual pay-ments) once made by clergy to the Pope but which had, since the Reformation, been made to the King. The func-tions and assets of the **Bounty** were passed to the new-ly-formed Church Commissioners in 1947. It has attracted controversy because in the 18th Century the **Bounty** had invested in, and profited from, the Atlantic Slave Trade.

From 1978 glebe lands ceased to belong to individual incumbents and became vested in Diocesan Boards of Finance. The (now limited) survival into the 21st Century of **'Chancel Repair Liability'** - a continuing obligation on own-ers of land that once had to pay tithes to pay for Chancel repairs - is an echo of this ancient means of funding church maintenance.

THE SAMUEL LEE CHARITY

Individual philanthropy remained important, the most no-table example being that of Samuel Lee, who was Ranger of Geddington Chase to the Duke of Montagu, a position of some standing locally, who left £100 for the benefit of the poor in 1708. His will read:

"I give to the use of the poor of Geddington in the County of Northamptonshire the sum of one hundred pounds

---

150 Lord Montagu of Beaulieu's archives, with thanks to Crispin Powell of the Buccleuch Living Heritage Trust

151 *An Abridged History of Geddington,* M J Harker (1956)

152 The Duke also had a handwritten copy of the Qur'an presented to him by his friend Ayuba Suleiman Diallo (1701-73), whose family were religious leaders in West Africa and who was trafficked as a slave in America before coming to England, eventually returning to Africa [with thanks to Crispin Powell, Buccleuch Archive].

153 The fields at Raunds were enclosed in 1800, and the Commissioners awarded alternative land nearby. Markham (op. cit.), pp 36 & 37 (1899).

to be laid out in a purchase or put to interest according as the Trustees I shall hereafter record shall think fit, the said rent or interest of the said money to be given to the Overseers or Churchwardens of the said Parish – which my trustees think most proper (to the poor of the said Parish upon every Christmas Day), the said one hundred pounds to be paid by my Executor to the Trustees I shall hereafter appoint or any three of them at twelve months after my death."

On 3rd March 1708, Samuel Lee died and his tombstone (Grade II listed) duly records his generosity to the village (see the description of his tombstone under 'Churchyard'). The Samuel Lee Charity is still active today and continues to help local residents facing difficulties. His tomb can be seen in the churchyard south of the church.

THE CHURCH IN 1719

In 1719 John Bridges (1666–1724), a Fellow of the *Society of Antiquaries*, commissioned the Flemish-born artist Peter Tillemans (1684-1734) to *"make about 500 drawings for a projected history of Northamptonshire"*, one of which was a view of Geddington Church from the north (*Fig. 67*). John Bridges comments[154] on this:

"At Geddington was antiently a royal seat, in a close to the north-east of the church, called the castle or hall-close. The surface of the ground is very uneven, and many foundations still visible." And later he says:

"a chapel on the north side of the Chancel, taken down some years since by the family of Maidwell, to whom it belonged."

Close inspection of Tillemans' drawing shows a blocked arch in the north side of the Chancel, confirming Bridges' observation. The drawing also shows a derelict house that once housed the village school. Bridges says that this schoolhouse was erected by Sir Robert Dallington and that over the door was an inscription:

"This schoole was built at the only cost and charges of Sir Robert Dallington Knight. He gave the great Bell of this Church and 24 three peny loaves everie Sunday unto 24 of the poore of this parish for eve

HE WAS BORN IN THIS TOWN AND IS NOW MR AND ONE OF THE GOVERNORS OF THE FAMOUS HOSPITALL IN THE CHARTER HOUSE AT LONDON AND IS ONE OF THE GENTLEMEN OF THE PRIVIE CHAMBER IN ORDINARY ANNO 1635. ÆT. SUAE 74. (Trans. = In the year 1635, in the 74th year of his age) DOCTRINA VITA VIRTUTIS." (Trans. = Teaching a life of virtue)

Bridges goes on to say that the school, being built on another person's ground, was never endowed and *"is now in ruins"*.

Figure 67: 'North Prospect of Geddington Church, 10 July 1719' by Peter Tillemans
The original drawing is in the British Library

---

154 Quoted in *Northamptonshire in the Early Eighteenth Century: the Drawings of Peter Tillemans and Others*, p. 75 (op. cit.)

THE VESTRY MEETING - COUNCIL TAX FORE-SHADOWED

The maintenance of the Nave and other areas of the church was, as it had been since medieval times, the responsibility of the parishioners. The Parish was entitled to levy charges on residents to fund the costs of repair, authorised at 'Vestry' meetings. For example, one such Vestry held on 21st December 1812 authorised a levy for the repair of the tower and spire[155]. The forerunner of parish councils, 'vestries' (so called because they often met in a vestry) evolved from medieval church governance and had both religious and secular functions. They were chaired by the Vicar. They were abolished in 1921.

THE COMMUNITY FIRE STATION

In the 18th and 19th centuries, the churchyard was also where the community fire engine was kept. In the days before powerful engines and electrically powered pumps, fire-fighting depended on a hand-pumped engine operated by volunteers organised by the Parish (Fig. 68).

This provision lasted into the 20th Century until the advent of motorised fire engines and a fire brigade provided by the County Council. Even then, the first line of defence was volunteers who could be called out to attend with a locally-housed engine. Only in the second half of the 20th Century did a fully-professional Fire Brigade provide complete cover.

The volunteer tradition has been sustained until the present day, however, in the shape of the **Geddington Volunteer Fire Brigade**. Formed during the national firemen's strike of 1977, it now has its own engine, the 'Queen Eleanor', and is a registered charity with a membership of more than 80. It carries out various community tasks to support organisations, groups, and individuals, including periodic clearances of church gutters and overgrowth in the churchyard.

THE COMMUNITY'S TIMEPIECE

The importance of the church clock and bells to the community is emphasised by the amounts listed in the accounts as paid to ring the bell (e.g. 4 shillings to John Dix in 1737) and to wind the clock (e.g. £1-12-6d to Edward Bullivant in 1741). This was the predecessor of the present clock, which was installed in 1766. The bells signalled not only the call to

Figure 68: Old fire engine (now in Kettering Museum)

worship but also the time for workers in the fields, and set the time for other clocks in the village.

Until 1881 a bell was rung every morning at 4 o'clock from St. Valentine's Day (Feb. 14th) to St. Martin's Day (Nov. 22nd) and at five o'clock for the winter period, except on Sundays. The daily bell at noon and the 8pm curfew bell were still being rung in the 1890s[156]. The custom of ringing the 'Pancake Bell' at 11am on Shrove Tuesday continued into the 20th Century.

The church bells have long also been used to signal important national events, notably the accession of new monarchs and their later deaths, great victories (e.g. Waterloo in 1815 and Alamein in 1942) and on news of peace - e.g. in 1801, 6 shillings were "**paid the Ringers when news of peace**"[157] and in 1918 and 1945. It is sobering to speculate that the two oldest bells in the tower would have been among those ringing to announce the defeat of the Spanish Armada in 1588!

---

155 From Churchwardens' accounts, recorded in Markham (op. cit.) p.74

156 Markham, op. cit. p.31

157 At the end of the French Revolutionary Wars, leading to the Treaty of Amiens.

PART III: A HISTORY OF THE CHURCH

A VICAR WRITES TO HIS FRIEND

On 19 Jan 1753 the Rev. William Sprigg, Vicar of Geddington, wrote to his friend William Folkes[158]:

William Sprigg, Geddington to William Folkes, Queens Square. Obliged for receipt sent by Mr Breese and for paper Mrs Folkes bought for him. Her good taste. Has finished parlour and divided yard, just needs a good wife to make him a happy man. Had a very warm contest about baking the bread given by Sir Robert Dallington for 24 poor people. Only given to members of the church so was determined a churchman should bake it. Does he want the book Ratten bound sent to Town?

Mr Brooke of Kettering declining and not expected to recover health. Mr Ekins at the club at Kettering and has severe gout. Will spend week in Oundle.

The Dallington Bread was clearly very much valued and fought over! Sadly, the Rev. Sprigg also died of 'floating gout' in the following year.

A CHURCH BAND

In this period (1798) the church seems to have had a full band: the Churchwardens' accounts include payments for *"strings for the violins and violincellos, and for mending the base viol"* and *"scrues of Jno Baker for the Base Viol".*[159] It is thought there was a musicians' gallery, probably in the North Aisle, until 1855.

THE 1794 ROOD SCREEN

Today there are few if any signs of this post-restoration period evident in the fabric of the church itself, although we know of a striking example of the church's growing sense of security: the great Rood Screen above the Chancel Arch, bearing the royal coat of arms and proudly proclaiming The Apostles' Creed, the Lord's Prayer, and the Ten Commandments. It was painted on plaster and we know this was created in 1794 because the accounts for that year include:

"July the 2 paid att town Meeting a bout the Court of Arms and Commandments…4 shillings"

and in August:

"Anthony Feary received for painting, two guineas; and in December he received for the commandments, four guineas."[160]

Although this great painted screen lasted barely 50 years before being removed, we still have a record of how it looked and what was inscribed on it, thanks to the drawings of Edward Bradley.

EDWARD BRADLEY, THE DUCHESS' PROTÉGÉ

Three of Edward Bradley's paintings hang in the church, the first depicting the view of the Nave in the first half of the 19th Century; a second the mural of Queen Elizabeth's cenotaph; and a third the late 18th Century painted rood screen. He painted several other scenes of Geddington, including The Cross and the exterior of the church.

Bradley, the son of a shoemaker, was born in Geddington on 2nd December 1802 and baptised in Geddington Church on 2nd January 1803[161]. He was taught reading and writing by Thomas Carley[162], the parish clerk and school master at Grafton Underwood, who was born without hands and had one deformed leg. Yet, with the aid of leather appliances Carley could wield knife and fork, write a beautiful hand, and 'perform with facility most of the functions which seemed to require two hands for efficient performance'[163]. He was a stern disciplinarian - if two boys were talking instead of working, he would go behind them and knock their heads together very roughly with his wooden extensions. Bradley remembered him, not with fondness, as *'Old Stumpy'* and later drew him (**Fig. 69**) in watercolour (now in the British Museum).

The school in Grafton

Figure 69: 'Old Stumpy' by Edward Bradley.
Courtesy of Trevor Harker.

158 From the Buccleuch Archive [M(B) 2/3/2/59], with thanks to Crispin Powell. William Foulkes (1725-68) was born in Oundle and was buried there.

159 Markham (op. cit.) p.74

160 From Rev. Richard Dorrington's notes (source unknown, probably the Churchwarden's accounts County Record Office)

161 *Parish Register* (1799-1812), accessible online via the *Ancestry* website.

162 *Northamptonshire Notes and Queries*, Taylor & Sons, Vol. 2 (1909) p.113*ff*

163 *Kettering History* from *https://www.townsontheweb.com/northamptonshire/kettering/local_visiting_history.htm*

was established by the Duke of Buccleuch in 1793 and Carley was appointed school master. Carley died in 1823, the same year that, on 16th June at St. Dunstan in the East, London, Bradley married a former ladies' maid to the Duchess of Buccleuch, Hannah Gould (1802-77) of Crux Eaton, Hampshire.

That same year also, at the prompting of Elizabeth, Duchess of Buccleuch, he obtained his release from 'menial services' by Thomas Christopher Hofland (himself an accomplished landscape artist and a founder-member of the Society of British Artists) so that, '*he shall be devoted entirely to employments connected with the art of drawing and painting*'[164].

Bradley later acknowledged Duchess Elizabeth and his Geddington roots, by naming one of his daughters 'Elizabeth' and another 'Eleanor'. He also named a son 'Montague'. For Duchess Elizabeth had helped establish Edward Bradley in his youth, and he received further patronage in her Will, providing annuities, pensions, legal assistance, voluntary allowances, clothing him and setting him up in business[165]. His print of the Eleanor Cross in Geddington was dedicated to the Duchess, and soon after his marriage he went to live at Putney, painting landscapes around Richmond, where the Duke had a villa, and exhibiting at the Royal Academy between 1824 and 1844. These works included: *Loch Gyle* (1832); *View from Cross Farm, Crux Easton* (1840); and *Landscape near Highclere* (1844). Many of his early works were collected by Thomas Dash and presented by his son to the British Museum. His *'View from Richmond Hill'* was sold from the Buccleuch collection in 1946[166]. Edward Bradley died at 9 The Terrace, Windsor Street[167] in Putney on 17 July 1883 and was buried at St. Mary's Church, Putney.

A 46-YEAR MINISTRY IN GEDDINGTON

Another character who loomed large in the Geddington story during this period was The Reverend James Hogg. Born in 1774, James Hogg became Curate of Geddington in 1798 with a stipend of about £45 a year. In 1801 he was appointed Master of Kettering Grammar School and two years later he married Mary Roughton of Kettering, where they set up residence in Gold Street. He became Rector of

Glendon in April 1814 and Vicar of Geddington and Newton in July that year. He was a remarkable man in his time, for not only did he teach at Kettering all week, but he was the incumbent of three country parishes. Every Sunday morning he drove to Geddington for a service at 10:30am, on to Great Oakley for a service at 1pm then to Newton-in-the-Willows for a 3:30pm service; and finally back to Geddington for a service at 6pm before returning home to Kettering after giving four services and sermons. He clearly had a zeal for 'modernising' reform too, for in 1830 he petitioned the House of Lords, praying their Lordships:

> "to turn their Attention to the State of the Agricultural Poor, and to apply such Remedies, either corrective or fundamental, as may be best fitted to change the present baneful Operations of the Poor Laws into such a one as may be beneficial."[168]

Rev. James Hogg was installed as Vicar whilst still in the reign of George III. By the time that he died on the 25th of November 1844, Victoria had been Queen for 7 years and the country was fast growing in prosperity. Change was in the air.

THE VICTORIAN CHURCH 1845 – 1914

When the newly-married Rev. William Montagu Higginson Church was installed as Vicar of Geddington in 1845, the parish had had but three Vicars in the preceding 90 years. We can see a good likeness of how the church looked when he arrived in Edward Bradley's painting that hangs in the church today (see the cover photo) - the old box pews, the tall timber pulpit, the Tresham Screen filling the central Chancel Arch, the Rood Screen above. We can just glimpse the medieval screen in the south aisle arch, with the painting of Elizabeth's tomb above, and in the distance we can make out the silhouette of the ancient reredos framed against a plain East Window. All this was about to change.

REV. CHURCH & RENEWAL OF THE CHURCH

Rev. William Church's theology was very influenced by the *Oxford Movement*, which sought to restore liturgical and

164 Henry Hoyle Oddie's vouchers 1822-1824 [Buccleuch Archive with thanks to Crispin Powell]

165 Duchess Elizabeth's executors' vouchers 1826-1827 [Buccleuch Archive, with thanks to Crispin Powell]

166 It was sold at Christie's, together with his 'View of the Star & Garter, Richmond Terrace' for £11,950 in 2002.

167 Now part of Upper Richmond Road. The Terrace was demolished in 1900 to make way for Kenilworth Court.

168 *House of Lords Journal* Volume 63: 30 November 1830 Pages 138-141. The *Poor Law Amendment Act* of 1834 abolished the old system of 'outdoor relief' that had existed since 1601 and introduced the new, and more punitive, workhouse system.

Figure 70: The Church in 1845, by Edward Bradley.

Picture courtesy of Jim Harker

devotional customs that borrowed heavily from traditions before the English Reformation as well as contemporary Roman Catholic practice.

The revival of religious devotion in this period meant that he also wanted to expand the seating available in church for his growing congregation. Not everyone shared this fervour. On 30th May 1848 an 'anti-church' meeting was organised at the Cross. The parish officers, with the aid of the village fire engine (now in the Kettering Museum), *'put to flight the whole troop of anti-churchmen.'* [169]

But Rev. Church's first priority[170] was a new school. Designed by the prestigious London architect, Benjamin Ferrey, this was completed on Grafton Road just south of the church in 1849 (it is now a private dwelling called *The*

Old School). In the same year, he had a dispute with David Townsend, village blacksmith, who ran an evening school for children. He told Townsend's pupils that if they continued to attend, he would not have them at the church Sunday School. Townsend responded with an *"Address to the Inhabitants of Geddington respecting Clerical Interference…"*!

The new school completed, William Church then turned his attentions to what, in his view, was the cramped and inadequate interior of the church. It was in *'dismal condition'* and he was *'obliged to huddle the children,'* making them impossible to train as a choir. As with the school, he went to a top London architect for the job of redesigning the interior: George Gilbert Scott, who had become

169 *Northampton Herald,* 3 June 1848.

170 This and the following description of the church renovations, draw heavily on correspondence between Rev. Church and the 5th Duke [Buccleuch Archive] with grateful thanks to Crispin Powell.

architect to Westminster Abbey in 1849. Scott prepared plans in 1852, but to keep prices down Rev. Church wanted local contractors: Mr Brown of Kettering for the woodwork and Edward Patrick, the Duke's estate master mason for the stonework. Brown said his men could do everything apart from the 'poppy head' ends of the pews. His estimate for the work totalled £566-50[171], which is roughly £80,000 at 2024 prices!

As well as the reorganisation, the work included the rebuilding of the eastern end of the north aisle, a new vestry east of it, a new porch, re-location of the font, removal of the medieval plaster and the heightening of the Chancel arch. This opening up of the view into the Chancel would help to draw the whole congregation visually and spiritually into the ritual and drama of the celebration of the Eucharist, but to achieve it meant removing the beautiful and rare Chancel screen. This accorded with Catholic practice: most churches having removed screens following the Council of Trent (1545-63).

Rev. Church sketched the height of the arch he wanted. This in particular he thought, **'will shock Mr Scott as it is against his monomania of non-restoration'**. This radical scheme had not been without its critics, for it swept away or re-located almost everything in Edward Bradley's pictures (other than the stonework). Bitterly opposed by Bradley and others, the scheme nevertheless went ahead.

Rev. Church complained that it was difficult to keep Mr. Scott's mind practical and focused on his maxim of, **'the paramount importance of room'.** Nevertheless, Mr. Scott's plans (Fig. 71) provided seating for over 400 people! Rev. Church was, however, keen to **'copy as much as I can of the old work',** ordering an exact facsimile of the old door in the south entrance; having the reredos and stone heads in the Chancel restored; and recreating the medieval inscription on the Chancel and south chapel steps - the gaps made good, **'by the father of one of my boys, a member of the Camden Society'.**

The renovated Church re-opened fully in 1857. Rev. Church was pleased overall despite Scott's high estimate, but he didn't like the Minton floor tiles. He told the Duke, who was sharing the costs of the renovations with Rev. Church:

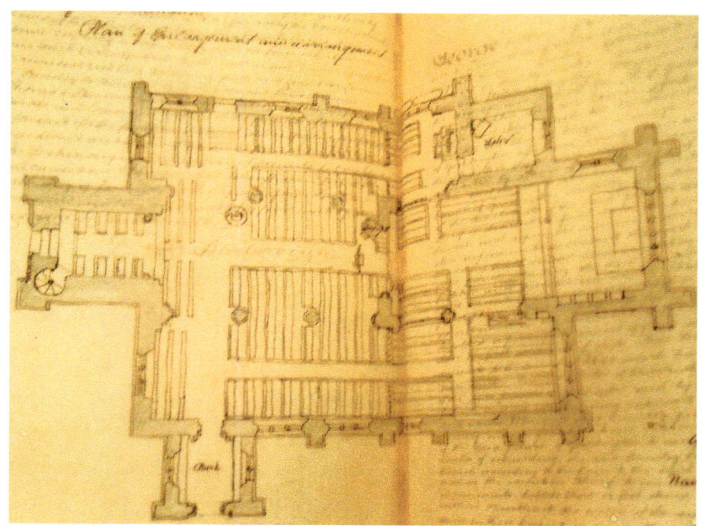

Figure 71: George Gilbert Scott's layout plan (1852).
By kind permission of the Boughton Archive.

'altogether the church looks very handsome and we have allotted the seats without creating discontent'; and noted, *'our choir is really quite sufficient now and took me quite by surprize with their singing'.*

As work on Geddington church was progressing towards its conclusion, the Rev. Church also began a restoration of his other church at Newton-in-the-Willows, where the Chancel was to be rebuilt in memory of his late wife, who had died in 1854. William Slater oversaw the work with the contractors again being Messrs. Brown and Patrick. The Duke must have questioned the expense, for Rev. Church assured him that Mr Slater always travelled second class!

Besides his energy in re-ordering the church, Rev. Church also ran a private school in part of what was then the new Vicarage (built in 1847)[172], but is now **Glebe House** in West Street. Future Prime Minister William Gladstone sent his sons there, as did the Duke. One description[173] says of the school:

"The headmaster, a Rev. William Montagu Church, was known to have a furious temper and the school was not academically renowned".

A former pupil[174] was rather more charitable, however, recalling:

"though he was no scholar, [Rev. Church] grounded us thoroughly in the elements of knowledge, especially in the Greek and Latin grammars and in the scriptures. But

---

171 A copy of Mr Brown's Estimate (1855) is shown at **Appendix 6**. With thanks to Crispin Powell and the Buccleuch Archive.

172 The previous vicarage stood in Queen Street nearly opposite Croft House. An even earlier one once stood on the east side of Wood Street.

173 *The Prime Minister's Son, Stephen Gladstone, Rector of Hawarden*, by Ros Aitken (2012)

174 A. C. Ainger: *Eton 60 Years Ago* (pub. 1917). Ainger was himself a pupil.

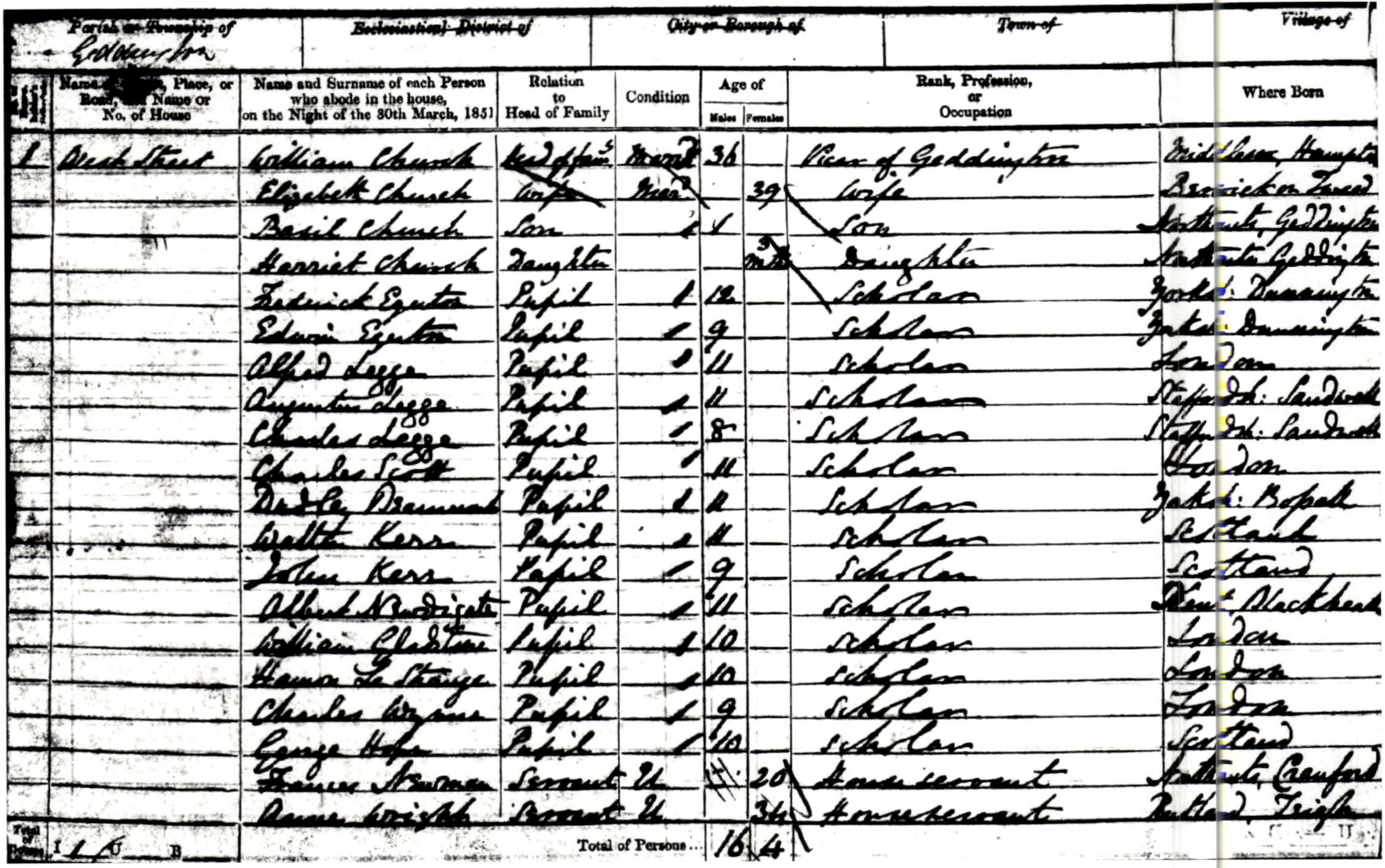

Figure 72: The 1851 Census return for Geddington Vicarage

these good qualities were seriously discounted by his ungovernable temper, and the instrument of flagellation, a sort of dwarf trace, was in constant use……… not far off was Boughton park, belonging to the Duke of Buccleuch, who gave us the run of it, and its miles of elm avenues. He was a patron of the living of Geddington, and I fancy he was a good friend to her church. At all events, he sent his son to the school and there were five or six Moore nephews of his there too. The school undoubtedly stood high in popular favour; it was always full and there was a strong flavour of aristocracy about it. The families of Cavendish, Kerr, Scott, Legge, Egerton, Lascelles, Beaumont, Talbot, Hope, Lyttelton, Moore, Needham, Boscawen were all represented there.'

Besides Admiral Lord Charles Scott, Admiral Lord Walter Kerr and General Lord Ralph Kerr, at least one future cabinet minister and two bishops attended. Fig. 72 lists the pupils present at the 1851 Census.

Rev. Church also wrote for **The Field** magazine, over the pen-name '**Peregrine**,' and flew merlins and sparrowhawks in Boughton Park, the Chase, and Weekley Hall Wood[175]. In the end the Rev. Church found the parish and two churches too big a job for the good of his health, and the father of one of his pupils found him a living at the seaside parish of Hunstanton in 1861. On leaving Geddington, he was presented with a richly-chased silver inkstand, a gold pen and silver pencil-case and an address handsomely illuminated on vellum. The inkstand was inscribed:

Presented to the Rev. WMH Church, vicar of Geddington-cum-Newton by his parishioners in affectionate remembrance of his ministration during a period of 16 years. March MDCCCLXI.[176]

On parting, he wrote to the Duke that: 'no parish can ever be the same to me that Geddington has been'.

RESEARCH AND (MORE) RENOVATION

Rev. Church was followed by Thomas Charles Brand Cornwell who, besides conducting extensive historical researches over the next 25 years, oversaw several improvements, notably the addition of a large organ and a new stone pulpit; and the Wetherall family made generous gifts, including

---

175 *Victoria County History of Northamptonshire* p377 (op. cit.)

176 *Northampton Herald* (23 March 1861)

a magnificent chair and a brass lectern. Rev. Cornwell took a great interest in the village and in church history: his historical notes formed the basis of Markam's 1899 book (op. cit.)

On leaving Geddington in 1885, Rev. Cornwell was presented with a drawing room clock and matching vases, and a parallel bible. His wife and daughters (who served as organists) were presented with a silver centre-piece for the dining table. A leather-bound book with the names of those who had contributed to the collection of £36-15s-9d[177] (worth approx. £6,000 in 2024) was also presented.

The Rev. Cornwell's successor, Rev. Nigel Nash, engaged a young architect just starting out on an illustrious career: Ninian Comper (later Sir) whose very first church restoration project, commissioned in 1888, was the restoration of the reredos of Geddington Church, soon followed, in 1892, by the glass of the great East Window. In commemoration of Queen Victoria's Diamond Jubilee in 1897, a new clock face was commissioned and dedicated on 21 November of that year[178]; heating improvements followed in 1899[179], and in 1900 a flagpole was fixed to the tower[180].

REPAIRS AND (YET MORE) RENOVATION

The arrival of the Rev. Benjamin Turton in 1901 began another phase of significant change. 1902 saw the restoration of the bells[181], replacement of the bell-frame and stonework repairs[182]. Before long, another prestigious architect, Sydney Gambier-Parry, had been engaged and a major programme of repairs and alterations was undertaken between 1903 and 1908[183].

This work (carried out by S.F. Halliday of Stamford and largely funded by the Duke of Buccleuch[184]) included extensive stonework repairs, especially to the tower; renewal of the Nave and Chancel roofs, including the replacement of the plaster ceilings with oak panelling[185]; the relocation of the pulpit from within the Chancel arch to its present position; and the insertion of three screens: the Tresham Screen in the South Aisle arch, a new screen designed by Gambier-Parry in the Chancel arch, and another new screen in the south arcade of the Chancel that replicated the medieval screen in the adjoining arch.

New choir stalls[186], designed by Comper, followed in 1912 and a new altar was installed in the Lady Chapel so that, apart from the Victorian pews, the position of the organ and acetylene lighting, the church was, by then, very largely as we see it today. Apparently the recently-installed acetylene lamps, which had replaced earlier oil lamps, failed during the singing of psalms, plunging the church into darkness![187] By this time people were legally allowed to sit anywhere in church, but many were used to sitting in their customary seats and this was recognised by the churchwardens. The works of 1904-06 prompted a revision of '*the present allotted seats with the object….of having one block of pews entirely free and unappropriated. The present arrangement has been in existence for a great number of years, and stands in urgent need of revision*'.[188]

In the summer of 1914, Geddington Church, both as a community and a building, was probably in better shape than it had been for a very long time. As well as a recently-renovated building, the choir, parish magazine, charitable work, school and church social activities were all thriving. All this was, once again, about to change.

THE WAR-TORN YEARS 1914 – 1953

Over one hundred years later, it is very hard to imagine the horrendous impact of the Great War on the village community and the church. By 1918, a great pall of grief had fallen on the village and the nation. 170 Geddington men served in the armed forces of whom 38 (more than 1 in 5 of those who served) never returned. Several more were left

177 *Kettering News* (27 November 1885)

178 *Kettering Leader & Observer* (21 November 1897). The Vicar's handwritten Order of Service is still held in the Parish.

179 *Kettering Guardian* (20 January 1899)

180 *Kettering Guardian* (24 August 1900)

181 By Taylors of Loughborough (*Kettering Leader*, 18 April 1902). The bells were in a very poor state (*Kettering Guardian* 18 October 1901).

182 The Dedication Service was held on 25th July 1902 (*Geddington Monthly Magazine*, August 1902)

183 The *Kettering Guardian* (11 May 1906) contained a lengthy article describing the work. Also see editions for 7 October & 18 November 1904, and 6 January and 10 February 1905.

184 *Kettering Guardian* (19 May 1905)

185 *Kettering Guardian* (31 March 1905)

186 see A Symondson & S A Bucknall (op. cit.).

187 The *Kettering Leader* (17 January 1913)

188 (*Geddington Monthly Magazine*, May 1905)

disabled by injury and another 7 died of war-related causes over the next five years; bringing total deaths to more than a quarter of those who left for war. The Vicar, Benjamin Turton, had known most of them as boys[189], many in the choir. The following extract from a letter sent by an army Chaplain to the grieving mother of Bertram Chapman in 1915 captures something of the mood of the time:

> "I buried your boy in Forquiére Cemetery. It is a lovely little place near Bethune, with a very pretty Churchyard. There are about thirty of our boys buried there, all together…Your boy died very quietly, quite unconscious, with no pain….. I am very sorry for you in your trouble. The tragedy of all these dear boys giving up their lives for justice and England is very real. We don't understand what it all means. All we can do now is to hold on to our Faith…"[190]

It was with a very heavy heart, but also a sense of great community pride, that a large crowd assembled in the churchyard on 28th July 1921 for a service of dedication for the new war memorial, which was unveiled by Major Wetherall (see Fig. 52). The memorial was designed by Mr. Talbot Brown, erected by Messrs. Patrick of Geddington at a cost of £227[191], and paid for by public subscription. It is today a Grade II listed monument. The shadow of this calamity hung over the village long afterwards, and the annual service of Remembrance every November became a fixture solemnly honoured to this day.

When the Rev. Ben Turton left Geddington for Newton Abbot, Devon in 1924, he had overseen a period of great change, not only in the visual appearance of the church interior, but also in the life of the village, and he must have been scarred and wearied by the loss of so many of his flock to war. He exchanged livings with Eugene de Romestin who was a very different character. The son of Auguste de Romestin, a priest and well-known religious writer[192] of French aristocratic background, Eugene de Romestin was married to Frieda Johanna Auguste Isa Elsbeth Von Reutter, a German countess who was more used to the salons of Paris than Geddington's rural tranquillity, eventually leaving

for the lights of New York. Rev. Eugene continued to minister to his flock through some very hard times, so that the holidays he provided for Geddington's children and adults at his estate, *Aber Bodirt* in Anglesey, were no doubt greatly appreciated.

The church stayed largely unaltered between the two world wars, the main change being the commissioning – from Ninian Comper - of a new east window in the Lady Chapel. The two central lights were installed in 1933 (as can be seen in Fig. 44), but it was to be another 25 years before the second pair finally completed the original conception; by which time the window's artist had been knighted.

When Rev. de Romestin resigned in 1938, the new Vicar, Wilfred Maxwell Opie arrived, having himself served as a private soldier in the Great War and as a Mission Priest in Oxford before coming to Geddington. Before long, he was ministering to a flock again facing the depredations and deprivations of war and its aftermath, with little opportunity to effect change on the church fabric. Thankfully, the church building itself emerged from the two wars very largely the same as it had been 30 years earlier, although repairs were needed to the top section of the spire, which were completed in 1955.[193] Rev. Opie's death in 1950 marked the end of a half-century of dramatic change, while the death of King George VI in 1952 seemed to many to mark the end of a long ordeal borne with fortitude, and the coronation of Queen Elizabeth II in 1953 to herald the dawn of a new, more optimistic, age.

THE SECOND ELIZABETHAN AGE: 1953 - 2022

For the church building, the middle decades of the 20th Century saw relatively little change but Rev. Guy Brodie, who had been an RAF pilot during the War and was Vicar between 1950 and 1962, presaged change when he protested:

> "Newton Church is very small. It is in the middle of a field. It is often surrounded by mud…. The Vicar does not see why he should go to Newton Church for service if there is no one there."[194]

---

189 Sunday School prizes were awarded in March 1905 to Bertram Chapman, Harry Higgs, Arthur Patrick, Ernest Rawson, and Fred Stanton. (*Geddington Monthly Magazine*, March 1905). Within 13 years, all would be dead.

190 Letter from Rev. Wilfred H. Abbot, Chaplain, to Mrs. Sarah Chapman of Church Gate, Geddington reproduced in the *Geddington and Newton Monthly Magazine, Dec. 1915*.

191 Worth approx. £15,000 today

192 *The Sacred Writings of St. Ambrose* which was co-authored by father and son, together with HTF Duckworth, is still in print today

193 The *Northamptonshire Advertiser* 1 October 1954 & 15 April 1955 carried pictures. As was common at the time, a Spire Fund was set up, and a 'thermometer' (made by John Hooper) was displayed showing progress towards raising the £700 needed. [*Geddington and Newton Monthly Magazine* August & November 1955.]

194 *Geddington & Newton Magazine*, November 1960. Earlier that year, Rev. Brodie also criticised Prime Minister Harold MacMillan's slogan 'You've

And so it was; the Church of St. Faith in Newton was de-consecrated in 1972, following which two of its most beautiful medieval floor monuments – the Mulsho Brass and the Tresham Alabaster – were brought to the north aisle of Geddington church. The Queen's Silver Jubilee in 1977 was marked by the making of many 'kneelers' or cushions on which to kneel during prayer. These were further augmented by another set made to mark the Golden Jubilee in 2002.

Towards the end of the Century, however, the Rev. Richard Dorrington led a period of greater activity. In 1989, the present altar rail was installed; and the flooring of the Nave and South Aisle was renewed in 1990, during which several burials dating from the 10th to the 12th centuries were discovered under the South Aisle. A new ringing floor was installed in the tower in 1994.

The 700th anniversary of Queen Eleanor's death was marked by a pageant, orchestrated by Rev. Dorrington and featuring a range of events including a re-enactment and service in the church[195], a peal of bells commemorated with a plaque in the Tower, and a walk by the Volunteer Fire Brigade (many dressed as medieval pilgrims) re-tracing the route of Eleanor's cortege. A second, smaller, pageant was held in 1994 to mark the 700th anniversary of the building of the cross.

This momentum was continued into the early years of the new Century with a real flurry of activity led by Rev. Giles Godber, including major roof repairs, the creation of a new servery in the base of the tower; a new bell frame and the addition of a sixth bell; the re-location of the organ to its present position; the replacement of most of the remaining old pews with chairs; and the introduction of a modern WC in the space vacated by the organ.

The cost of new chairs was substantially defrayed by sponsorship in memory of deceased loved ones, their names marked by small plaques affixed to chairs. A full list of names commemorated is given in Appendix 4. These changes have substantially added not only comfort and convenience, but also improved the church's capacity to host a much wider range of events and activities of benefit to the community.

FRIENDS OF THE CHURCH

Crucial to helping the church make these improvements have been not only some very generous bequests (notably a very large gift by the Towndrows) but most especially the work of **The Friends of Geddington Church**, founded in 1997 with the aim of raising funds for the maintenance and improvement of the fabric of the church. It was established as a charity separate from the church (although the church does nominate a trustee to represent it on the Friends' Committee) so that non-churchgoers who nevertheless value the building itself can play a part in conserving and improving its wonderful heritage.

The Friends raise funds through various events, including an annual garage sale around the village, murder mystery plays, occasional lunches, annual Twelfth Night celebrations, and quizzes. They have raised well over £100,000 for the church since their foundation and in the past few years alone, their generosity has funded, either in whole or in part, a beautiful new mobile altar, a display case for the Book of Remembrance, curtains for the servery and ringing floor, repairs to the Lady Chapel roof, and a major contribution to the conservation of the medieval reredos and aumbrey carried out in 2023.

THE CHURCH TODAY

If those who attended church in 1914 could have travelled forward in time then (apart from the physical changes of the past 30 years) perhaps the biggest differences they would notice would be in the life of the church itself: the liturgy (no longer is the Book of Common Prayer in general use); the broadcasting of services online; and above all, the admission of women to the priesthood. Geddington's first woman incumbent in a history of more than 1,000 years – Rev. Gillian Gamble - was installed in 2019.

Yet for all the changes of recent decades, the church today is more recognisably the church of our great-grandparents' day than would have appeared the church of their day to their great-grandparents from the early 19th Century. Let us hope and pray that, in another Century our great grand-children will be able to speak well of our stewardship of this beautiful gem of a building.

---

never had it so good' and 'I'm all right Jack' attitudes when so many were landless and malnourished in the world – "we should all be ashamed of the tepid Christianity that allows [this to continue]'

195 A video of the 1990 Pageant is available at **https://www.youtube.com/watch?v=0aUIK7K0PNA**

Part IV: A Building built for Worship

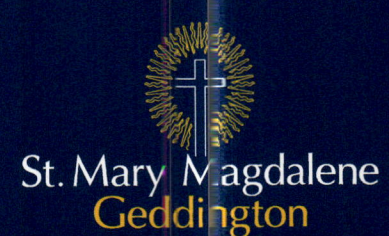

St. Mary Magdalene
Geddington

The ways in which Christians have worshipped – the words, music, and rituals, and their theological significance – have evolved down the centuries. These changes have in turn influenced the church building itself. A larger or smaller Chancel; the creation of side aisles and chapels; the positioning of font and altars; the images on walls and in window glass; the presence or absence of rood screens; the styles of wall and floor monuments and the languages and lettering employed in inscriptions – all these and more have been influenced by the character and content of Christian worship and belief. The following is very far from a comprehensive account of Christian worship, but attempts to outline the main ideas and movements that have helped to shape Geddington Church.

THE MASS IN SAXON TIMES

Worship in the early English church was almost entirely shaped by monastic practice and followed the form used in most of continental Europe: the Roman Mass. This was said and sung in Latin by the priest officiating from within the Chancel and the body of worshippers standing in the Nave. Although only the nobility and wealthier citizens would have been able to speak Latin, the rest of the congregation would have been expected to learn the main prayers by heart – the *Paternoster* (Lord's Prayer); the *Ave Maria* (Hail Mary); and *Gloria in Excelsis Deo* (Glory to God in the highest, or 'The Gloria').

This was well before printing made books more widely-available, so the Bible was always hand-written in Latin on parchment, and would only have been available to the clergy and very wealthy people. Ordinary people would have absorbed Christian teaching mainly from their priest and their parents.

Anglo-Saxon, or Old English, was sometimes used in private prayers at home or in the fields, however, and the following Old English and Latin forms of the Lord's Prayer – which would have been said by virtually everyone at least once, and often several times, each day in one or other language - give a tiny glimpse into the daily rituals of life in Geddington in the century before the Norman Conquest:

Fæder ure þu þe eart on heofonum si þin nama gehalgod. Tobecume þin rice. Gewurþe ðin willa on eorðan swa swa on heofonum. Urne gedæghwamlican hlaf syle us to-dæg. And forgyf us ure gyltas, swa swa we forgyfað urum gyltendum. And ne gelæd þu us on costnunge, ac alys us of yfele. Soþlice.

Pater noster, qui es in caelis, sanctificetur nomen tuum. Adveniat regnum tuum. Fiat voluntas tua, sicut in caelo et in terra. Panem nostrum quotidianum da nobis hodie, et dimitte nobis debita nostra sicut et nos dimittimus debitoribus nostris. Et ne nos inducas in tentationem, sed libera nos a malo. Amen.

In the later Saxon period, reforms inspired by St. Benedict led, in 973, to the adoption by the English church of the *Regularis Concordia* [the Rule of Peace] - a document that served as a rule for how monastic life should be conducted. Compiled by Æthelwold, Bishop of Winchester, and aided by continental monks, this included the rule of the divine service (or *quem quaeritis* – 'whom you seek') which served also as the liturgy for services held in parish church settings. It stressed the importance of theatrical ritual to aid those who could not read or understand Latin in the understanding of the liturgy. [196]

196 See *The Liturgy of the Late Anglo-Saxon Church*, ed. H Gittos and MB Beddingfield [Henry Bradshaw Subsidia Series. London 2005]"

As an example, the rule includes the theatrical recital to be performed the night before Easter Day. Concerning the scene where Mary Magdalene, Mary the mother of James, and Salome visit Jesus' tomb, it requires that:

"An alternating song between the three women approaching the grave, and the angel watching on it, shall be recited; the friar who sings the words of the angel is to take his seat, clad in an alb and with a palm-twig in his hand, in a place representing the tomb; three other friars, wearing hooded capes and with censers in their hands, are to approach the tomb at a slow pace, as if in quest of something".

The angel then converses with the women:

"Quem quaeritis in sepulchro, o Christicolae?"…" Jesum Nazarenum cruifixum, o caelicolae"…."Non est hic, surrexit, sicut praedixerat. Ite, nuntiate, quia surrexit de sepulchro".

This translates as :

Angel: *'Whom are you looking for in the tomb, O Christians?'*

Women: *'Crucified Jesus of Nazareth, O heavenly ones'.*

Angel: *'He is not here, he has risen, as he had predicted. Go, tell them that he has risen from the grave'.*

From the perspective of today, with its proliferation of sophisticated methods of communication, it is difficult to comprehend the impact of a well-conducted performance of dramatic liturgy such as this on a largely illiterate audience for whom church attendance was one of the very few communal activities open to all.

THE MEDIEVAL MASS

In the 12th and 13th centuries, worship was very similar across Europe, although each Diocese developed its own liturgies for Cathedral worship (known as '**the Use of**…') that were then adopted by priests officiating in parish churches. In time, the **Use of Sarum** (Winchester Diocese) came to dominate in the south of England and would probably have been the form used in Geddington throughout most of the medieval period until the Reformation. The Cathedral Mass was performed by three clergy – the Priest, assisted by a Deacon and a sub-Deacon – with servers to carry candles, incense and holy water and the support of a choir

(often also composed of clergy). Parish priests were expected to follow this liturgy very closely.

Figure 73: King Edgar with St. Æthelwold and St. Dunstan. *11th Century manuscript of the Regularis Concordia [British Library].*

Most parish churches didn't have this number of priests and would have had to adapt accordingly, but at Geddington, royal patronage, the size of the Chancel and the provision of 3 Sedilia (seats) in the Sanctuary all suggest that – particularly by the mid-13th Century – there would have been enough clergy to at least undertake the principal roles – something that the monks of Pipewell would no doubt have striven to maintain after 1357. The principal Mass on Sundays[197] was intoned or sung in plainsong, except for certain parts (mainly the prayer of consecration) which were said in a low voice.

The Mass was preceded by a rite called the 'blessing of salt and water'. The priest was presented with water in a small pot which he exorcised with prayers, throwing the salt into the water with the sign of the cross, and blessing the mixture. He then sprinkled the altar, his assistants and any privileged laity who had been allowed into the Chancel. He then processed clockwise around the church with his assistants sprinkling any side altars and the lay congregation before returning to the Chancel. Reciting the hymn **Veni Creator Spiritus** [Come, Creator Spirit], the prayer **Deus cui omne cor patet** [O God to whom all hearts are open], and the **Kyries** [Lord have mercy], he would then don a chasuble (a vestment – often elaborately decorated - that went over his alb or robe).

He then went to the altar on which would be two lighted candles signifying Christ as the light of the world. Facing eastwards towards the altar, he would begin with the 'office' or introit, a short Biblical text which would be repeated by the choir if there was one. He would then offer the **Confiteor** (prayer of confession) to his assistants, who reciprocated; then absolve them and exchange a kiss of peace. Following further prayers, he kissed the altar, made the sign of the cross and blessed a thurible of burning incense that had

---

197   This account of the medieval Mass is taken from *Going to Church in Medieval England*, by Nicholas Orme (Yale University Press, 2021)

been brought to him and used it to cense the altar, following which an assistant would cense him. The priests and/or the choir would then sing the early Christian hymn *Gloria in excelsis* ['Glory to God in the highest'], after which the priest turned to face the people and intoned the Collect (the special prayer for the day).

Next an assistant, standing at the south end of the altar, prepared the vessels and elements for the eucharist whilst intoning an epistle. The priest sang the '*gradual*' – a short text usually from the psalms – together (except in Lent and times of penitence) with the *alleluia*, followed by the gospel reading. The priest with his assistant holding the holy text aloft, would process to a position at the western end of the Chancel or the east of the nave, where the priest would intone the reading. The congregation stood during this and bowed when Jesus was named. During Advent, the Christmas and Easter seasons and certain major festivals, this gospel sequence would be preceded by a rhythmical hymn.

After the gospel, the priest and/or choir sang the Nicene Creed, bowing 3 times at the words affirming that Christ was born incarnate by the Holy Spirit of the Virgin Mary, followed by the offertory (another short, sung text). At this point – switching to the use of English for the benefit of the congregation - announcements might be made or a sermon preached, during which time donations might be collected. Donations were a matter of choice, but were expected at Candlemas, weddings, funerals, and certain other occasions. Some churches also took periodic collections for the poor.

Then, the priest prepared for the central part of the Mass: the Eucharist. First he placed the paten (a small plate) on which lay the 'host' (a circular wafer of unleavened bread), and a small chalice of wine mixed with water. An assistant then passed him the thurible with which he censed the altar, the paten, and chalice, following which he washed his hands and passed the thurible to his assistants to cense each other and the congregation. Lowering his voice, he would then say the 'secret' (a short prayer to God) and another to the Virgin. The choir and/or the priest then sang *Sursum Corda* ['Lift up your hearts'], followed by the 'preface'

Figure 74: A Sanctus Bell in a bell-cote

(a prayer of praise that varied according to the occasion) and the '*Sanctus*' ['Holy, holy, holy, Lord God of hosts'], accompanied by the ringing of the *sanctus* bell – a bell usually hung in a bell-cote on the church roof (Fig 74).

The prayer of consecration – the holiest part of the Mass - would then begin with the priest facing east towards the altar. It was usually said quietly or even silently. It began with prayers for the living: the Pope, the Bishop, the King, the priest himself, those present and any others thought appropriate. Paying reverence to the Virgin Mary, the apostles, and other early saints, the prayer recalled how Christ broke bread at the Last Supper with the words *Hoc est corpus meum* ['this is my body']. Some priests broke the bread at this point, but the Sarum Missal condemned this as foolish. Venerating the host, the priest then took it from the paten and held it aloft accompanied by the ringing both of the sanctus bell and of smaller hand-held bells[198] – known as the 'first sacring'. Those hearing the sanctus bell at home or in the fields were expected to genuflect. The priest continued by repeating Christ's words over the wine ('Drink this all of you') and raised the chalice aloft.

He then bowed, kissed the altar, and prayed for the dead, following which he elevated the host and chalice together above his head – known as the 'second sacring'[199]. The priest then took the host and with it made the sign of the cross 5 times over the chalice, followed by the singing of the Paternoster, to which the choir (and perhaps the congregation) responded with the last line: *sed libera nos a malo* ['but deliver us from evil']. He would then break the host into 3 pieces, replicating Christ's actions at the Last Supper – first into half and then the left half into two quarters.

After another prayer, the choir and/or the priest sang: *Agnus Dei, qui tolis peccata mundi miserere nobis* (x2). *Agnus Dei, qui tolis peccata mundi, dona nobis pacem.* ['Lamb of God you take away the sins of the world, have mercy on us (x2). Lamb of God you take away the sins of the world, grant us peace'.] He placed one of the parts of the host into the chalice of wine as a sign of the mingling of Christ's body and blood, and kissed the chalice.

Then, taking the pax or 'pax-brede' (a table of ivory, wood

---

198 Usually in the form of 3 or 4 small brass bells held in a single frame. Geddington still possesses such hand bells that date from the mid-Victorian period. They have been used sometimes in recent decades, depending on the liturgical leanings of the priest at the time.

199 Prior to about 1200, there had normally been only one elevation of the host and wine, but a 'first sacring' was added around that time -a practice that grew out of the doctrine of the Real Presence (praying Christ's words transformed the bread and wine into his physical body and blood).

or metal marked with a symbol of Christ) he kissed it and said *pax tibi* ['Peace to you'] to his principal assistant, who took the pax, kissed it and then either he or another assistant priest took it first to those in the Chancel, and then also to everyone in the Nave to be kissed by each person. Meanwhile, after more prayers, the priest bowed or genuflected before the host and wine, and consumed them himself. Normally nobody else shared this communion, even other priests, except on Easter morning, when everyone was required to receive. This explains why pre-Reformation chalices are small compared with later ones.

Next came the ablutions, when an assistant poured un-consecrated wine over the priest's fingers into the chalice, followed by water to wash the fingers, paten, and chalice – a mixture that the priest then consumed so as to clean the vessels before washing and drying his hands. He then offered a post-communion prayer appropriate to the day, returned the paten and chalice to the altar and intoned *Dominus vobiscum* ['The Lord be with you'] to which his assistant replied *et cum spiritu tuo* ['and with your spirit']. Whilst the priest and his assistants then faced the altar, a Deacon would sing in plainsong the words *Benedicamus Domino* ['Let us bless the Lord'], to which the response was *Deo gracias* ['Thanks be to God']. The clergy then turned to face the congregation, and a Deacon sang; *Ite, missa est* which was taken to mean 'Go! The Mass is ended', although this dismissal was not quite the end, because before everyone left, there would be a further reading from John's Gospel.

Although the Latin, the distance between priest and congregation, and the inaudibility of many of the words make this Mass seem very inaccessible today, any Roman Catholic or any 'high' Anglican would instantly recognise all the essential elements. However, by the late 14th Century, this inaccessibility of the Mass, among several other things, was stoking demands for reform across Europe.

In England, the theologian John Wycliffe and associates translated the Bible into English (1384) and he was a leading proponent of reforms that became known as 'Lollardy'. Some 100 years later, William Tyndale made an English Bible translation[200] that formed the bedrock of what, another century on, became the 'King James Bible'. We don't know how these tensions played out in Geddington but, although

it is reasonable to believe that the clergy and educated gentry would have known about, and perhaps taken a close interest in, the theological debates that swirled around Europe in the 15th and early 16th centuries, the limited evidence available suggests the probability of a mostly conservative outlook. The leading family (the Treshams) were very piously Catholic, the bequests made to the church in the years just before the break with Rome, and the delay in removing the Rood Screen (until 1558), all suggest there was no widespread hunger for change locally. In the end though, it was the monarchy that played the decisive role in changing the way people worshipped in England.

POST-REFORMATION WORSHIP

By the time that the 1559 version of the *Book of Common Prayer* (BCP) was adopted, the conduct of services in Geddington Church would have looked and sounded very different from the way it had been 25 years earlier. The BCP required that:

> "*The Table at the Communion time having a fair white linen cloth upon it, shall stand in the body of the Church, or in the Chancel….*"[201].

This meant that the High Altar would either have fallen into disuse or been removed.

The Rood Screen with its Cross and figures of Saints Mary and John were removed in 1558; medieval wall paintings were supposed to be whitewashed over, stained-glass and figures removed – all stressing a new simplicity and severity. There are, however, hints that Geddington Church may not always have been rigorous in the application of these strictures. For example, it was upbraided in 1619 because "*the Chancell wall wants whyteninge*"; an Altar Rail was installed in 1635, no doubt along with the return of the High Altar to its pre-Reformation position[202]; and until 1855-57 the east Chancel wall still bore the Latin "*Ave Maria…*" and "*Ecce Ancilla Domini…*"- both invoking Mary the mother of Jesus. Whether these latter inscriptions were medieval survivals is unknown, but it seems quite possible that Catholic ideas were not completely eliminated from this church's practice for much of the post-Reformation period; or if they were, it was not for long.

One very noticeable change, however, would have been

---

200 The translation cost him his life – convicted of heresy and burnt at the stake in the Duchy of Brabandt in 1536, though he was strangled first as an act of mercy.

201 *The Book of Common Prayer*: Order for the Administration of the Lord's Supper, or Holy Communion.

202 see letter from Edmond Vialls (op. cit.) For the wider context, see *The Restoration of Altars in the 1630s* by Kenneth Fincham (op. cit.)

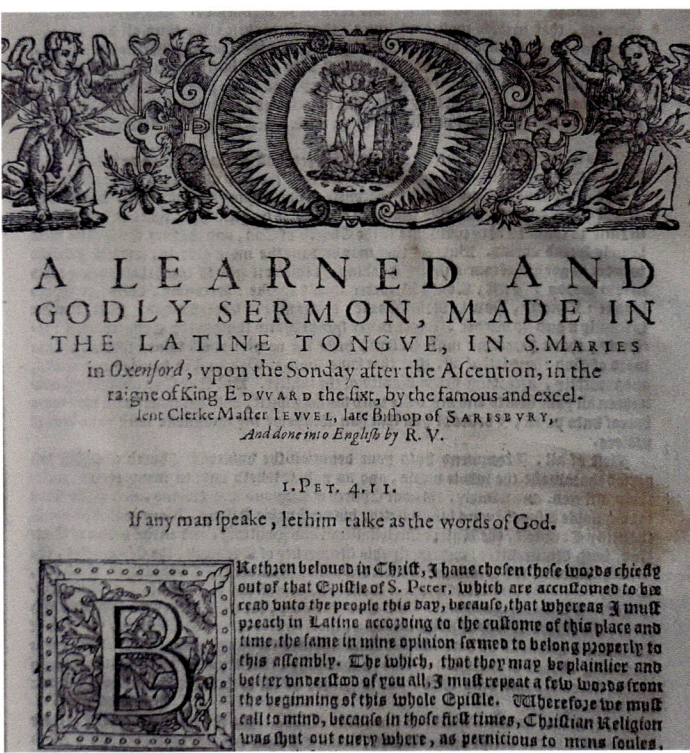

Figure 75: Extract from a book of sermons (c1550) by Bishop John Jewel

the use of English throughout, with the priest (now mostly called the Minister) addressing the congregation both directly and audibly. And, from 1548, priests in the Church of England were also permitted to marry.

Theologically, it was in the celebration of the Eucharist that the most significant change was to be found:

"When the Priest, standing before the Table, hath so ordered the Bread and Wine, that he may with the more readiness and decency break the Bread before the people, and take the cup into his hands, he shall say the Prayer of Consecration…." and later -

"Then shall the Minister first receive the communion in both kinds himself and then proceed to deliver the same to the Bishops, Priests and Deacons (if any be present) in like manner and after that to the people also in order, into their hands, all meekly kneeling…and the Minister that delivereth the Cup to any one shall say…".

Gone was the doctrine of the Real Presence of Christ – instead the receiving of bread and wine was symbolic:

"in remembrance that Christ's Blood was shed for thee…"[203]

Again, we don't know how these changes were received in Geddington, but it seems likely that, alongside those who welcomed the new ways, there would have been at least as many, if not more, who were deeply unhappy. That Archbishop Bancroft felt it necessary in 1509 to order a folio of the works of the 16th Century anti-Catholic protagonist Bishop John Jewel (Fig. 75) to be placed in every church, chained to the lectern[204] and read out regularly suggests a lingering reluctance in many congregations to embrace the reforms wholeheartedly.

Yet, for all this change in the style, language, and directness of worship, ***almost*** all the key theologically important elements of the Mass were there – it was what the reformers deemed unfaithful to the practices of the early Christian church that had been stripped away from the liturgy and from the fabric of the church building.

Later, however, we do get a glimpse of how more radical dissent from even the 'reformed religion' manifested itself in Geddington church, because in 1662 the Minister, Thomas Elborowe was ejected from his living for refusing to 'conform' to the revised version of the ***Book of Common Prayer*** that, alongside other measures[205] to repress puritan influence, had been adopted in 1662 following the Restoration of the monarchy.

Figure 76: Vincent Alsop

Although Thomas Elborowe later conformed, there were many who didn't, one such being Vincent Alsop, who lost his living at Wilby in the 'Great Ejection' of 1662 and lived in Geddington for some time, applying for a licence to preach in his own house here in 1672 and also preaching at Wellingborough, being imprisoned for six months for praying with a sick person. He later achieved national prominence as a preacher and writer, suffering significantly in the process.

This strict enforcement of the ***Act of Conformity*** established 'non-conformism' not only as a legally disabling fact but as an enduring identity that persists even to this day.

---

203 ***The Book of Common Prayer***: Order for the Administration of the Lord's Supper, or Holy Communion.

204 A copy of this large book is held by Geddington Church, still with its chain attached – though no longer chained to a lectern.

205 Several Acts, collectively known as the 'Clarendon Code', prevented puritans from holding public office and severely restricted the activities of dissenting ministers.

METHODISM

'Methodism' began as an 18th Century Christian revival movement within the Church of England, based very largely on the teachings of John Wesley (1703-91), with George Whitfield and John's brother Charles also being very prominent within the movement. They were called 'Methodists' for "*the methodical way in which they carried out their Christian faith*" [206].

Although this led to the creation of a separate church after John Wesley's death, it nevertheless left a lasting legacy within the Anglican Church. For a time, there was a Wesleyan Chapel in Geddington near **Croft House** in Queen Street, but it fell into disrepair and was sold before being demolished in the mid-19th Century. In 1875 it was replaced by the Union Chapel which still stands in Queen Street today.

In doctrine, the Methodists have influenced the evolution of the 'evangelical' wing of Anglican theology, with an emphasis on simplicity rather than ritual. The vigorous singing of hymns (many composed by the Wesleys) became a notable part of Anglican worship too, and in recent years there have been moves to try to re-unite the Methodist and Anglican churches. Although many of the features of methodist worship have been very evident in worship at Geddington at various times, and especially in the early 21st Century, Methodism does not appear to have had any significant impact on the building's architecture, except perhaps in the introduction of a mobile altar in the Nave for the celebration of Holy Communion.

THE SOCIETY OF FRIENDS ('QUAKERS')

In the mid-17th Century a young George Fox was dissatisfied with the teachings of both the Church of England and nonconformist groups of the time. He claimed that one could have a direct relationship with Christ without the need of a clergyman's authority or intercession. Travelling around England and overseas he preached and taught with the aim of gaining converts to his view, and claimed to be restoring a 'pure' Christian church. 'Quaker' was originally a term of ridicule – Fox having bade magistrates hearing a charge of blasphemy brought against him to '*tremble at the word of the Lord*' – but it later became accepted.

In teaching, Quakers generally believe in each person's capacity to experience a light within that answers God's call; many adopt the idea of the 'priesthood of all believers'; and most avoid set creeds, liturgy, and authority structures. The movement has influenced the modern Anglican church through the practice of Christian meditation and the development of 'house groups' where people meet in private houses to pray and discuss matters of faith and morality.

In Geddington, the Friends' Meeting House was in Grafton Road, almost opposite **The Priory**, and still stands today as 'Quaker Cottage', a private house. According to Markham, burials were still taking place in the back garden as late as the 1850s.

EVANGELICALISM

Evangelicalism [from Greek εὐαγγέλιον, meaning 'gospel' or 'good news'] is a theological approach practiced across a range of Protestant denominations. It stresses the importance of being "born again" through an experience of personal conversion; the authority of the Bible as God's revelation to humanity; and spreading the Christian message. As early as 1517 Martin Luther[207] had emphasised that scripture and gospel preaching should determine Church practices, but modern Evangelicalism grew out of various movements, notably Pietism (a movement within the Lutheran Churches), Puritanism, Quakerism and Methodism among others.

Originally largely confined to English-speaking churches, the Evangelical movement has gained ground well beyond the Anglosphere. A substantial proportion of Anglicans today would describe themselves as 'evangelical' and, though never an avowedly 'evangelical' church, Geddington's congregation has usually included a proportion of folk for whom evangelical beliefs, worship styles and missionary interest hold a strong appeal. In terms of shaping the building we see today, however, evangelical ideas have had no substantial impact.

THE OXFORD MOVEMENT

As the name implies, the *Oxford Movement* was centred in the University of Oxford. It sought a renewal of 'catholic' thought and practice which had been largely suppressed, both within the Church of England and in wider society, since the Reformation. Catholic Emancipation in 1829 meant that public bodies and officials no longer had to be

---

206 *Probationer's Handbook*. Stephen O. Garrison, (1908). [Eaton and Mains] referenced in Wikipedia article on Methodism.
207 Martin Luther: *Ninety-Five Theses*.

observant Anglicans, and nearly all restrictions that previously prevented Catholics from participating fully in civic life were removed. For a time it seemed that the Church of England might lose its position as the 'established' church and, with it, the many endowments that flowed from that status. This led to many emphasising that the church's authority came not from its dependence on the State, but from its teachings, and especially from the 'apostolic succession' that meant its bishops could trace their offices and authority back in an unbroken line to Christ's Apostles.

The Movement's protagonists therefore argued that the Anglican church, though no longer part of the Roman church, was nevertheless 'catholic' in its history and identity. Leading members of the movement included John Henry Newman, a clergyman who eventually converted to Roman Catholicism and became a cardinal; Richard Hurrell Froude, a clergyman; John Keble, a clergyman and poet after whom Keble College, Oxford is named; and Edward Pusey, a clergyman and professor at Oxford, after whom Pusey House, Oxford is named. The ideas of the Movement were published in 90 *Tracts for the Times* between 1833 and 1841 with Newman as editor. Those who supported the *Tracts* were known as 'Tractarians' who asserted the doctrinal authority of the catholic church to be absolute, and by "catholic" they understood that which was faithful to the teaching of the early and undivided church. They believed the Church of England to be such a catholic church.

The *Oxford Movement* had a profound effect on Geddington Church as a building – principally through the changes made in the mid-19th Century, notably by opening up the Chancel and restoring the high altar and reredos. Apart from the re-introduction of a screen in the Chancel arch in 1908, the church we see today is essentially the building bequeathed to us by the 19th Century Tractarian priests. And, although not continuously practiced, the ringing of bells[208] and the use of incense during the eucharist have periodically been adopted from time to time over the past 170 years, depending on the views of incumbent priests and the inclinations of the congregation. The number of embroidered 'kneeler' cushions made for the Silver and Golden Jubilees of the late Queen Elizabeth II in 1977 and 2002 bears witness to the Anglo-Catholic practice of kneeling to pray during the Eucharistic prayers being common within living memory, as parishioners of a certain age can attest.

---

208 A practice that arose when the Mass was in Latin, said very softly and almost hidden from view. The bells (usually a linked set of 4 small hand bells) were rung to let people know at the point of consecration. Though no longer needed for this reason, it remains in both Roman Catholic and Anglo-Catholic traditions as a reminder of the importance of what is happening.

Note: the information in this Appendix has been taken from Christopher Markham's 1899 book, from documents held in the Buccleuch Archive, from currently-living persons, and from Longden's *Northamptonshire & Rutland Clergy*.

1222	**Nicholas de Breaute**, Clerk, was presented by the King to the church of Gedinton
unknown	Dom. **Phil. de Subaudia**; on his resignation
1245	**Guydo de Palmere**, Sub-Deacon, was presented by the King
1282	**Jacobus de Aquablanca**, Chaplain of the Pope, and Rector of this parish; on his resignation
16th October 1282	Mag. **Hugo de Camera**, Chaplain, was presented by the King; on his death
25th August 1283	**Hymbertus de Vienna**, Chaplain, was presented by the King. In August 1289, the Bishop granted him a year's leave of absence. He died before the year elapsed
17th March 1290	**Galfridus de Gropes**, Clerk, was presented by the King. On the 30th January 1292 the churchyard was re-consecrated because blood had been shed therein. On the resignation of this Vicar
1333	In 1333 King Edward III granted the advowson of Geddington to his mother Queen Isobel (or Isabella) of France for her lifetime.
28th April 1334	**Simon de Greppo**, S. Petro Diac., was presented by the Queen Isabella. On 30th September 1337 he exchanged with
30th September 1337	**Robertus de Kildesby**, Clerk, of Essenden exchanged to Geddington by permission of Queen Isabella. On his death
3rd December 1350	**William de Walcote** (probably incumbent of Cotterstock 1341-49) was presented by Queen Isabella. On his death
31st January 1357	The Crown gave the living to the Abbot and Convent of Pipewell
1st February 1357	**William Freman**, Priest, of Little Newton, was presented by the Abbot and Convent of Pipewell. He exchanged with William Mareschall, and was probably afterwards the incumbent of Little Bowden.
8th March 1363	**William Mareschall**, Rector of Colwick, co. Nottingham, exchanged to Geddington, and later exchanged with John Curteys
15th May 1371	**John Curteys**, Vicar of Bodekesham exchanged to Geddington by permission of the Abbot and Convent of Pipewell
1371	**Henry Clipsham**, Priest, presented by the Abbot and Convent of Pipewell. In February 1373 he exchanged with Thomas Batteley, incumbent of Blatherwyck by permission of the Abbot and Convent of Pipewell
February 1373	**Thomas Batte of Batteley**, Priest, of Blatherwyck exchanged to Geddington. He then exchanged with Roger Champeneys, Rector of Little Oakley, by permission of the Abbot and Convent of Pipewell
10th October 1374	**Roger Champeneys**, Rector of Little Oakley, exchanged with Thomas Batte by permission of the Abbot and Convent of Pipewell
unknown	**William Taylor**; on his death
9th May 1425	**John Anneys**, Priest, was presented by the Abbot and Convent of Pipewell.
unknown	**John Jay**. On his resignation
15th June 1429	**John Palmer** was presented by the Abbot and Convent of Pipewell.
unknown	**John Coventree**. On his resignation
2nd August 1437	**Nicholas Welles**, Priest. On his resignation
7th October 1439	**William Berkeley**, Priest, formerly incumbent of Little Barton. On his resignation
30th April 1447	**Thomas Balle**, Chantry Priest of the Blessed Mary of Sapcote. On his death
22nd July 1467	Dom. **Henry Draper**, Priest. On his resignation
18th December 1468	**Richard Draper**, Priest. On his death
2nd March 1487	**Richard Johnson**, Priest. On his death
27th August 1491	**William Preston**, Monk of Pipewell
28th August 1494	**John Langton**, Abb. Mon. de Grat. juxt Tur. Lond. [Abbot of St. Mary Graces Abbey, Tower Hill[209]] On his resignation
8th April 1497	**Henricus Foster**, Priest. On his death
12th February 1510	**Henricus Bisshopp**, Clerk.
1538	The Monastery of Pipewell was suppressed and the advowson granted to Sir George Tresham of Newton.
18th November 1545	**Richardus Freman**, Clerk was presented by George Tresham of Newton, Knight, and Elizabeth, his wife. On his death
20th March 1561	**Anthonius Chesseldene**, Clerk, was presented by the Bishop by reason of lapse
1600	**Henricus Hull**
1601	**Thomas Jones**
1607	**Richardus More**
1613	**William Allen**
23rd September 1626	**Thomas Chaloner** presented by Sir Thomas Tresham, Knight
14th June 1637	**Nathaniel Cole**, presented by William Tresham, esq.
1650	**John Dodd** supplied the cure. The vicarage had a value of £13-6s-8d. An augmentation to it of £40 had been granted out of the impropriated tithe of Weldon, the property of Lord Brundell, which it was recommended be continued. Mr. W. Tresham was the Impropriator and Patron

---

209 also known as Eastminster, like Pipewell, a Cistercian House. Dugdale, *Monasticon Anglicanum* (1718) Vol. 5, p717 says that: 'JOHN LANGTON Abbot of Graces was presented by the Abbot and Convent of Pipewell to the vicarage of Geddingham August 28, 1494.'

1662   **Thomas Elborowe** was ejected from his living, but afterwards conformed. He is recorded as 'Robert Elborough' in Henry Isham Longden's biographical dictionary[210]. He died in 1675.

1675   **Rev. Perkins** was probably Thomas Perkins, vicar of Naseby between 1633 and 1640, a nonconformist, who was ejected from Burley on the Hill, Rutland in 1647. He died about 1678.

1679   **John Barton**, Clerk, was at Leicester School, and on becoming vicar at Geddington oversaw repairs to the church in 1680. He was also rector of Glendon between 1687 and 1719. The Bartons were a Brigstock family of many generations, related to the Dukes of Montagu. His daughter Martha married John Balgay the land steward at Boughton in 1711. Rev. John Barton continued as Vicar of Geddington and Newton for 40 years and was buried at Geddington on 6th March 1719.

1719   **Isaac Bassett** was from Daventry and vicar of Cold Ashby between 1704 and 1706. He was Vicar at Geddington for about two years and was buried at Newton on 14th October 1721.

1721   **Philip Sone** was the son of John Sone, a pauper of Empshott on the Hampshire Downs, and became the Duke of Montagu's steward for his Beaulieu estate, but he was in poor health and not up to the job. Having taken Holy Orders, in 1699 he became rector of Morestead, Hants., and letters from Hampshire survive in the Buccleuch archives. The Duke sent him to Bath for his health before settling him in Northamptonshire. He was Vicar of Geddington and Newton for about eighteen months and then translated to the living of Barnwell St. Andrew in March 1722 where he died on Tuesday 30th August 1637. He was buried on Friday 2nd September, aged 67. His son (also named Philip) was curate of Barnwell All Saints 1730-1742, rector of Warkton 1742-1756, rector of Scaldwell 1742-1758, and chaplain to the Prince of Wales and to the Duke of Montagu.

23rd April 1723   **Francis Groleau** came from a family of London Huguenot printers. He spent much of his time at the Bristol hot wells drinking the mineral waters for his health. He was instituted as vicar of Geddington and Newton on the presentation of John, Duke of Montagu and "not having an opportunity of residing at his Parishes at present does employ as curate his very humble servant W:Scriven." During the incumbency of Mr. Groleau the living was augmented by the donation of £200 from Queen Anne's Bounty. This money was laid out in the purchase of land and by deed dated the 12th May 1724, certain lands known as "Collier's ffreehold" situate in the fields of Raunds, and containing by estimation 40 acres, were conveyed to the Rev. Francis Groleau and his successors, Vicars of Geddington. He was buried at Newton 17th December 1726.

5th January 1726   **William Scriven** "who on acct. of his excellent merit succeeded yᵉ sᵈ Mr. Groleau" and became Vicar. He came from Woodford Halse near Daventry and had been proposed for Geddington instead of the Rev. Groleau. In 1735 he was presented to the Rectory of Church Lawford, co. Warwick - a living on the Montagu Warwickshire estate. He died in 1736.

7th July 1735   **Michael Broughton** MA was the son of an apothecary and was presented to the living of Geddington and Newton by John, Duke of Montagu. The 'very agreeable' Mr. Broughton was a member of the 2nd Duke of Montagu's circle of 'house party' friends, participating in their experiments, debates, and entertainments. He was 'electrified by the new method of the wheel.' Several of his colourful letters to the Duke of Richmond have been published and more survive in the Buccleuch archives. He was presented to Barnwell All Saints in October 1737 and in 1742 was further presented to Barnwell St. Andrew on the resignation of Philip Sone, Jnr. He died in 1756 and was buried at Barnwell on 8th October that year.

6th May 1742   **William Sprigg** was the brother of a successful Kettering plumber and glazier who worked at Boughton. He studied at Clare College, Cambridge and was also rector of another Montagu living at Luddington. His amusing letter (1753) about the Callington bread charity survives in the Buccleuch archives. He died from 'floating gout' on 28th September 1754.

8th January 1755   **Samuel Quincy** was presented to the Donative of Newton and inducted into the vicarage of Geddington on 1st February 1755 on the presentation of Sir Edward Montagu, having had the misfortune to be robbed on his way to Geddington. He died on 27th August 1777 and was buried at Geddington two days later.

29th November 1777   **Joseph Knight** served his curacy at Kettering, was presented to Newton, and instituted to Geddington on the 15th December being presented by George, Duke of Montague. He was Chaplain to the Duke and Dowager Duchess of Buccleuch and Queensbury. He was instituted Rector of Kettering on the 17th of July 1783 and retained the three livings until his death. He died at Kettering in July 1814 aged 67.

1st July 1814   **James Hogg** was inducted to the vicarage of Geddington and the Donative of Newton, having been Curate of Geddington since February 1798 and rector of Glendon between 1808 and 1814. He was Headmaster of Kettering Grammar School and married Mary Roughton, who was from a family of Kettering doctors. James Hogg died on 25th November 1844.

31st January 1845   **William Montagu Higginson Church** was presented to Geddington and Newton by Walter, Duke of Buccleuch. In 1861 he was presented to the living of Hunstanton co. Norfolk, and he was Vicar of Hickleton in co. Yorkshire between 1877 and 1880. He died in Highgate, London on 8th April 1902, aged 88.

19th April 1861   **Thomas Charles Brand Cornwell** was presented to the Vicarage of Geddington by Walter, Duke of Buccleuch, having been ordained priest in 1852 and serving as Curate at Geddington. He resigned from the living of Geddington in 1885 and became Rector of Scaldwell Co. Northampton. He died at Cambridge on 21st July 1893.

1886   **Nigel Fowler Nash** was presented as Vicar by William, Duke of Buccleuch having been ordained a priest in 1867. He resigned in 1896 and moved to Newbury co. Berkshire

---

210 *Northamptonshire & Rutland Clergy from 1500*, by Rev. Henry Isham Longden pub. Archer & Goodman, 1942

APPENDIX 1: INCUMBENTS OF THE PARISH OF GEDDINGTON

17th November 1896 — **Stanley Daws Dewey** was presented by William, Duke of Buccleuch to the living, having been ordained priest in 1892. In 1901 he accepted the living of Moreton Hampstead in Devon. He later became Sir Stanley Dewey in 1926 on the death of his father, who had been President of the Prudential Assurance Co., and served as Prebendary of Exeter Cathedral from 1935 to 1943. He died in 1968.

1901 — **Benjamin Turton** was presented by William, Duke of Buccleuch in Geddington, having been previously Vicar of Dunton cum Doughton co. Norfolk. Born in Westmoreland in 1862, he married his wife Louise in 1892. In 1924 he exchanged livings with Eugene de Romestin, He died in Newton Abbot, co. Devon in 1941.

1924 — **Eugene de Romestin** was presented by John, Duke of Buccleuch in Geddington having exchanged with Benjamin Turton. He was born on 12th May 1863 in Dresden, Germany, and was educated at Warrington Grammar School and New College, Oxford. His father, Augustus, was a Priest and author. Of French nationality, he was independently wealthy. He married Frieda Johanna Auguste Isa Elsbeth Von Reutter in Germany in 1921. He had an estate at Aber Bodirt in Anglesey where he provided holidays to children and adults from Geddington. He retired in 1938 to Burton Latimer and died in Northampton on 16th January 1942.

1938 — **Wilfred Maxwell Opie** was presented by Walter, Duke of Buccleuch in Geddington. Born in Plymouth on 14th July 1877. He married Marie Eugenie who divorced him in 1918. He served in the Great War and was wounded. His army record said 'he looked old for his age'. He spent time in Australia and South Africa before returning to England in 1930 and becoming a mission priest in Oxford. He rented out rooms in the Vicarage (former school premises). He died in Geddington in 1950 and is buried in the churchyard, just east of the Lady Chapel.

1950 — **Guy Trevor Brodie** was presented by Walter, Duke of Buccleuch in Geddington. He was born in London on 25th November 1893 and served as an RAF pilot in World War II, acquiring a cache of headed notepaper from the wrecked Reichskanzlei in Berlin along the way![211] His last service in Geddington was on 14 October 1962. He died at the St. Barnabas Care Home in Lingfield, Surrey on 18th February 1964.

1963 — **Thomas Woolfenden** was presented in Geddington by Walter, Duke of Buccleuch. He was born 26 August 1911. During his time at Geddington, he wrote a short guide to the church in pamphlet form, which is still available today. He died at 135 Headlands, Kettering on 31st May 1994.

1988 — **Richard Bryan Dorrington** was born on 16th May 1948 in Bodmin, Cornwall. He was presented by Walter, Duke of Buccleuch in Geddington in 1988 having been Rector of Beckbury from 1985 to 1988 and became very active in village as well as church life, compiling extensive notes on the history of both and being a leading organiser of the 700th anniversary celebrations of Queen Eleanor and the Cross. He left Geddington in 1998 to become Priest-in-Charge of Abbots Bickington and Bulkworthy (1998-99) and then Rector of Bradworthy, Sutcombe, Putford, Abbots Bickington and Bulkworthy (2000-13); becoming Rural Dean of Holsworthy from 1999 to 2011. He retired to his home town of Bodmin, where he died on 10th May 2020 aged 71.

2000 — **Francis Giles Godber** (known as 'Giles'). He was born in Bedford in 1948. An accountant before his ordination, he was presented by Walter, Duke of Buccleuch in Geddington in 2000 and was Diocesan Ecumenical Officer in addition to his parish duties, building good relations with the Chapel in Geddington. He led a series of major projects that updated the church building. He retired to Somerset on 31st March 2013.

2013 — **Robert Thomas Parker-McGee** was born in Soham, Cambridgeshire, in 1978 and was a mill manager before training as a priest at Mirfield. He was presented in Geddington with Weekley by Richard, Duke of Buccleuch in January 2014 after serving as Curate in Worcester Diocese. He restored many church traditions and made extensive use of digital communications to help build the congregation. He left Geddington in March 2018 to become Vicar of All Saints', Orpington, then later became Rector of Boxford, Edwardstone, Groton, Little Waldingfield and Newton in Suffolk.

2019 — **Gillian Florence Gamble** was born in Newry, Northern Ireland in 1978 and worked in Christian youth ministry before taking Holy Orders; training at Ripon College, Cuddeston and serving as Curate at Oadby, Leicestershire. She was presented in Geddington with Weekley by Richard, Duke of Buccleuch on 3 February 2019. As the first female incumbent in over 1,000 years, the early years of her ministry have seen a strong emphasis on pastoral care (of special importance during the Covid outbreak) and the restoration of the medieval reredos.

---

211 Information courtesy of Jim Harker who knew Rev. Brodie.

AGER Percy John Private 31296, 5th Battalion, Northamptonshire Regiment. Died 12 May 1917. Aged 23. Son of Thomas and Charlotte Ager, of Geddington, Kettering, Northants. No known grave. Commemorated on ARRAS MEMORIAL, Pas de Calais, France. Bay 7.

ALLEN John Edward L/Cpl died 30 December 1914 aged 29. 1st Bn., Northamptonshire Regiment. Resident of Grange Road, Geddington. Husband of Ethel Allen. Buried at BOULOGNE EASTERN CEMETERY, France Section III Row A Grave 82.

ALLETT Arthur Private 13048, 6th Battalion, Lincolnshire Regiment. Died 15 August 1915. Aged 32. Born Geddington, Kettering. Son of William Allett; husband of Kitty Bell (formerly Allett), of 49, Silverton Rd., Coventry. Buried in ALEXANDRIA (CHATBY) MILITARY AND WAR MEMORIAL CEMETERY, Egypt. Section J. Grave 103.

ALLSOPP Levi [Charles] Lance Corporal 200914, 1st/5th Battalion, Durham Light Infantry formerly 3648, Northamptonshire Regiment. Killed in action 23 April 1917. Born Geddington, Northants, resident Woodford Lodge, enlisted Thrapston. Son of Mr. L. J. Allsopp, of "Sunnyside," Geddington, Kettering, Northants. Buried in WANCOURT BRITISH CEMETERY, Pas de Calais, France. Plot IV. Row D. Grave 32.

ALLSOPP Wilfred [John] Private 353207, 12th Battalion, Royal Scots (Lothian Regiment) formerly 15502, Northumberland Regiment and 15081, Essex Regiment. Died of wounds 13 April 1918. Born Geddington, Northants, enlisted Kettering, Northants. Buried in LIJSSENTHOEK MILITARY CEMETERY, West-Vlaanderen, Belgium. Plot XXVI. Row H. Grave 19A.

BERRIDGE Arthur Private 16091, 2nd Battalion, Northamptonshire Regiment. Died 4 January 1915. Aged 24. Son of Elizabeth Abbot (formerly Berridge), of Wood Rd., Geddington, Kettering, Northants, and the late George Berridge. No known grave. Commemorated on LE TOURET MEMORIAL, Pas de Calais, France. Panel 28 to 30.

BUTLER Albert Thomas Pte.14452. Died 29 December 1915 aged 19. 6th. Bn., Northamptonshire Regiment. Resident of Stamford Road, Geddington. Half-Brother of Frank Dainty. Buried at MEAULTE MILITARY CEMETERY, Somme, France Row A. Grave 27.

CATT Arthur F Pte. G/58775. Died 19 September 1917 aged 39. 32nd Bn., Royal Fusiliers. Resident of Newton and brother of Horace Catt of Newton. Buried at TYNE COT CEMETERY, Belgium Section LVII. Row F. Grave 36.

CHAPMAN Bertram Private 15071, "A" Company, 11th Battalion, Essex Regiment. Died of wounds 29 September 1915. Aged 23. Resident of Geddington. Son of Isaac and Sarah Elizabeth Chapman, of Church Gate, Geddington. Buried in LA PUGNOY MILITARY CEMETERY, Pas de Calais, France. Plot I. Row D. Grave 49A.

CLIPSTONE Frederick Private 14th London Regiment. Died I June 1920. Aged 33. Son of Charles and Amelia Clipstone. Buried in GEDDINGTON (ST. MARY MAGDALENE) CHURCHYARD.

COLES Steven Gnr 55154. 90th Siege Bty., Royal Garrison Artillery. Died 24 December 1917, aged 22. Resident of Newton. Grandson of Agnes Coles. Buried at MENDINGHEM MILITARY CEMETERY, Belgium VI. BB. 40.

COOPER Thomas William Pte. 15064, 11th Battalion, Essex Regiment. Died 15 October 1916. Aged 36. Resident Geddington, Northants. Son of John and Rebecca Cooper; husband of Mary Elizabeth Cooper of Geddington. Buried in BANCOURT BRITISH CEMETERY, Pas de Calais, France. Plot VIII. Row D. Grave 1.

CRICK Harold Ernest Pte. 268502, 1st/7th Battalion, Royal Warwickshire Regiment. Died 16 June 1918. Aged 23. Son of Ernest and Emma Crick, of Geddington. Buried in CAVALLETTO BRITISH CEMETERY, Italy. Plot 1. Row F. Grave 6.

DAINTY John Bertram Private 49827, 2nd Battalion, Lincolnshire Regiment. Died 19 October 1918. Son of Mr. J. T. Dainty, of Red House, Geddington. Buried in TERLINCTHUN BRITISH CEMETERY, WIMILLE, Pas de Calais, France. Plot VIII. Row C. Grave 18.

DARKER Cecil George Private 203547, 7th Battalion, Bedfordshire Regiment. Died 10 August 1917. Aged 19. Son of William J. and Sarah Ann Darker, of 22, Grafton Rd., Geddington. No known grave. Commemorated on YPRES (MENIN GATE) MEMORIAL, West Vlaanderen, Belgium. Panel 31 and 33.

ELSON W H Pte. 22919. Died 16 August 1916, aged 21. 1st Bn., Northamptonshire Regiment. Resident of Northampton. Son of William and Agnes Elson of Queen Street, Geddington. Buried at BAZENTIN-LE-PETIT COMMUNAL CEMETERY EXTN, France. Sp. Mem. Row A Grave 6.

HANNAN George Giles 2nd Lt. Died 17 August 1917 aged 20. 8th Bn., Suffolk Regiment. Resident of Geddington. Son of Alfred George and Rosetta Hannan, of Kettering, Northants. From 1914 to 1916 served with "B" Sqdn. Northants Yeomanry. Buried in BRAND HOEK NEW MILITARY CEMETERY NO.3, Belgium. Section I. Row A. Grave 21.

HECTOR Thomas Robert Pte. 65901. Died 4 October 1917, aged 22. 13th Battalion, Royal Fusiliers (City of London Regiment) formerly 32423, Northamptonshire Regiment. Resident of Chapel Lane, Geddington. Son of Thomas & Harriet Hector. Buried in ZANTVOORDE BRITISH CEMETERY, West-Vlaanderen, Belgium. Plot I Row D. Grave 16.

HIGGS Harry James Pte. 9142, 2nd Battalion, Oxfordshire & Buckinghamshire Light Infantry. Died 12 November 1914. Aged 19. Son of George and Eliza Higgs, of Grange Rd., Geddington. No known grave. Commemorated on YPRES (MENIN GATE) MEMORIAL, West Vlaanderen, Belgium. Panel 37 and 39.

HIPWELL George Ashton Pte. 016199, Royal Army Ordnance Corps. Died 23 April 1917. Aged 28. Husband of Grace C Hipwell, of "Redcliffe," Geddington. Buried in GEDDINGTON (ST. MARY MAGDALENE) CHURCHYARD.

JOHNSON James William Pte. SPTS/5330. Died 13 April 1917. Aged 24. 10th Battalion, Royal Fusiliers (City of London Regiment). Son of Mary Jane Clipston, of Star Lane, Geddington, Kettering. Buried in DUISANS BRITISH CEMETERY, ETRUN, Pas de Calais, France. Section III. Row G. Grave 6.

MILLER George Pte. 13301, Died 9 May 1915. Aged 21. 1st Battalion, Northamptonshire Regiment. Resident of Malting Lane, Geddington. Son of William & Rebecca Miller. No known grave. Commemorated on LE TOURET MEMORIAL, Pas de Calais, France. Panel 28 to 30.

MOORE Alfred Pte. 7085, 2nd Battalion, Lincolnshire Regiment. Died 17 April 1918. Aged 33. Son of Henry and Eleanor Moore. Resident of Geddington. Buried in HARINGHE (BANDAGHEM) MILITARY CEMETERY, West-Vlaanderen, Belgium. Plot V. Row D. Grave 7.

MOORE Sydney George Pte. 17643, 6th Battalion, Northamptonshire Regiment. Died 17 February 1917. Aged 19. Son of Harry and Mary Jane Moore, of Kettering Rd., Geddington. No known grave. Commemorated on THIEPVAL MEMORIAL, Somme, France. Pier and Face 11 A and 11 D.

OSBOND Sidney James Pte. 45791, 2nd Battalion, South Wales Borderers formerly M/225697, Royal Army Service Corps. Died 1 July 1917. Aged 19. Son of Thomas and Clara Osbond of Queen Street, Geddington. Buried in MENDINGHEM MILITARY CEMETERY, West-Vlaanderen, Belgium. Plot II. Row E. Grave 43.

PATRICK William Arthur Pte. 6135, 4th Battalion, Yorkshire Regiment. Died 21 December 1916. Aged 24. Son of William and Catherine Beatrice Patrick, of Stone House, Queen Street, Geddington. Buried in CONTAY BRITISH CEMETERY, Contay, Somme, France. Plot VII. Row B. Grave 1.

PATRICK Harry Arthur. Royal Army Service Corps. Wounded in action 4 Jul 1916, discharged 17 Mar 1919, died of wounds 20 January 1920, aged 37. Resident of 16 Queen Street, Geddington. Son of John T & Ellen Patrick. Buried in GEDDINGTON (ST. MARY MAGDALENE) CHURCHYARD.

PATRICK Lionel John George. Royal Horse Guards Machine Gun Regiment. Son of George Henry Patrick. Resident of Park View, Kettering Rd., Geddington. Enlisted 1916, discharged in 1919 to Eastbourne, and died of wounds 1 March 1920. Buried in GEDDINGTON (ST. MARY MAGDALENE) CHURCHYARD.

PATRICK Roland Charles Pte. 15117, 11th Battalion, Essex Regiment. Died 22 April 1917. Aged 22. Son of John T & Ellen Patrick. of 16, Queen St., Geddington, Kettering. No known grave. Commemorated on LOOS MEMORIAL, Pas de Calais, France. Panel 85 to 87.

PIDDINGTON George William Pte. 202387, 2nd Battalion, Northamptonshire Regiment. Died 24 March 1918. Aged 39. Son of the late John and Mary Piddington; husband of Agnes E. Piddington, of Geddington. No known grave. Commemorated on POZIERES MEMORIAL, Somme, France. Panel 54 to 56.

RAWSON Ernest Charles. Air Mechanic 2nd Class 10096, 47th Squadron, Royal Flying Corps. Died 7 April 1917. Aged 20. Son of Charles and Elizabeth Rawson, of Grange Rd., Geddington. Buried in SARIGOL MILITARY CEMETERY, Kriston, Greece. Plot B. Grave 253.

RAWSON John George. Private 37476, 2nd Battalion, Princess Charlotte of Wales's (Royal Berkshire Regiment). Died 16 August1917. Aged 22. Son of Charles and Elizabeth Rawson, of Grange Rd., Geddington. Buried in HOOGECRATER CEMETERY, West-Vlaanderen, Belgium. Plot IV. Row D. Grave 4.

REECE Henry William Acting Sergeant 3/11042, 1st Battalion, Northamptonshire Regiment. Died 3 July 1915. Aged 33. Son of late John George & Emma Reece; husband of Edith M Durrant (formerly Reece), of Grange Road, Geddington. Buried in QUARRY CEMETERY, VERMELLES, Pas de Calais, France. Row A. Grave 28.

RICH Sidney. Pte. 2269, 9th Bn., East Surrey Regiment. Died 26 September 1915, aged 34. Husband of Rebecca Rich of Wood Street, Geddington. Buried at CABARET-ROUGE BRITISH CEMETERY, Souchez, France. Section XI Row E. Grave 1.

SIMONS Frederic John Pte. 13285, Northamptonshire Regiment. Died 9 May 1915, aged 21. Son of Mrs. Eleanor Elizabeth Simons who was originally from Geddington and was a servant (linen maid) at Buckingham Palace in 1911. No known grave. Commemorated at LE TOURET MEMORIAL, France. Panel 28 to 30.

SLOUGH Ernest William. Pte. 33582 6th Bn., Bedfordshire Regiment. Died 19 February 1917, aged 19. Resident of West Street, Geddington. Buried at ST. PATRICK'S CEMETERY, Loos, France. Section III. Row A. Grave 30.

STANTON Arthur Frederick Aubrey. Pte. 15113, 11th Battalion, Essex Regiment. Died 26 September 1915. Aged 24. Son of Arthur & Ellen Stanton of Grafton Road, Geddington. No known grave. Commemorated on LOOS MEMORIAL, Pas de Calais, France. Panel 85 to 87.

STANTON Roland Charles. Pte. 15112, 11th Battalion, Essex Regiment. Died 26 September 1915. Aged 23. Son of Arthur & Ellen Stanton of Grafton Road, Geddington. No known grave. Commemorated on LOOS MEMORIAL, Pas de Calais, France. Panel 85 to 87.

TABRUM Frederick James. Pte. M2/202134 Army Service Corps. Died 8 November 1918, aged 27. Husband of Daisy Tabrum of 2 Wood St., Geddington. Buried at TINCOURT NEW BRITISH CEMETERY, France. Section VI. Row D. Grave 5.

TOWNLEY Charles. Driver 234526, 210th Brigade H.Q., Royal Field Artillery. Died 9 November 1918, aged 24, at York General Hospital of pneumonia following wounds. Son of Ruth Townley and the late Samuel Lee Townley, of Wood St., Geddington. Buried in GEDDINGTON (ST. MARY MAGDALENE) CHURCHYARD.

TOWNLEY Frederick Pte. G/25267, 1st Battalion., Queen's (Royal West Surrey Regiment). Died 14 April 1918. Aged19. Son of Ruth Townley and the late Samuel Lee Townley, of Wood St., Geddington. No known grave. Commemorated on PLOEGSTEERT MEMORIAL, Hainaut, Belgium. Panel 1 and 2.

WALPOLE Harold Edgar. Able Seaman R/6329, Anson Battalion, Royal Naval Division, Royal Naval Volunteer Reserve. Died 11 November 1918. Aged 19. Son of Henry Francis and Mary Ann Walpole, of 26, Wood St., Geddington. Buried on the east side of NOUVELLES COMMUNAL CEMETERY, Hainaut, Belgium.

WHITE Frederick Joseph. Rifleman P/99,16th Bn., Rifle Brigade. Died 4 July 1916, aged 21. Son of Emma White, of Wood Street, Geddington. Buried at LE TOURET MILITARY CEMETERY, Richebourg-l'Avoue, France. Section III. Row J. Grave 27.

WHITE William Turner Pte. 20172, 2nd Battalion, Norfolk Regiment. Died of wounds in Mesopotamia 26 February 1917, aged 37. Resident of Queen Street, Geddington. Son of Joseph and Mary White (dec'd). Buried in AMARA WAR CEMETERY, Iraq. Plot XXIX. Row B. Grave57/66.

The following died of war-related causes in the years following the War:

BLACK John Thomas Grenadier Guards. Badly wounded in 1916. Discharged. Died 9 July 1922, aged 27. Resident of West. St. Geddington. Buried in GEDDINGTON (ST. MARY MAGDALENE) CHURCHYARD.

HIGGS Stephen Royal Artillery. Died 03 September 1921, aged 24. Buried in GEDDINGTON (ST. MARY MAGDALENE) CHURCHYARD.

HIPWELL Samuel Henry. Royal Engineers. Resident of West Street, Geddington. Discharged with shell shock November 1916. Died 17 February 1922, aged 41.

MOORE Frank Roy Machine Gun Corps. Developed TB as a Prisoner of War. Died of Typhoid fever at Wellingborough Isolation Hospital 31 May 1924 aged 27. Burial place unknown.

PIDDINGTON Joseph Levi Pte. 202197 Nottinghamshire and Derbyshire Regiment. Badly wounded in 1916. Discharged. Died 19 July 1923, aged 42. Burial place unknown.

1939-1945

ABBOTT John Thomas Rifleman 14660169, 6th Battalion, The Cameronians (Scottish Rifles). Died 8 March 1945. Aged 33. A resident of Church Hill, Geddington. He is buried in REICHSWALD FOREST WAR CEMETERY, Nordrhein-Westfalen, Germany. Plot 49. Row C. Grave 9.

BAKER Henry John Sergeant 5669993, 3rd Battalion, Coldstream Guards. Died 12 November 1943. Aged 29. Son of William and Alice Amelia Baker; husband of Annie Meikle Baker, of Geddington. A resident of Kettering Road, Geddington. No known grave. Commemorated on the CASSINO MEMORIAL, Italy. Panel 3.

BLANCHARD Harry Lance Corporal 5886956, 2nd Battalion, Northamptonshire Regiment. Died of wounds 22 January 1944. Aged 26. Son of Charles Blanchard, and of E.E. Blanchard, of Geddington. Buried in MINTURNO WAR CEMETERY, Italy. Plot III. Row B. Grave 25.

CHAPMAN Edward Brooks Cecil Sergeant 563626 RAF. Died 20 December 1941. Aged 28. Son of Mr. and Mrs. J. Chapman, of Newton. Commemorated on the SINGAPORE MEMORIAL. Column 410.

GREEN James William Aircraftman 2nd Class 1157782, 930 Balloon Squadron, Royal Air Force Volunteer Reserve. Died 15 September 1940. Aged 32. Son of William and Eliza Green, husband of Alice Grace Christine Green. Resident Queen Street, Geddington. Buried in GEDDINGTON (ST. MARY MAGDALENE) CHURCHYARD.

HOPKINS Alfred George Marine PO/X 103550, 18th Bn. Royal Marines. Died 15 June 1942. Aged 30. Resident of Kettering. Son of Arthur and Annie Hopkins of Geddington and wife of Lucy. Died in Northampton following an accident at Tenby, Wales. He sustained a fractured skull when the carrier he was in overturned. Buried in LONDON ROAD CEMETERY, KETTERING. Row OO. Grave 15.

JARMAN Thomas Robert Hector Stoker 2nd Class 102394 Royal Navy HM Trawler Tamarisk. Died 12 August 1940. Aged 21. Resident of Grange Road, Geddington. Husband of Harriet Hector. Commemorated on PORTSMOUTH NAVAL MEMORIAL. Panel 42, Column 3.

MITCHELL Ernest John Thomas Pte. 5888999, 2nd Battalion, Northamptonshire Regiment. Died of wounds in Sicily 11 August 1943. Aged 29. Son of Ernest and Betsy Mitchell of Queen St. Geddington. Husband of Gladys Elsie Mitchell. Buried in SYRACUSE WAR CEMETERY, Sicily, Italy. Plot IV. Row D. Grave 12.

RAWSON Margaret Elsie. Women's Royal Air Force. Died 24 June 1944, aged 23 in Bradford, Yorkshire. Buried in GEDDINGTON (ST. MARY MAGDALENE) CHURCHYARD.

SWAN Ronald Charles Ord. Smn. Royal Navy # P/JX 553417 - H.M.S. Chanticleer. Died 18 November 1943. Aged 22. Resident of Newton. Son of Harold John and husband of Mary Swan. Commemorated on PORTSMOUTH NAVAL MEMORIAL. Panel 76, Column 3.

TEBBUTT Allen Parker Sergeant (Navigator) 1583675, 103 Squadron, Royal Air Force Volunteer Reserve. Died 26 August 1944. Aged 21. Son of William Parker Tebbutt and Gertrude Jessie Tebbutt, of Geddington. Buried in GEDDINGTON (ST. MARY MAGDALENE) CHURCHYARD.

WALKER Charles Alexander Flight Sergeant 875132, 260 Squadron, Royal Air Force. Died 26 November 1944. Aged 21. Son of William and Catherine Fanny Walker, of Geddington. Buried in NAPLES WAR CEMETERY, Italy. Plot IV. Row C. Grave 4.

WALKER George William Sergeant (Wireless Operator/Air Gunner) 1212018, 106 Squadron, Royal Air Force Volunteer Reserve. Died 31 March 1944. Aged 24. Son of William and Catherine Fanny Walker, of Geddington. Buried in HANOVER WAR CEMETERY Niedersachsen, Germany. Joint grave 8. A. 15-16.

WHITBREAD William Ellis Leslie Flying Officer (Pilot) 178540, RAF Volunteer Reserve 10 Sqdn. Died 17 January 1945. Aged 34. Son of Mr. and Mrs. W. Whitbread and husband of Mary L. Whitbread. No known grave. Commemorated on RUNNYMEDE MEMORIAL, Surrey. Panel 268.

COMMONWEALTH WAR GRAVES

There are four war dead commemorated by the Commonwealth War Graves Commission (CWGC) who are buried in the churchyard at St. Mary Magdalene, Geddington:

James William Green d. 15 September 1940, Age 32. Grave D 35

George Ashton Hipwell d. 23 April 1917, Age 28. Grave A 103

Allen Parker Tebbutt d. 26 August 1944, Age 21. Grave A 34

Charles Townley d. 9 November 1918, Age 24. Grave C 118

In addition, there are seven men who are commemorated elsewhere by the CWGC and also by their families on memorials in Geddington churchyard.

Harold Ernest Crick d. 16 June 1918. Commemorated by his family at Grave A64 & buried by the CWGC at Cavalletto British Cemetery, Italy

Harry James Higgs d. 12 November 1914. No known grave: commemorated by his family at Grave A88 & by the CWGC on the Ypres (Menin Gate) Memorial, Belgium

Sidney George Moore d. 17 February 1917. No known grave: commemorated by his family at Grave C93 (missing) & by the CWGC at the Thiepval Memorial, France

Sidney James Osbond d. 1 July 1917. Commemorated by his family at Grave D30 & buried by the CWGC in Mendinghem Military Cemetery, Belgium

Roland Charles Patrick d. 22 April 1917. No known grave: commemorated by his family at Grave A98 & by the CWGC on the Loos Memorial, France

Frederick Townley d. 14 April 1918. No known grave: commemorated by his family at Grave C117 & by the CWGC at the Ploegsteert Memorial, Belgium

Harold Edgar Walpole d. 11 November 1918. Commemorated by his family at Grave A37-A42 & buried by the CWGC in Nouvelles Communal Cemetery, Belgium

Although not commemorated by the CWGC, the following men died after the end of the Great War of war-related causes and are buried in the churchyard:

Harry Arthur Patrick d. 20 January 1920, aged 37. Grave A 98

Lionel John George Patrick d. 20 January 1920, aged 22. Grave A 93

Frederick Clipstone d. 1 June 1920, aged 33. Grave C 97

Stephen Ernest Higgs, d. 3 September 1921, aged 24. Grave A 88

Samuel Henry Hipwell, d. 17 February 1922, aged 41. Grave E 15

John Thomas Black, d. 9 July 1922. Aged 27. Grave C 77

Joseph Levi Piddington, d. 19 July 1923, aged 42. Grave A 100

- Communion set made in 1855. The cup is hallmarked 'E.B.' with a Lion Passant; 'J.B.' with a Leopard's Head; a Queen's head and the words: 𝕮𝖆𝖑𝖎𝖈𝖊𝖒 𝖘𝖆𝖑𝖚𝖙𝖆𝖗𝖎𝖘 𝖆𝖈𝖈𝖎𝖕-𝖎𝖆𝖒 𝖆𝖙 𝖓𝖔𝖒𝖊𝖓 𝕯𝖔𝖒𝖎𝖓𝖎 𝖎𝖓𝖛𝖔𝖈𝖆𝖇𝖔 (I will receive the cup of salvation and call upon the name of the Lord). The Paten is hallmarked as the cup and inscribed: 𝕬𝖌-𝖓𝖚𝖘 𝕯𝖊𝖎, 𝖖𝖚𝖎 𝖙𝖔𝖑𝖑𝖎𝖘 𝖕𝖊𝖈𝖈𝖆𝖙𝖆 𝖒𝖚𝖓𝖉𝖎 𝖉𝖆 𝖓𝖔𝖇𝖎𝖘 𝖙𝖚𝖆𝖒 𝖕𝖆𝖈𝖊𝖒 (Lamb of God who takes away the sins of the world, grant us peace). The flagon likewise with the words: 𝕻𝖆𝖘𝖈𝖍𝖆 𝖓𝖔𝖘𝖙𝖗𝖚𝖒 𝖎𝖒𝖒𝖔𝖑𝖆𝖙𝖊𝖘 𝖊𝖘𝖙 𝕮𝖍𝖗𝖎𝖘𝖙𝖚𝖘 (Christ the Passover Lamb is sacrificed for us). #

- Alms dish also made in 1855 inscribed: 𝕿𝖔 𝖉𝖔 𝖌𝖔𝖔𝖉 𝖆𝖓𝖉 𝖉𝖎𝖘𝖙𝖗𝖎𝖇𝖚𝖙𝖊 𝖋𝖔𝖗𝖌𝖊𝖙 𝖓𝖔𝖙. *

- A pewter alms basin made in London circa 1700 by "Francis....oft" *

- Small silver/pewter chalice with lid made c. 1570 inscribed only with an elliptical fish* #

- Silver/pewter paten lid inscribed: 𝕱𝖔𝖗 𝕲𝖊𝖉𝖊𝖓𝖙𝖔𝖓, 1570* #

- Silver 'tulip' chalice marked with Cross Keys and 'I.H.S. In Glory'; #

- Silver 'cake stand' paten marked with Cross Keys and 'I.H.S. In Glory'; #

- Silver flagon marked with Cross Keys and 'I.H.S. In Glory' #

- Silver paten marked with Cross Keys and 'I.H.S. In Glory' #

- Silver chalice marked with the Tresham Arms and inscribed: *The Guift of Henry Tresham to the Church of Newton, who dyed the 15th April 1672* [formerly in St. Faith's Church, Newton] #

- Silver paten with hallmark and inscribed: *Newton Church 1923* [formerly in St. Faith's Church, Newton] #

- Silver-plated paten inscribed: *St. Dunston Church Craft* #

- Unmarked silver plate wafer box

- Electroplated silver paten (unmarked)

- Brass Lectern and Altar Cross given by Captain and Mrs. Wetherall of Geddington Priory and members of their family, together with a brass Alms Dish inscribed: and on the rear: *To the Glory of God in memory of John William Wetherall.* These items were all donated in October 1885.*

- Silver Altar Cross and two silver candlesticks.

- Six brass candlesticks.

- Wooden Cross with brass figure of Christ mounted thereon.

- Pair of scales*. These were purchased in 1802 for 14 shillings and were kept in the Parish Chest in 1899. Some parts were stolen in the 1970s.[212]

- Five-branched altar vesper lights were the gift of Mrs. Isaac Smith in 1890*.

- Baptismal Shell engraved with the Holy Nativity: the gift of Mrs Bowman in 1898, it came from Jerusalem.[213]

- A White oak prayer desk and chair with open panel work, the gift of Mrs. Wetherall (1885) with a brass plate on the rear inscribed: "*To the Glory of God in memory of John William Wetherall*".

---

212 A note made by Brian Leaton in 1993 records that some parts remained in 1993.

213 *Kettering Guardian* (16 September 1898)

Dedication	First Name(s)	Surname	YoB	YoD	Other
In memory of	John	Abraham	1908	1985	
	Margaret	Abraham	1912	1977	
Donated in memory of	Michael	Allaway			by the Trustees of the Samuel Lee Charity
In loving memory of	David Gordon	Allison	28th December 1944	June 15th 1990	
In memory of	Mr & Mrs D.J.	Allsopp			Former Church wardens
Donated by	Arthur	Bagley			
Donated by	Betty D	Bagley			
Donated by	Carolyn Marjorie	Bagley			
	Annie Augusta	Bagshaw			for her 90th Birthday
	Thomas S.	Bale			One-time Server
In loving memory of	Evelyn June	Banks (nee Goodwin)			
In loving memory of	Newland Grandsire	Bennett			
In loving memory of	Winifred E.E.	Bennett	1898	2008	
In loving memory of	Barbara	Bishop			
Donated by	Cynthia & Barbara	Bishop and family			
In loving memory of	Ivy Miriam	Blackwell who died		1994	aged 74
In Memory of	Edith Mary	Chamberlain	1901	1986	
In Memory of	Evelyn	Chapman	1892	1989	
In memory of	Albert Samuel	Clipstone	1912	1989	
In memory of	Emily	Clipstone	1908	1990	
In loving memory of	Horace James	Clipstone	1910	1991	
In loving memory of	Jane and	Clipstone	1910	1982	
	Sydney	Clipstone	1904	1967	
In loving memory of	Esther Lydia	Coldham	1909	1988	
In loving memory of	Philip Walter	Coldham	1905	2004	
In memory of	Albert Ashton	Coles	1906	1975	
In memory of	Frederick William & Miriam	Coles			
In loving memory of	John Charles (Jack)	Dainty	1915	1995	
In Memory of	George William	Digby	1902	1960	
In Memory of	Graham Ellis	Digby	1946	1987	
In Memory of	Winifred	Digby	1907	1990	
In loving memory of	Alfred & Ethel	Essam			
In loving memory of	A.	Evans			
In loving memory of	Grace	Fetch	1921	2008	
In memory of	Ronald Andrew	Fetch			
In loving memory of the		Field Family	1912	1995	of Church Hill
Beloved Son	Steven	Field-Smith	1955	1981	
In loving memory of	Olive (nee Redhead) and Cyril	Foulds			
In loving memory of	Jean & Frank	Gordon	1901	1988	
In loving memory of	Doris (nee Redhead)	Graves			
In loving memory of	Robert Charles (Bob)	Green	14th November 1932	5th May 1984	
In loving memory of	Anthony	Griffin			
In Memory of	H.W. & F.E.	Harborne			
In loving memory of	Matthew James	Harker	1921	1984	

APPENDIX 4: PERSONS COMMEMORATED ON CHAIRS

Dedication	First Name(s)	Surname	YoB	YoD	Other
In Memory of	Matthew Rowland	Harker	1915	1983	
Donated by	Miss Barbara	Harker			
in memory of	Bertha	Hawes			
In memory of	Janice	Higgs			
In memory of	Richard & Violet	Higgs			
In memory of	Richard & Violet	Higgs			
In memory of	Eva & Ernest	Hopkins			
In loving memory of	Florence E.M.	Hopkins	1920	2007	
In loving memory of	George & Gertrude	Hopkins			
In loving memory of	Gordon Henry	Hopkins			
In loving memory of	Harold	Hopkins			
Donated by	Bob & Valda	Horton			
In memory of	George William	Hotson	1898	1985	
In memory of	Reginald J.A.	Hotson	1905	1988	
In memory of	Samuel Flavel	Hughes			
in memory of	Elsie & William	Hutchings			
In loving memory of	Edith & Joseph	Jackson			
In Memory of	Sylvia & Fred	Jackson			
In Memory of	Charles & Beatrice	Jarman			
In loving memory of	Ernest Dudley (Tim)	Jarman			
In loving memory of	Ernest Henry	Julian	1907	1941	
In loving memory of	Winifred E.E.	Julian	1909	1993	
In loving memory of	George	Julyans	1899	1960	
In loving memory of	Karen Sara	Liddington			
Donated by	Mr & Mrs W.L.	McLaughlin			
In loving memory of	William Luke	McLaughlin	1919	1990	
In thanksgiving for 40 happy years together	Jack & Ivy	Middleton	1930	1970	
Presented by	Jean & Jack	Miller			to commemorate their Golden wedding
In loving memory of	Samuel Frederick	Miller	1914	1983	
In memory of a dear Uncle	Arthur	Neale			
In loving memory of	William Edward	Newbold			Died August 28th 1986 Aged 70 years
In loving memory of	Donald Arthur	Osborne	1929	1990	
In loving memory of	Raymond	Parry	1908	1981	
In loving memory of	Hugh and Emily	Patrick			
In loving memory of	Joseph James (Jim)	Patrick	19th July 1909	3rd Feb. 1994	
Donated by	Valerie and Brian	Peel			
Donated by	Valerie and Brian	Peel			
In memory of	Albert & Alice	Pettit			
In loving memory of	George	Pettit			
In loving memory of	John Thomas & Ruby	Pettit			
In loving memory of	Ivy	Plummer (Walpole)	08-Jan-09	04-May-96	
	P & V	Richardson	06.09.69	06.09.09	
In loving memory of	Bernard Arthur	Rogers			
In loving memory of	Pamela Mary	Rowlatt	1931	2005	
In loving memory of	John Thomas	Russell	26th November 1909	31st May 1990	
Donated by	Winifred, wife of Jack	Russell	1990		

APPENDIX 4: PERSONS COMMEMORATED ON CHAIRS

Dedication	First Name(s)	Surname	YoB	YoD	Other
Donated by	Richard & Violet	Saltmarsh			
In loving memory of	Joseph Karl	Schramm	10-Dec-21	28-Apr-68	
In loving memory of	William & Grace	Searle			
In loving memory of	Bertha Emma	Semark (nee Allsopp)	1902	1986	
In loving memory of	Donald Christopher	Shiells	1946	2006	
In memory of	J.T.	Shuttleworth			
In memory of	J.T.	Shuttleworth			
In Memory of	J.T.	Shuttleworth			
In memory of	Robert Lewis	Slough	1903	1975	
In loving memory of	Albert	Smith			
In loving memory of	Fanny	Smith	31st January 1892	13th September 1985	
In loving memory of	Peter James	Smith	1920	1996	
In memory of	Liz	Spencer	1969	1988	
In memory of	Elizabeth & John	Spriggs			
In loving memory of	Arthur & Ellen	Stanton			
In loving memory of	Ivy Lilian	Stanton			who loved the church
In Memory of	Hilda M.	Staples	1896	1958	
In memory of	Walter	Staples	1894	1972	
In Memory of	Debbie Leigh	Tarleton		Died 1989	aged 22 years
Donated by	Brian & Maureen	Thompson			in 2000
In loving memory of	Albert	Toseland	August 2nd 1905	March 26th 1984	
In memory of	Ernie and Ada	Toseland			
In loving memory of	Gertrude May	Toseland	1912	1995	
Donated by	Keith and Pat	Toseland			
In memory of	Alfred	Towndrow			Benefactor of this church
In memory of	Marjorie	Towndrow			Benefactress of this church
In loving memory of	Leslie Marshall	Vickers			
In memory of	Alf and Minnie	Walpole			
In loving memory of	Edgar (Dick)	Walpole	1906	1976	At rest
In loving memory of	Mary	Walpole	1919	1989	
In loving memory of	Reginald	Walpole	1917	1992	
In memory of	William J.A.	Walpole			
In loving memory of	Fred	Ward	1909	1990	
In loving memory of	Annie	Warren	8th July 1902	11th Sept 1991	
In memory of my husband	Arthur Edward	Warren	1902	1964	
In loving memory of	Herbert G.	Weekley	1909	1989	
In thanksgiving for 40 happy years together	Jimmy and Dorothy	Welsh	1940	1980	
In loving memory of	Mabel (nee Redhead) and Claude	Wilson			
In loving memory of	Irene & Arthur	Wooldridge			Beloved Mum & Dad of Joyce Clipstone
In loving memory of	John (Jack)	Wright			

CHURCH OF ST. MARY MAGDALEN: (GRADE I)

List Entry Number: **1052076**

Date first listed: **25-Feb-1957**

Details: GEDDINGTON SP8883 GRAFTON ROAD 1337-0/12/259 (North side) 25/02/57 Church of St. Mary Magdalene GV I Parish church. Anglo-Saxon origin, late C12 north aisle C13 south aisle, C14 Chancel tower, perhaps C12 heightened C15, other C15 alterations (especially windows), restored C19 and 1904-6. Coursed limestone rubble and ashlar roofs probably of lead. West tower and spire, aisled nave, Chancel flanked by chapels, C19 north-east vestry and south porch. 4-stage west tower has moulded plinth clasping buttresses quatrefoil frieze with gargoyles at angles and castellated parapet. Twin 2-light Perpendicular bell-openings with transoms. West face has moulded pointed entrance arch with C19 double doors, 2-light Perpendicular window, and tiny stair-light. South face has clock face and stair lights. Recessed octagonal spire with finial and weathervane. Plain parapets with gargoyles, to nave and aisles. South aisle has buttresses and sill band and from left to right, C19 gabled porch, 3 3-light square-headed windows with cusped lights, a blocked window, and a lancet. North aisle has similar windows, one of 3 lights and 3 of 2 lights, a simple pointed-arch doorway, and a chimney at east end. Chancel has angle buttresses and Decorated windows, of 5 lights to east, 3 lights to south end, 2 lights to north. Clerestory windows, 3 to nave and 3 to Chancel, square-headed with 3 cusped lights at south aisle. Pointed south doorway with C19 door.

GEDDINGTON WAR MEMORIAL: (GRADE II)

List Entry Number: **1425141**

Date first listed: **10-Mar-2015**

Reasons for Designation: Geddington War Memorial, which stands in the churchyard to the south-west of the church of St. Mary Magdalene, is listed at Grade II for the following principal reasons: * Historic interest: as an eloquent witness to the tragic impact of world events on the local community, and the sacrifice it made in the conflicts of the C20; * Design: an elegant limestone cross; * Group value: it stands alongside the Grade I-listed church of St. Mary Magdalene.

History: A memorial committee was formed in July 1919, and reported its proposals in January 1920 for a memorial cross and a tablet carrying the names of all 170 Geddington men who had served to be erected in the churchyard. Construction took a month and immediately afterwards, on 28 July 1921, the memorial was unveiled by Major Wetherall of Northampton. An additional inscription was made following the Second World War.

Details: The Geddington memorial stands within the churchyard, south-west of the church of St. Mary Magdalene (listed Grade I). It comprises a c9m high floriated Latin cross with IHS in a shield at the top. The cross-head is set on an hexagonal pillar which rises from a square plinth set on a two-stepped octagonal base. On the plinth is inscribed 1914 – 1918/ IN UN-DYING MEMORY OF/ THE MEN OF GEDDINGTON/ WHO IN THE GREAT WAR/ GAVE THEIR LIVES FOR US. The inscription ALSO/ 1939-1945 has been added below, to the top step of the base. Nearby, on the outer west wall of the south aisle of the church are three tablets bearing names and additional inscriptions. The outer concrete path around the memorial is excluded from the listing.

GROUP OF 3 CHEST TOMBS, INCLUDING THAT OF SAMUEL LEE CIRCA 10 METRES SOUTH OF CHURCH OF ST. MARY: (GRADE II)

List Entry Number: **1052077**   Date first listed: **19-Jun-1992**

Details: GEDDINGTON SP8883 GRAFTON ROAD 1337-0/12/258 (North side) Group of 3 chest tombs, incl. that of Samuel Lee c.l0m S of Church of St. Mary GV II Chest tombs. Early/mid C18. Limestone ashlar. 3 tomb chests, each with moulded plinth, and cambered lid. That to Samuel Lee has fielded panels, to south inscribed *"Here lieth interred the body of/Mr SAMUEL LEE/ who died March the 3rd, 1708. He was/Ranger of Geddington Chase to His Grace the/Duke of Montague and bequeathed to the Post/of Geddington the profits of a Piece of/land lying in Cranford St. John".* 2 similar tomb chests to west, with recessed panels. Any inscriptions on them are no longer legible.

CHEST TOMB OF SAMUEL ROWLATT, CIRCA 10 METRES SOUTH OF CHURCH OF ST. MARY MAGDELENE (GRADE II)

List Entry Number: **1286938**   Date first listed: **19-Jun-1992**

Details: GEDDINGTON SP8883 GRAFTON ROAD 1337-0/12/256 (North side) Chest tomb of Samuel Rowlatt, c.10 metres S of Church of St. Mary Magdalene GV II Chest tomb. Early C18. Limestone ashlar. Moulded plinth and cornice, corner pilasters with drops of flowers. Flat lid. Recessed panels with egg-and-dart moulding to north, and south, cherub's head to east, cartouche, and cherubs' heads to west. Inscription to south in memory of Samuel ?Rowlatt, d. ?1710, barely legible.

CHEST TOMB CIRCA 15 METRES NORTH-EAST OF WEST END OF ST. MARY MAGDELENE (GRADE II)

List Entry Number: **1052075**   Date first listed: **19-Jun-1992**

Details: GEDDINGTON SP8883 GRAFTON ROAD 1337-0/12/257 (North side) Chest tomb c.15m NE of W end of Church of St. Mary Magdalene GV II Chest tomb. Early/mid C18. Limestone ashlar. Moulded plinth and cornice, slightly cambered lid. Corner pilasters with foliage drops. Moulded recessed panels between fielded panels to south, 2 fielded panels to north. Cherub's head above swag to east and west. Inscription no longer legible.

The following are the different items for Mason
=work & Plastering, Excavator &c proposed
to be done Geddington Church Namely

	£ s D
Taking up the floors & Monumental Stones &c	2 " "
Excavating the Earth internally	12 " "
Concrete all over the Ground 6 inches deep	5 " "
Underpinning all Foundations useing good Cement	4 " "
Excavating the ground externally including Carting	10 " "
York Channel out-side the walls & Buttresses of the Church	
100 ft of earthenware pipes as specified	
Laying Drains side of Foundation	5 " "
Cleaning off all pillars, Arches, Doorways, Strings,	
and all Stonework inside & repairing all defective parts	50 " "
with weldon Stone to match including Bases & Caps	
Repairing the Font & refix the Same	" 10 "
Laying drain from font	1 " "
remove all mural monuments & refix afterwards	2 " "
Flooring Chancel between Seats with Mintons Tiles	8 " "
Laying the altar with encaustic do	38 " "
reworking old floor & finding Ketton Stone to make	
good the deficiency	40 " "
reworking all the Steps as Specified finding new	
to make good of the Same description	5 " "
Building new Aisle	100 " "
Building new Vestry	40 " "
Brick for all flues and Labour	4 " "
Cramps & copper dowels for Stone work & Lead to fasten	3 " "
Taking down end of East Aisle & prop the roof	1 " "
to repair the triangular window & refix	" 5 "
Raising Arch leading into the Chancel as plan	25 " "
restoring ancient window in South Aisle Chancel	1 " "
Building up modern Doorway	" 10 "
opening out Archway in Tower & repairing	3 " "
making good walls of Tower for Plastering	" 15 "
restoring west Doorway	2 " "
the reredos to be Carefully restored & the Ancient Heads	
in the Chancel	" " "
	£370 " "

	£		
Brought over	371	"	
Stone Pulpit			
Doorway into Vestry new	6	"	"
to Chop off all Plastering from all walls throughout the Church & Stucco	90	"	"
to Build a new Porch			
floor the Porch with Stone			
Slating the Porch with white Slate	70	"	"
Clean off all whitewash from all woodwork	3	"	"
Finding Scaffolding for all works & props for Shoring	20	"	"
A new arch for South Aisle Leading into recumbent Chancel including Stone &c	35	"	"
the North Doorway to be Arched to suite the Plan	1	10	"
	596	10	0

GEDDINGTON ✦ PARISH ✦ MAGAZINE. 1891.

An apology is due to our subscribers for the omission to supply them with the numbers of the Magazine for the months of September and October, which we send out with the current number.

THE EAST WINDOW.

We are glad to be able to state that the East Window is no longer being thought about and collected for, but is actually in hand.

The artist selected is Mr. Comper, who has already done work in the Church, having decorated the sanctuary some years since.

Our readers will like to have a description of the design for the window.

The main idea running through the window is the power of Divine love, on the one hand in overcoming evil; and, on the other hand, the power of human love, when touched by the Grace of God, in enabling men and women to answer to Divine love.

This idea is thus worked out: —The great manifestation of Divine love took place when the Word was made Flesh, i.e., when by the mystery of the Incarnation, God was made Man. Accordingly, the central light of the window will contain a figure of our Blessed Lord as an Infant in the arms of His Mother.

Then, as a most notable instance of the power of Divine love in overcoming evil, and of human love in answering to the Divine, we shall have pourtrayed our Patron Saint, Mary Magdalene, out of whom, S. Luke tells us, our Lord cast seven devils, and who thenceforth devoted herself to His service.

And, again, as another instance of the same thing, we shall have in another light of the window, S. Peter, the Patron Saint of this Diocese, whom, when he had thrice denied Him, His Master recalled to his allegiance by a look of loving tenderness that made him go out and weep bitterly.

The other two lights will be filled with S. John Baptist, the great Forerunner of our Lord, and S. George, the Patron Saint of England, trampling under foot the dragon, the emblem of evil.

Underneath the figures of the Holy Child and His Mother there will be an angel bearing a scroll with the words: "The Word was made Flesh"; and underneath the other figures will be the symbols of the four Evangelists, bearing scrolls with words taken from their writings, applicable to the figures above.

Over the side figures will be four of the Prophets with scrolls bearing words from their writings.

The head of the window will contain Cherubim and Seraphim attending upon our Lord, represented in the central light.

We hope that the window will be in its place by next Easter. We have worked and waited patiently for it, and shall find our reward in the great addition that it will make to the beauty of our Parish Church.

Our readers will be interested in hearing that the Rummage Sales, that have been held have added no less than £100 to the Window Fund.

GEDDINGTON CHURCH MONTHLY.

JANUARY, 1893.

The great event of the year just ended has been the Dedication of the East Window, and the Reredos, which took place on December 17th.

The general opinion is that these, the latest adornments of our ancient and interesting Parish Church, are not unworthy of the position that they occupy; and this is saying a great deal.

The Window has been worked and waited for with much energy and patience, and it is a great relief and happiness to see it in its place. The approbation of it that is experienced on all sides would seem to show that the expectations that had been formed respecting it have not been disappointed; and this again, is saying a great deal.

Messrs. Bucknall and Comper, architects, of 7, Queen Anne's Gate, London, S.W., who designed and executed the Window (the whole of the glass having been painted in their office), are to be congratulated on the highly successful result of their efforts. The design, which is very thoughtful, and reverently treated, has been most carefully and beautifully executed.

It is unnecessary to remind our readers that the story which the Window is designed to tell, is "the power of Divine Love shown in overcoming evil."

The way in which the Window fulfils its purpose, was most ably and beautifully pointed out by the Preacher on the occasion of its being dedicated, the Rev. Canon Ingram, Vicar of St. Matthew's, Leicester, (who, by the bye, we are pleased to see, has been appointed Dean of our Cathedral), his text being Genesis, chap. 6, verse 16.—"A window shalt thou make to the ark." There was a large gathering of the neighbouring Clergy and Church people. The service, which was choral, was very well rendered.

It is very satisfactory and gratifying to be able to state that the Window is paid for. A Rummage Sale held on Dec. 19th realised close upon £10; the effect of which was to leave a balance of upwards of £12 on the East Window Fund, after payment of all expenses.

advowson	the right of presentation to the Bishop of a priest for installation to the living (q.v.) of a church
alb	a long white robe worn by priests
altar	the table or slab at which the bread and wine are consecrated by the priest during Mass or Holy Communion.
aumbrey	recess, cupboard or safe for the storage of consecrated bread, wine, and oils. See tabernacle.
apse	rounded extension of church building, normally of the Chancel
baptistry	the part of a church reserved for performing baptisms
benefice	a permanent Church appointment, commonly a rector or vicar. Originally the grant of land and income to support a rector in carrying out their ministry in a parish
breviary	book containing daily church masses or services (Catholic or Anglo-Catholic)
cassock	close-fitting ankle-length priest's garment
catechumen	person undergoing instruction prior to reception into the Christian church (Catholic)
censer	vessel for burning incense, usually hung, or swung on a chain
Chancel	part of church, normally at the eastern end, containing the high altar and seats for the choir
Chancel arch	the arch separating the Chancel from the nave (q.v.)
Chancel screen	a screen dividing the Chancel and the nave, sometimes called a 'rood screen'.
chapel	a small building, room or area of a church set aside for worship, usually with its own altar.
chantry	chapel where prayers for the dead are said, often for a benefactor who may maintain or have built it.
chasuble	sleeveless priest's garment, normally worn over an alb (q.v.)
Christogram	a combination of Initials that stand for Christ; e.g. the two Greek letters Chi-Rho (CR) together; or IHS (Jesus Hominum Salvator, 'Jesus Saviour of Men')
clerestory	upper storey or windows near the roof of a church
compline	prayer service held at the end of the day, often at dusk
cornice	Horizontal decorative moulding on top of a feature or piece of furniture (from Italian for 'ledge')
credence	a small table for placing sacred vessels for use in the Eucharist (from Latin credo: 'I believe')
crenel	opening between 2 solid pieces of wall, (as in battlements). 'crenelated' = with a series of crenels
crosier	a staff resembling a shepherd's crook carried by bishops and abbots as a symbol of office
crucifer	Literally 'cross-bearer'. Person who carries a cross (usually mounted on a staff) in procession.
curate	a recently-ordained priest who assists a parish priest for a period before being presented to a parish of their own
donative	a benefice (q.v.) presented to a church without reference to the bishop
font	a container, usually of stone, mounted on a low pillar, containing holy water for baptism. Sometimes set within a baptistry (q.v.) and normally located near the west door.
frontal	cloth hanging over the front of an altar. In different colours according to the liturgical 'season' (Easter, Lent, Advent, etc.)
genuflect	the act of bending the knee in submission (often accompanied with the sign of the cross)
glebe	church land granted to a rector to support their ministry and the maintenance of the Chancel
INRI	Iesus Nazarenus Rex Iudaeorum (Jesus of Nazareth, King of the Jews)
interregnum	Period between the resignation or death of one vicar and the institution of the next
jamb	the side-post or lining of a doorway or other opening (from French jambe 'leg')
jubé	ornamental choir-screen. In medieval churches, usually with the rood (q.v.) above
kirtle	a one-piece garment worn by men and women across Europe in the Middle Ages (sometimes called a cotte or cotehardie)
lectern	desk or stand from which Bible readings are given
liturgy	The public ritual of religious worship. [Greek: 'work of public service']. The 'Order of Service' used by worshippers sets out the liturgy for them to follow.
living	see benefice
lucarne	more commonly known as a 'dormer' window or opening
matins	service of prayers held in the early morning
minster	a church associated with a monastery (q.v.)
misericord	a pivoting wooden bracket within a choir stall that lifts up to provide relief for (medieval) clergy who had to stand during long church services. From the Latin word for 'mercy'. Often ornately carved and decorative.
missal	book containing complete service for mass
mitre	high headwear worn by a bishop or archbishop
monastery	a building or complex of widely varying size housing the quarters, workplaces, and place(s) of worship of monks, nuns or other religious orders living in communities or as hermits.
narthex	small entrance or porch to a church, usually at the western end
nave	the main body of a church where the congregation sits
ogee	Architectural feature comprising a double-curve in a serpentine shape
orientation	the compass alignment of the church, normally east-west, with the altar at the east end
parvise	enclosed space at the front of a church, or room over a church porch
paten	a small plate, usually silver, used to hold Communion bread
pax	tablet decorated with sacred figure(s) and kissed by the congregation during mass (medieval). From the Latin word for 'peace'
peculiar	a parish or church exempt from the jurisdiction of the bishop of its diocese
pews	wooden seats or benches in a church, often with 'poppyheads' (q.v.)

piscina	a basin set within the wall of church to wash vessels used in the mass (medieval). From the Latin for 'fish pond'.
poppyhead	raised ornament on top of the upright ends of seats or pews
presbytery	the part of a church reserved for officiating clergy
pulpit	a raised and enclosed stand, usually with steps up, from which a preacher addresses the congregation. In older churches, often covered by a carved canopy.
pyx	a small round container used to carry consecrated bread
quatrefoil	Architectural feature taking a 4-lobed form (e.g. in a frieze or a stone column)
recusant	a Roman Catholic who refused to renounce their faith or the Pope as head of the church
reliquary	a small box or shrine used to hold relics of a saint
requiem	a Mass for the dead or a lament
reredos	a screen behind the altar, often elaborately decorated and often depicting the Last Supper or the Crucifixion
rood	a cross or crucifix above the entry or archway to the Chancel (q.v.)
rosary	a string of beads by which to count sequences of prayers
sacristan	Lay person who arranges the liturgical books, vestments, and other things necessary for the celebration of Mass.
saltire	an X-shaped cross
sanctuary	the holiest part of the church where the high altar is placed, normally at the eastern end and raised up by a step or two.
sedilia	recessed stone seats within the wall of the Chancel for officiating clergy. From the Latin 'to sit'
sepulchre	a receptacle for holding sacred artefacts, usually on or near the altar. Sometimes recessed in a wall. An 'Easter Sepulchre' represented Jesus' tomb (medieval)
sexton	church caretaker or bellringer
stalls	segmented spaces where the choir sit during services. Often richly carved and fitted with misericords (q.v.)
stoup	a vessel for holding holy water with which people cross themselves on entry and departure, usually located near the church entrance door
synod	an ecclesiastical assembly or council.
tabernacle	an ornamental container or a recess in a wall for storing consecrated bread and wine. See aumbrey.
thurible	an incense-holder suspended from chains used during the Mass
tonsure	a small shaved area on the crown of head of a priest or monk
transept	a part of a church off to one side of main structure, normally to the north or south
transom	horizontal beam or cross-piece separating an opening from another opening above (e.g. a window over a door)
transubstantiation	the miraculous changing of bread and wine into the body and blood of Christ
trefoil	Architectural feature taking a 3-lobed form (e.g. at head of window)
triduum	the period of three days of prayer preceding Easter Day
tryptich	a picture (such as an altarpiece) or carving in three panels side by side
tympanum	a semi-circular or triangular decorative wall surface over an entrance, door or window, bounded by a lintel and an arch. (from Latin, meaning "drum")
verger	a church usher or attendant
vestry	the priest's robing room. Also 'choir vestry' where the choir robe before services
voussoirs	Wedge-shaped stones used in the building of an arch

INDEX

ADDITIONAL ACKNOWLEDGEMENTS

Made possible with
Heritage Fund

www.heritagefund.org.uk

With grateful thanks to the **National Lottery Heritage Fund** and to all our funding Partners

SOCIETY OF ANTIQUARIES OF LONDON

www.sal.org.uk

ChurchCare

www.churchofengland.org /resources/churchcare

The Francis Coales Charitable Foundation

franciscoales.co.uk

The Friends of Geddington Church

geddingtonweekleychurch.org.uk

Northamptonshire Historic Churches Trust

nhct.org.uk

The Leche Trust

lechetrust.org

John Warren Foundation

The Benham Charitable Settlement

'Geddington': in 'Report of the Summer Meeting at Leicester', Archaeological Journal 90 (1933) by Prof. A. H. Thompson, See also *Archaeological Journal 69 (1912)* by the same author.

Transactions of the Leicestershire Archaeological and Historical Society Vol. X: Notes on Buildings visited by Leicestershire Archaeological Society in June 1907 (led by Prof. A.H. Thompson)

Pevsner Architectural Guides (Buildings of England Series) Northamptonshire (2013) Ed. Bruce Bailey, Nikolaus Pevsner & Bridget Cherry.

Victoria County History of Northamptonshire Ed. By Rev RM Serjeantson & Sir WRD Adkins (1906) Vol. II

Anglo-Saxon Architecture by I, H. M. and J. Taylor (1965) pp.248-50.

The History and Antiquities of Geddington, Northamptonshire by Christopher A. Markham (1899).

The Chancel of English Churches by Francis Bond, OUP (1916)

The Church of St. Mary Magdalene Geddington by Rev. T. Woolfenden (1972).

An Abridged History of Geddington by M J Harker (1956)

Geddington as it Was: the Social History of a Rural Community by Monica Rayne (1991) ISBN 0-9518775-0-X

Geddington: A Diary of a Village 1086-1914, M L Hopkins (Ed), pub. by the author (1986). This work includes the principal references to Geddington to be found in the History of the King's Works; the Calendar of Liberate Rolls; the Curia Regis Rolls; and the Calendar of Fine Rolls during the medieval period. It also gives the many 19th & 20th Century newspaper references quoted.

Sir Ninian Comper: An Introduction to his Life and Work with Complete Gazetteer by Anthony Symondson and Stephen Arthur Bucknall (2006).

The History and Antiquities of Northamptonshire. (Compiled from the manuscript collections of the late learned antiquary J.Bridges, Esq.) by the Rev. Peter Whalley. Oxford 1791, II, pp 310-11.

The History and Antiquities of Northamptonshire by the Revd. Thomas James (London, 1864)

An Inventory of the Historical Monuments in the County of Northamptonshire, Volume 2, Archaeological Sites in Central Northamptonshire (RCHME) pub. HMSO (1979)

Sepulchral monuments in Great Britain : applied to illustrate the history of families, manners, habits, and arts, at the different periods from the Norman Conquest to the seventeenth Century by Richard Gough Vol. II, Part II, (1796)

Churches Built for Priests? The Evolution of Parish Churches in Northamptonshire from the Gregorian Reform to the Fourth Lateran Council by Paul Barnwell pub. in *Ecclesiology Today*, January 2004

The Corpus of Romanesque Sculpture in Britain & Ireland See https://www.crsbi.ac.uk/ and search for 'Geddington

Letter from King James I to Lord Montagu, Buccleuch Archives

Annales Cestrienses: Chronicle of the Abbey of S. Werburg at Chester ed. Richard Copley Christie (London, 1887)

The Archaeology of the Medieval English Monarchy by John Steane (1994)

Old English Churches by George Clinch, and Christopher Markham (1903).

Estate Letters from the Time of John, 2nd Duke of Montagu, transcribed by Alan Toseland, pub. Northamptonshire Record Society, 2013. ISBN 978-0-901275-70-7

Northamptonshire in the Early Eighteenth Century: The Drawings of Peter Tillemans and Others, pub. Northamptonshire Record Society (1996), Ed. Bruce Bailey   ISBN: 0 901275 60 3

The Parish Churches and Religious Houses of Northamptonshire : Their Dedications, Altars, Images and Lights. By R. M. Serjeantson, MA. F.S.A. and the Rev. H. Isham Longden, M.A. Archaeological Journal Vol LXX No. 277 (March 1913)

A History of Ecclesiastical Architecture in England by Rev. George Aycliffe Poole (1848). Pub. Joseph Masters, London.

The Puritans in Peterborough Diocese 1558-1610 by WJ Sheils (Northants Record Society, Vol. 30)

Geddington: A Village at War, complied, edited and published by M L Hopkins (1989) - ISBN 0-9515029-0-5

Geddington Chase – The History of a Wood by Burl Bellamy (1987) ISBN 0951211706

The Magna Carta King in Geddington and the Rockingham Forest by Vic Crouse (2016) Pub. Logan Press ISBN No: 9780946988273

The Architectural Development of Geddington Church: draft of an unpublished paper by PJ Ellis (1986)

The History of Pews by John Mason Neale: a paper read to the Cambridge Camden Society (Nov. 1841).

English Church Screens by Aymer Vallance (Batsford, 1936)

A Topographical Dictionary of England Edited by Samuel Lewis (1848) p.287. See https://archive.org/details/topographicaldic00lewi2/page/286/mode/2up?q=Geddington

QUEER AS
Folklore

QUEER AS Folklore

The Hidden Queer History of Myths and Monsters

SACHA COWARD

unbound

First published in 2024

Unbound
c/o TC Group, 6th Floor King's House, 9–10 Haymarket, London SW1Y 4BP
www.unbound.com

Text design by Jouve (UK), Milton Keynes

A CIP record for this book is available from the British Library

ISBN 978-1-80018-336-0 (hardback)
ISBN 978-1-80018-337-7 (ebook)

Printed and bound in Great Britain by Bell & Bain Ltd, Glasgow

1 3 5 7 9 8 6 4 2

This book is dedicated to every person who has ever walked around a museum and wondered if they belong there.

With thanks to the patrons of this book:

Bert Aerts
Michael Caddy
Shaun Parry